Researching and Writing Dissertations

A complete guide for business and management students

ROY HORN

The Chartered Institute of Personnel and Development is the leading publisher of books and reports for personnel and training professionals, students, and all those concerned with the effective management and development of people at work. For details of all our titles, please contact
the publishing department:
tel: 020 8612 6204
e-mail: publish@cipd.co.uk
The catalogue of all CIPD titles can be viewed on the CIPD website:
www.cipd.co.uk/bookstore

Researching and Writing Dissertations

A complete guide for business and management students

ROY HORN

Chartered Institute of Personnel and Development

Published by the Chartered Institute of Personnel and Development, 151, The Broadway, London, SW19 1JQ

This edition first published 2012
© Chartered Institute of Personnel and Development, 2012

Typeset by Fakenham Prepress Solutions, Fakenham, Norfolk

Printed in Great Britain by CPI Group (UK) Ltd, Croydon, CR0 4YY.

British Library Cataloguing in Publication Data
A catalogue of this publication is available from the British Library

ISBN 978 1 84398 302 6

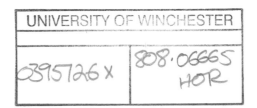

Chartered Institute of Personnel and Development, CIPD House,
151, The Broadway, London, SW19 1JQ

Tel: 020 8612 6200

E-mail: cipd@cipd.co.uk Website: www.cipd.co.uk

Incorporated by Royal Charter. Registered Charity No. 1079797

Contents

List of Figures

Walkthrough of textbook features and online resources

At the beginning of each chapter a bulleted set of learning outcomes summarises what you can expect to learn from the chapter, helping you to track your progress.

What will I learn in this chapter?

- Strategies for finding a successful topic
- Ways to check out whether the topic will succeed
- How to audit my own desires, motivations and skills
- The common habits of high achievers
- How to audit my time and make time to complete a dissertation

These boxes contain interesting questions and activities designed to get you reflecting on what you have just read and to test your understanding of important concepts and issues.

REFLECTIVE ACTIVITY

PRACTICE IN ANALYSING

Choose one of the following topics:

- Motivation
- Diversity
- The glass ceiling
- Leadership

Spend exactly 60 minutes investigating your chosen topic, using 20 minutes to read textbooks, 20 minutes searching websites, and 20 minutes reading journal sources. As you read, summarise using a mind map, so that at the end of the 60-minute period you have an outline of the theory, knowledge and approaches used in the study of the chosen topic. It is important to only skim-read and record the headline theory, research and ideas.

PETRA

CASE STUDY

Petra is a postgraduate student carrying out her research in training and development. She also works part-time at Concorde Industries, a large IT and engineering provider. One of the directors, Mrs Jade Gemini, asks if she would like to carry out some research for the company. Each year the company spends in the region of £1.5 million on training and development activities. Some of this is in-house training and most of it is supplied by about eight external agencies. The board of directors has become concerned at the sums being spent and has asked Jade to justify these amounts and the benefits of training and development to the company. As one part of the review strategy, Petra is asked to research the views of departments using the training and development service – this has not been done before. The outcomes of the research are likely to lead to great poor research findings. 'This has to be dead right,' she says.

The departments who use the training and development service vary in size from five people to the large engineering groups of over 100 people. There are 22 departments in total. There have been no complaints about the training and development service, but Jade feels 'We need to know what they think.' Jade is pretty sure Petra can do this with a survey. Jade's view is that she should avoid getting 'bogged down in too much theory'.

To think about ...

1 Comment on how useful a survey will be in discovering the views of the departments. If you were to use a survey, would one survey be suitable for all departments?

CASE STUDIES

A range of case studies illustrate how key ideas and theories are operating in practice, with accompanying questions or activities.

 EXPLORE FURTHER

Emmett, R. (2007) 'Oral history and the historical reconstruction of Chicago Economics'. Interview transcript in *History of Political Economy*, Vol. 39, Supp. 1: 172–92

Eriksson, P. and Kovalainen, A. (2008) *Qualitative Methods in Business Research* (*Introducing Qualitative Methods* series). London: Sage

Fransella, F., Bell, R. and Bannister, D. (2003) *A Manual for Repertory Grid Technique*. Chichester: John Wiley & Sons

Israel, M. and Hay, I. (2006) *Research Ethics for Social Scientists*. London: Sage

Watson, T. (2000) *In Search of Management*. London: Thompson Learning

Weblinks

The Oral History Society, home page: http://www.oralhistory.org.uk/

The Data Protection Act (1998): http://www.legislation.gov.uk/ukpga/1998/29/contents

ESRC Framework of ethics: http://www.esrc.ac.uk/_images/Framework_for_Research_Ethics_tcm8-4586.pdf

Google docs YouTube tutorials: http://www.youtube.com/watch?v=OBh8bMC7XEU

Google docs overview tour: http://www.google.com/google-d-s/tour1.html

Policy and Code of Conduct on the Governance

EXPLORE FURTHER

Explore further boxes contain suggestions for further reading and useful websites, encouraging you to delve further into areas of particular interest.

ONLINE RESOURCES

- Lecturer's Guide – practical advice for lectures with feedback on in-text features
- Guidance on chapter activities
- PowerPoint slides – build and deliver your course around these ready-made lectures, ensuring complete coverage of the module
- Annotated web links - a series of annotated web links point you in the direction of important articles, reviews and research guides.
- Screenshots, checklists and templates – practical tools from text are provided as electronic files for your use.

For Online resources, please visit **www.cipd.co.uk/orl**

CHAPTER 1

Preface and Introduction

What will I learn in this chapter?

- Why this book was written
- The readership level of the book and thus who can use it successfully
- The features of the book
- How to use different parts of the book for the different stages of your dissertation
- The general layout of the book
- To distinguish between quantitative and qualitative research
- Why dissertations are used to determine university degrees
- Which are the key skills that are assessed in a dissertation
- How your work is assessed
- What plagiarism is and how to avoid it
- The process by which you and your work are supervised
- Ten top tips for successfully completing on time
- The characteristics of excellent and of poor dissertations

1.1 INTRODUCTION

This preliminary chapter explains why this book was written and how the book can be used. A dissertation is put together in stages, and the chapter presents a guide to those parts of the book most useful for specific stages. The book includes many learning features, and these are outlined here too.

You are probably reading this book because you want to successfully complete your dissertation within a reasonable time frame while yet maintaining your sanity – there is a section in this chapter that features the ten top tips for completing on time. Other sections look at why dissertations are used to determine the university degrees that are awarded, at how your work is assessed, at the supervision process, and at the dangers of plagiarism. A further section introduces the nature of quantitative and qualitative research. There are in addition sections that explain how this book may be particularly useful for various specific courses.

Perhaps the best way to use this chapter is to read it through a couple of times. Try to establish how subsequent chapters may be most valuable to you, and match your reading of the book to the progressive production of your dissertation. Writing will be central to the successful completion of your dissertation, so I would advise an early look at Chapter 10 – *The craft of writing*. This will allow you to integrate these writing ideas into your work from an early stage.

1.2 WHY THIS BOOK WAS WRITTEN

I have supervised and assisted many undergraduate and postgraduate students as they carried out dissertation research and general research, and I wrote this book to help them. I hope it will help you. On a more personal note, I tend to find myself having to answer the same questions over and over again: the answers to all those questions are contained in this book. I have tried to make it as friendly and welcoming as possible so it may eventually seem like an old friend to be consulted when you are not sure of how to do something. Its limited size means that you might read it from cover to cover in a weekend – and you may wish to do this – but you will find it most useful if you read it in sections that are related to the stage of the dissertation you are completing.

The organisation of this book is based on the stages and the sequence of work that is required to complete a piece of research. You will therefore find that the first sections are about getting started and the research proposal. The sections in the middle are about methods and carrying out the research. Finally, the later sections are specific to writing and reviewing your work.

At my university we use the following dissertation stages:

- **The proposal stage**: around 1,000 words. This stage checks that you are proposing to write a dissertation on a viable topic and that you have identified a context, the appropriate literature and an appropriate method. The proposal as submitted is used to allocate a suitable supervisor.
- **The extended synopsis stage**: between 3,000 and 5,000 words. This stage ensures that you have a critical literature review and a well-reasoned and evaluated method.
- **The final submission stage**: between 12,000 and 20,000 words, depending on the degree award.

At *the proposal stage* I would advise reading the following chapters and sections:
Chapter 1 – Introduction
Chapter 2 – Finding a topic
Chapter 3 – The skills that are tested
Chapter 4 – The research proposal
Chapter 5 – Managing and completing on time

Skim read:
Chapter 6 – Theory and literature
Chapter 7 – Methodology
Chapter 10 – The craft of writing, and introductions and conclusions

The aim of the proposal stage is to develop and communicate to your supervisor your enthusiasm for a well-thought-out and do-able research topic.

At the *extended synopsis stage*, I would advise reading the following chapters and sections:
Chapter 6 – Theory and literature
Chapter 7 – Methodology
Chapter 10 – The craft of writing, and introductions and conclusions

The aim of the extended synopsis stage is to ensure that your research is grounded in a critical debate of the literature and to guarantee that a well-reasoned and evaluated method is being followed.

At the point of *data analysis*, when you have collected data and may not be sure what to do with it, read:
Chapter 8 – Data and how to analyse it
Chapter 9 – Data analysis and representation

Remind yourself of:
Chapter 10 – The craft of writing introductions and conclusions

At the point of *completing the research*, read:
Chapter 11 – Reviewing and evaluating your dissertation

Remind yourself of:
Chapter 10 – The craft of writing, and introductions and conclusions
Chapter 3 – The skills that are tested

Researching and Writing Dissertations has been designed and organised to be friendly and easy to use. Each chapter deals with a separate aspect of carrying out research. At the beginning of each chapter is an *introduction* beneath a bullet list of *learning objectives* that answer the question 'What can I learn from this chapter?' The main body of each chapter is *structured in sections* for ease of navigation. At the end of each chapter is a *summary* that highlights the key points of the chapter. There is also a bibliography of sources, a list of suggested further reading and a brief section of web links.

1.3 FEATURES OF THIS BOOK

LEARNING OBJECTIVES

Under the question *What can I learn from this chapter?* you will find a bullet list of the main aspects covered in the chapter. This is useful for navigating the chapter and as a refresher when you return to a chapter.

REFLECTIVE ACTIVITY

Each Activity invites you to pause and reflect on an aspect of the dissertation process and/or to carry out a practical activity to help you develop or consolidate your learning.

STUDENT COMMENT

A student comment represents a student view of the dissertation process related to the chapter topic. It is designed to provide a valuable insight into personal aspects of the dissertation process.

SUPERVISOR COMMENT

A supervisor comment represents a tutor view of the dissertation process. It is effectively a tutor tip to assist you in your dissertation.

EXAMPLES AND ILLUSTRATIONS

Examples and illustrations are provided to display and illuminate important aspects of a chapter. Some practical examples develop ideas within a section and illustrate an aspect of dissertation research.

KEY LEARNING POINTS

At the end of each chapter is a summary of the main ideas contained within the chapter both for reinforcement and to help you take action. An additional topic summary may occur in the main body of a chapter and reinforce complicated or interpretative aspects of the text.

SCREENSHOT

Where it is important to illustrate a computer-related example, a screenshot is included.

These also help you to carry out practical activities using software, and give you confidence that you are replicating the same input and obtaining the same output. All screenshots can be downloaded from the companion website.

CASE STUDY

Case studies are included to provide a practical context for you to explore the ideas and techniques presented in a chapter.

EXPLORE FURTHER

At the end of each chapter is a bibliography, a list of suggested further reading, and web links to encourage wider reading and direct you to useful sources of information.

COMPANION WEBSITE

Comprehensive and interactive websites for students and tutors include a range of features such as lecture notes to help guide you through the book and develop your understanding. www.cipd.co.uk/tss for tutors and www.cipd.co.uk/sss for students

1.4 THE LEVEL OF THIS BOOK

This book was written with university students as its main intended readership. It follows the chronological order of the tasks undertaken to complete a dissertation, and that means it will be very useful to all business, leisure, tourism, sport and social science students. Throughout the book I have related the chapters and sections to undergraduate dissertations and postgraduate dissertations (often known as master's awards). Both undergraduate and master's research must carry out the same basic steps to achieve completion. In many respects there are two major differences between these levels. One is the size of the research task – more data is normally collected for master's-level research. The other is the level of critique and evaluation expected: a more critical stance is expected at master's level.

The book is also specifically designed to be used with two CIPD modules: 'Using Information in Human Resources' and 'Investigating a Business Issue from a Human Resources Perspective'.

USING INFORMATION IN HUMAN RESOURCES

The *learning outcomes* for this unit are listed below, and I have indicated the most appropriate chapters relating to each learning outcome.

On completion of this unit (Using Information in Human Resources), learners will:

1   know how to identify and scrutinise appropriate HR data sources.

    Chapter 6: *Theory and literature* is the most appropriate starting point for this learning outcome – particularly
      Section 6.3 The Literature Review process
      Section 6.4 Sources of theory and literature

2   be able to conduct small-scale research and analyse the findings.
    Chapter 7: *Methodology* and Chapters 8 and 9: *Data analysis* will be most useful in organising and conducting a small-scale research project – particularly
      Sections 7.4 and 7.5 Creating questionnaires and conducting interviews
      Section 8.2 Preparing data
      Section 9.3 Describing quantitative data
      Sections 9.6 and 9.7 Qualitative data analysis

3 be able to draw meaningful conclusions and evaluate options for change.
   Chapter 9: *Data analysis and representation* provides advice on how to create a data story. Chapter 10: *The craft of writing, and introductions and conclusions* looks at creating conclusions – particularly
   Section 9.2 Analysis and explaining: an overview
   Section 10.6 Introductions and conclusions

4 know how to deliver clear, business-focused reports on an HR issue.
   Chapter 10: *The craft of writing* is the most suitable chapter for this learning outcome.

INVESTIGATING A BUSINESS ISSUE FROM A HUMAN RESOURCES PERSPECTIVE

The *learning outcomes* for this unit are set out below, and I have indicated the most appropriate chapters relating to each learning outcome.

The learning outcomes of this module are that the learner will be able to:

1 identify and justify a business issue that is of strategic relevance to the organisation
   Chapter 2: *Strategies for finding and developing a topic*

2 critically analyse and discuss existing literature, contemporary HR policy and practice relevant to the chosen issue
   Chapter 6: *Theory and literature*

3 compare and contrast the relative merits of different research methods and their relevance to different situations
   Chapter 7: *Methodology*

4 undertake a systematic analysis of quantitative and/or qualitative information and present the results in a clear and consistent format
   Chapters 8 and 9: *Data and how to analyse it* and *Data analysis and representation*

5 draw realistic and appropriate conclusions and make recommendations based on costed options
   Chapter 9: *Data analysis and representation* and Chapter 10: *The craft of writing*

6 develop and present a persuasive business report
   Chapter 10: *The craft of writing*.

The book is designed to take you logically through all the major operations required to produce a dissertation. It answers virtually all of the questions that might arise as you progress through the research stages. There will be specific areas in which you may need guidance from your supervisor. But do not expect a supervisor to make decisions for you – a good supervisor will point out that it is *your* dissertation and *your* responsibility. I hope this book provides you with all the support you need to succeed.

1.5 THE LAYOUT OF THIS BOOK

- Chapter 1 introduces some of the features of the book and research, and explains the composition of the book.
- Chapter 2 explores approaches to finding a suitable and do-able topic.
- Chapter 3 investigates in detail the skills that you will need to display in the final work.
- Chapter 4 looks specifically at the first output of dissertation research – the research proposal.
- Chapter 5 offers ideas for getting organised and motivated to successfully complete on time.
- Chapter 6 takes a detailed look at theory and literature, and at how these create a foundation for your own research.

- Chapter 7 examines what is appropriate methodology and lists a range of methods for dissertation research.
- Chapter 8 sets out the basic tasks required for data preparation and analysis.
- Chapter 9 details some important techniques of analysing quantitative and qualitative data.
- Chapter 10 suggests ways to develop and manage the writing process.
- Chapter 11 describes techniques to review and evaluate your work prior to submission.

1.6 DISSERTATIONS AND UNIVERSITY DEGREES

Dissertations are a common component of the assessment strategies of universities. Undergraduate and postgraduate degrees use dissertation research as a major element of the assessment process – typically, 25% of the third year of undergraduate awards, and 33% of the total credits in postgraduate awards. CIPD qualifications use management reports and projects to test the autonomous project management and research skills of students. Employers want graduates with a range of skills, but an important area that employers feel is missing in many graduates is the ability to be proactive, to initiate things, to complete tasks, to plan and organise, and to display self-motivation. The dissertation is designed to develop and assess this set of skills. It also contributes to assessing what are described as the 'higher-level' skills of critique, analysis, synthesis and evaluation. It is essentially the independent nature of the dissertation task that enables these skills to flourish and develop and ultimately be displayed in the finished work.

Research skills are highly prized in the general business context as well as in the academic environment. Dissertations are the start of a development process that builds important workplace skills which can mark you out as an effective employee. The topic of candidates' dissertations often comes up at job interviews because employers recognise that it is an independent learning outcome achieved with only limited support from tutors.

Dissertations are a substantial and independent piece of work for which the outcome – in terms of the grade awarded – is to a great extent under the control of the student. Universities want a means of assessment that clearly separates students into groupings for the differential awarding of degrees. Research has proved to be a very good arbiter of student ability over many years. The well organised, skilled, critical and thoughtful student will be awarded a high grade, and a student who has few of these behaviours and abilities will be awarded a low grade.

1.7 QUANTITATIVE AND QUALITATIVE RESEARCH

There are many ways to characterise research. One popular and enduring way is to characterise research as either quantitative or qualitative.

Quantitative research collects predominately numerical data and opinion, and often relies on deductive reasoning. Deductive reasoning forms a view about the likely nature of a thing, and then tests whether the view is correct. It often reports findings in terms of the relationship between one variable and another. This type of research requires a sound base in literature and theory. The main method of quantitative research is the questionnaire. The analysis of the data is mostly statistical.

Qualitative research is carried out from a very different perspective. It assumes that areas being researched are 'rich' and context-based, and require exploration to uncover the nature of a thing or a process. No theory or view is formed before the research is undertaken, but theory and models of how things change or behave develop as the research progresses – this is called inductive reasoning. The outputs from qualitative research tend to be rich accounts of participants' views or emergent theory-driven categories of behaviour. Interviews are a common method of investigation in qualitative studies.

There is a general trend in research to move towards what is known as multi-method approaches. In this approach a number of different methods are used to collect data on the phenomena under investigation. Sometimes, but not always, the multi-method approach pairs up a quantitative method with a qualitative method. It is argued that using a multi-method approach can increase the reliability and validity of the outcomes. When three methods are used, it is often known as triangulation.

1.8 WHAT SKILLS ARE ASSESSED IN DISSERTATIONS?

Chapter 3 provides details of the skills that are assessed. However, it might be worth setting out at this point the skills that are tested. Having a clear focus throughout the dissertation process on what skills are to be assessed is vital if you are planning to achieve a good grade. The essential top-level skills assessed through a dissertation are:

- *knowledge and understanding* – your ability to use relevant knowledge and display that you understand this knowledge by applying it appropriately
- *analysis* – your ability to separate the component parts of arguments, problems, findings, theories and research to better explain the connections and relationships
- *critique* – your ability to explore and express the underlying assumptions and foundations of theory, research, findings and models
- *evaluation* – your ability to express judgements about the worth or value of findings, theory, research and data
- *synthesis* – your ability to combine parts of theory, findings, research and data to present new ideas, solutions or theories.

1.9 HOW IS YOUR WORK MARKED?

The key skills listed in the section above are positioned on a grid that also shows the percentages of each skill that the university considers are appropriate for the subject discipline. Your work is marked by comparing your dissertation with the grid and awarding a mark for each of the key skills. The total of these marks then becomes your grade. Typically, dissertations are expected to display knowledge and understanding in the ratio of approximately 33%, critique and analysis in the measure of approximately 33%, and finally, evaluation and synthesis in the measure of approximately 33%. Universities communicate these proportions in a document entitled *Dissertation marking criteria*; such documents also contain broad descriptions of how these skills should be displayed in a dissertation. Note that if evaluation is expected to make up 33% of the finished dissertation, it is important that around 33% of your dissertation contains sentences, statements and paragraphs that are evaluative in nature.

A common problem with university dissertations is that they contain too much description and knowledge and too little critique, analysis and evaluation.

1.10 PLAGIARISM, AND HOW TO AVOID IT

Plagiarism is a form of academic cheating. It is possible to cheat openly and knowingly, but it is also possible to plagiarise others' work without being aware of it. Universities are beginning to phrase their plagiarism regulations to take this distinction into account. Many have penalties for 'major' and 'minor' plagiarism.

Major plagiarism occurs when you take others' work and claim it as your own – such as cutting and pasting from Internet sources, other students' work, or academic papers. In major plagiarism there is always intent to pass off others' work as your own: you intended to cheat at the point of plagiarising the work. Cheating occurs for many reasons among people who cheat at many things, the habitual cheats. There is very little that can be done to help the habitual cheat. But people who do not normally cheat can be drawn or pushed into cheating behaviour through poor planning and/or a sense of desperation. For this group, avoiding plagiarism would involve careful planning and organising so that they do not get into a situation where they are tempted to cheat. The penalties for major plagiarism are specific to each university, but are severe.

Minor plagiarism occurs when poor academic practice leads you to fail to acknowledge the contribution from another's work. If you use the words of another person, the quoted material should be clearly marked as a quotation, and a reference for the source should be clearly cited. There should never be any words in your dissertation that are not your own unless they are distinctly and visibly quoted, with or without quotation marks around them. Even when properly referenced and with quotation marks, material quoted from published sources should not be over-used. Quotations should illustrate your argument – they are not a substitute for your argument. Dissertations with substantial amounts of material quoted from published sources are often very poorly argued and commonly receive very low marks.

The distinction I drew above was 'published quotations' – using the words of your participants as evidence and to illustrate your findings is good practice. They still require quotation marks but can be used extensively to evidence your research.

Another problem arises with the ideas of other writers. When your writing is paraphrasing or developing a line of argument, the original idea or ideas must be referenced. So if, for example, we want to develop an idea to explain our research based on 'border theory', we must be sure to reference the original author of the idea (Clark, 2000), and if other writers have developed the work further, then they must be acknowledged as well (Desrochers, 2003). Most of your academic writing will require extensive referencing: failure to do it may be regarded as minor plagiarism. Minor plagiarism is regarded as poor academic practice – the penalties are less severe than for major plagiarism, but they are penalties nonetheless.

It is quite often necessary to paraphrase the arguments of other writers as a description and summary of research or academic ideas. Literature reviews typically require extensive paraphrasing of original ideas, research and critical views of others' research. Minor plagiarism is committed when you use the expressions and simply change a few words or the order of words. Never copy the form of words used in other sources. Read, reflect, relate to your research – and then write a summary.

Minor plagiarism is easily avoided if you:

- resist using large numbers of quotations from published works
- clearly differentiate any quotation published elsewhere (this includes the Web) from the rest of the text and give it a proper reference
- ensure that all your writing contains extensive references acknowledging the ideas on which your text is based
- do not paraphrase too closely the work of others.

Consult your university regulations regarding plagiarism, and if you are in doubt, ask one of your tutors.

TURNITIN™

Turnitin is a plagiarism detection system that is used by universities. You may be asked to send your work electronically, and it may then be submitted to the Turnitin system, where it will be compared with hundreds of thousands of other assignments already submitted and with hundreds of thousands of web sources. Pattern recognition may then determine if your work has been, shall we say, 'borrowed' from other source material. Be sure that if you have fallen into the temptation to cheat, this system will expose that cheating. Turnitin is also much more than a plagiarism-checker – it has facilities for the electronic marking of work and for student peer review.

WriteCheck™ is a student product that correspondingly allows you to check your dissertation before submission. It will indicate any areas of your writing that might be regarded as plagiarism.

1.11 THE SUPERVISION PROCESS

This is just a brief introduction to the supervision process: the process is described in much more detail in Chapter 5.

It is important to realise early on in the supervision process that your supervisor has only a set amount of time to help you. This is typically between four and eight hours across the whole year. Use this time wisely – it can make a real difference to the ease of completing a dissertation. In some cases, poor use of the supervisor's time will lead to failure.

You will be allocated a supervisor early in the research process. Quite often this is a random process, unless you intervene and express a preference. By the research phase of a degree you will know your tutors quite well. If you want to work with a specific tutor, you will have to devise a strategy by which they are made aware of your interest in being supervised by them. Clumsy approaches often do not work, so it is essential to use comparatively subtle and planned techniques. Read the chapters that relate to the research proposal and then prepare, early, a proposal for your topic.

Ask your preferred supervisor if they would have a look at your draft proposal. If they like the topic area and are sympathetic to your efforts at being organised, they may well suggest that they supervise your research.

Supervisors like:

- people (students) who are organised
- topics in their own subject area
- specific questions
- clarity
- a willingness to listen and take advice
- sound use of English
- brevity.

Try to ensure that your draft proposal displays all of the above things. If you don't make a preferred connection before the allocation process, you will be allocated a supervisor randomly.

The supervision process is essentially one of getting advice from your tutor. Advice is most useful early in the research process. The key areas in which supervisor advice can make a real difference are:

- the topic area and the precise aspect that is to be researched
- framing research questions and hypotheses
- finding literature appropriate to the topic, and knowing how to be critical of the literature
- choosing a suitable method and methodology
- data analysis.

Do not waste your valuable supervision resources on:

- English, and the use of English
- getting organised
- getting motivated
- choosing the broad area of your research
- proofreading.

Supervisors dislike:

- people who are lazy
- people who are poorly organised
- people with poor punctuality
- general chats
- people who won't take advice
- people who are argumentative
- poor use of English.

Dissertation supervision can be a really helpful resource – but you must be organised and strategic about how you use it. Do not ask your supervisor a question until you have read the chapter in this book related to the question.

1.12 TEN TOP TIPS FOR ON-TIME COMPLETION

1   Spend time developing a clear, do-able topic – Chapter 4.

2   Be organised from Day 1 – Chapter 5.

3   Follow the pattern of regularly reading, thinking and writing – Chapters 6 and 10.

4   Make the best use of your supervisor – Chapter 5.

5   Start writing early, and try to write every day– yes, every day! – Chapters 5 and 10.

6   Carefully plan your days and weeks. Set and meet deadlines – Chapter 5.

7   Pay careful attention to word counts and use word counts for each chapter of your dissertation. Review your work regularly to keep it within the word count – Chapter 10.

8   Develop techniques and work habits that motivate you – Chapter 5.

9   Make sure you have a dissertation friend or buddy: join or create a study group.

10 Try to enjoy the experience – it *is* possible!

1.13 EXCELLENT AND POOR DISSERTATIONS

Excellent dissertations:

- have (a) clearly stated research question(s) and argue these questions precisely
- have a clear well-planned structure
- display a range of knowledge and understanding of the literature associated with the topic area
- include analysis, critique, synthesis, argument and evaluation, rather than simple description
- display correct referencing and acknowledgement of ideas
- are well written and couched in the appropriate academic style
- use a range of sources and make particular use of journals
- produce sound and reliable data that leads to appropriate and convincing outcomes.

Poor dissertations:

- display (a) weakly-focused research question(s)
- are poorly planned and structured
- are predominantly descriptive
- display little critique, analysis, synthesis and evaluation
- contain inconsistent referencing and acknowledgement of ideas
- display small amounts of unreliable data that are weakly associated with the findings
- feature an unconvincing argument
- use a limited range of sources
- are poorly written, with errors in English usage and an inappropriate academic style.

KEY LEARNING POINTS

SUMMARY

This book is designed to help you complete research on time. How you use it may make a big difference to the ease with which you complete your dissertation.

- Understand the research stages for your own degree. At my own university we use:
  - the proposal stage
  - the extended synopsis stage
  - the final submission stage.
- Understand the learning features of the text:
  - reflection points
  - activities and exercises
  - student and tutor comments
  - worked examples
  - case studies.
- Get to know the structure of the book so you can navigate easily to any part of it for advice on the phase of the research you need:

- Chapters 1, 2 and 3: dissertation research
- Chapter 4: the proposal
- Chapter 5: getting organised
- Chapters 6 and 7: theory and method
- Chapters 8 and 9: data analysis
- Chapters 10 and 11: writing.
- Understand why dissertations are used and how they are marked:
  - They represent your abilities and skills.
  - They test knowledge and understanding, critique, analysis, synthesis and evaluation.
  - They are marked against assessment criteria.
  - Develop sound referencing habits that avoid plagiarism.

CHAPTER 2

Strategies for finding and developing a dissertation topic

What will I learn in this chapter?

- Strategies for finding a successful topic
- Ways to check out whether the topic will succeed
- How to audit my own desires, motivations and skills
- The common habits of high achievers
- How to audit my time and make time to complete a dissertation

2.1 INTRODUCTION

Many students look on the choosing of a dissertation topic with excitement and enthusiasm – but they also feel quite a bit of dread and worry. Choosing the right topic area and developing the proposal is a vital part of completing the dissertation. If you get this process substantially correct, the rest of your work will be enjoyable and fulfilling. This chapter aims to guide you through the stages required to start a dissertation.

The best way to use this chapter is to start at the beginning and work your way through each of the ideas, worked examples and activities. By the end of the chapter you should have a very workable dissertation topic.

2.2 STRATEGIES FOR FINDING A TOPIC

It is quite possible to stumble into a good dissertation topic. But by adopting a more systematic approach, you should find a topic that can be completed, that is suitable for your degree award, and that should be enjoyable to complete. Set out in the following sections is a range of strategies together with the benefits and drawbacks of each strategy. The list is not exhaustive but it does cover the main approaches to finding a suitable topic.

THE BURNING DESIRE STRATEGY

The Burning Desire strategy is based on an issue or a problem that you have wanted to investigate for a long time. The topic is important to you, although you may at the same time think it not specially important to the academic world or the professional world.

Typical topics include:

- an investigation into stress relief at work
- research into the length of holiday time in relation to work motivation
- a statistical analysis of retirement age and gender
- a study of sexual orientation and work commitment.

These are all worthy topics to investigate and a dissertation could be completed on each of them – but they do not feature in any list of important academic or practical problems. The topic area could be more closely specified and the aims and objectives could be developed to the point where the dissertation could go ahead, and with the normal care and commitment would return results and eventually become a dissertation that would pass the requirements for a higher degree. So if your topic is not very central to an academic discipline but is important to you, then proceed to develop it – it is an academic right to pursue any area of life or work.

REFLECTIVE ACTIVITY

'PETS' AND 'STRESS'

Use a search engine with the following two terms: 'pets' and 'stress'.

How many hits did you find?

If you are able to use Athens™, carry out an advanced search using the same two terms – filter the output to scholarly outputs.

How many articles did you find?

Reflect on why there were so many search engine hits but so few journal hits!

There is a whole range of issues and problems to be addressed with this strategy, as there is with all the strategies here. Perhaps the largest hurdle that will occur – and it will occur early – is the lack of relevant literature dealing with your chosen topic.

In the Reflective Activity you probably found that there was very little scholarly work relating to either topic, but quite a lot of website hits. This is an indication that there is very little academic interest or theory in the topic area. To solve this problem you would have to use more general theory relating maybe to stress, and interpret the theory to your chosen area. This is not impossible to do, but it does take time and is a slightly more demanding task than working in a well-established area of research. Another area of difficulty may be your supervisor's lack of knowledge or interest in your topic. This can be solved by communicating clearly and developing the areas of your dissertation more fully before your supervisor is invited to give feedback. There may also be some difficulty in getting your supervisor to sign off on the topic (see the section on supervision if you are unsure of this process).

Don't be too despondent if you intend to follow this strategy, for it has one huge advantage. Because the topic is something you have wanted to do for a long time, your motivation to get the investigation completed will outweigh a lot of the problems you will encounter.

THE REPLICATION STRATEGY

The Replication strategy works by finding some published research in an area that interests you or your organisation, and adjusting the scope and context, and then repeating the research. This is a fairly common approach in commercial and academic research because it directly builds on existing knowledge and data and represents a saying that is often heard in academia: 'standing on the shoulders of giants'.

STANDING ON THE SHOULDERS OF GIANTS

Meaning:

Using the understanding gained by major thinkers who have gone before in order to make intellectual progress.

Origin:

Twelfth century AD (in Latin)
The best-known use of this phrase is by Isaac Newton in a letter to his rival Robert Hooke, in 1676.

The one drawback with this strategy is that your own personal motivation to complete the research may not be as high as it would be with the Burning Desire strategy above.

There are a number of positives aspects to this strategy, including:

- The literature is well defined.
- The literature is well critiqued.
- The method may have been developed and tested.
- The possible lines of analysis are already established.
- A survey instrument or a set of interview questions may already exist.
- The research data can be compared with other studies.
- Access and ethical issues will have been investigated.

There will be some work to be completed in adjusting the existing study to your own context, and the scope of the research will have to be realigned with your access arrangements.

 THE REPLICATION STRATEGY: A WORKED EXAMPLE

CASE STUDY

Alison was interested in looking at examination anxiety. She searched the Athens database and found the following article:

Ravi Chinta (2007) 'Influencers of exam performance: an empirical replication in the Middle East', *Journal of American Academy of Business, Cambridge*, Vol. 10, Issue 2, March; 177.

She quickly discovered that this article was a replication of an earlier study:

David J. Burns (2004) 'Anxiety at the time of the final exam: relationships with expectations and performance', *Journal of Education in Business*, No. 80 (November/December); 119–24.

This gave her confidence that the topic was a sound and well-researched area, and she decided that her dissertation would replicate these two studies but in her own university.

She read the article several times and made copious notes relating to:

- the literature
- the method
- past research in the area
- critique of the method and areas of difficulty, mainly around the self-reporting aspect
- the five hypothesis that were used in the Chinta study.

She noted the data analysis approach and the results, and the limitations of the study as expressed by the author. She also imported the bibliography into her bibliographical index.

One problem still remained in that the questionnaires that were used in the study were not included in the article. She tracked down the author using Google™ and sent him an email asking if she could look at the questionnaires and possibly use them in her study. Some days later he replied, saying he was pleased that she would be carrying out a similar study, attaching the two questionnaires and asking her to send him the dissertation when it was completed.

After thinking about this study and considering how she would carry out the study in her own university, she wrote a dissertation proposal incorporating a number of the elements above. Her tutor was very pleased with it and gave her the OK to proceed with the research.

She still had some worries about the ethical position and made a note to see her tutor later about these.

THE CAREER GOALS STRATEGY

The Career Goals strategy requires you to do some analysis of where you think your career path will lead in the next five years, and to develop a dissertation that will assist that career. When using this strategy, it is also worth discussing with your line supervisor the developmental potential of any study you may undertake. In some circumstances your work organisation may have a very particular area of its business that needs research to be carried out. Researching an organisational problem may also gain some useful support from your employer, frequently in the form of time away from your normal duties or of finance to assist with the research costs.

Many of the difficult-to-solve issues around carrying out research are avoided using this strategy. Access to most or all parts of your organisation should be granted once you have organisational support. The support your employer can provide will prove invaluable in finding the time and motivation to complete the research. You may well receive assistance from your colleagues and superiors in dealing with the practical and intellectual issues around the research.

There are, on the other hand, some significant downsides to this strategy that must be weighed against the benefits. Your dissertation performance will quickly become part of your work role and may well be assessed along with your work performance. This is fine if all is going well – but research tends to have a life and path of its own. Your workplace line manager may well be looking for scope and results beyond what can be delivered in a dissertation. The outcomes expected by the university for the award of a higher degree may be substantially different from the outcomes expected by your organisation.

THE PRACTICAL PROBLEM STRATEGY

Practical organisational problems exist everywhere and can provide useful dissertation topics. They are especially useful as the subject of a management report. This approach is also a sound strategy when completing either of the CIPD modules, 'Investigating a Business Issue from a Human Resources Perspective 'or 'Using Information in Human Resources'. Such topics may relate to your own organisation or may be represented in the professional press. Practical problems generated from within your own organisation may have many characteristics of those aimed at by the Career Goals strategy, and should benefit from the advantages of following that strategy. There is one major issue to be overcome with basing your dissertation on a practical problem from your own organisation, and that is the need to untangle the problem and place it in a theoretical context. This clarifying, untangling, and placing in theoretical context is vital if the dissertation is to succeed in fulfilling the requirements of your degree. If you follow this strategy, you must allow for a substantial amount of time in the proposal development stage to address this issue.

If the practical problem derives from professional literature, the authors of the published work will have already completed much of the contextual grounding. There may also be supporting material related to critical theory, method, analysis and data. The outstanding issue then becomes one of access to carry out the research. Practical problems outside of your own organisation can present serious issues of access because many practical organisational problems are of a personal or commercially confidential nature. (See also the strategy below.)

THE CONVENIENT ACCESS STRATEGY

This strategy focuses on securing one of the most difficult aspects of dissertations first and then fitting the research around the access you have acquired. The routes to access are many and varied, and include:

- a family member or acquaintance who has a senior position in an organisation
- organisations where you have previously worked and with which you have maintained good contacts
- the organisation in which you currently work
- organisations that have traditionally been used for research – schools, hospitals, universities
- family-owned organisations in general
- your own university (often used as the access of last resort)
- access through your personal networks to organisations.

The Convenient Access strategy always requires some compromises in relation to the research as planned from a theoretical or practical standpoint. You may be able to get access to look at reward management in general, but not access to data about individual rewards. As a general rule, the more confidential aspects of organisations and employees will be restricted. This requires that you follow the strategy as stated, in that you negotiate the access rights and then develop the research proposal.

THE TUTOR-DRIVEN STRATEGY

Your supervising tutor will probably be involved in a number of research areas and will generally be responsive to developing those areas through your dissertation. There is also scope to do replication studies from the tutor's research or a former student's research. Tutors who are managing research studies will also be responsive to developing dissertations on some aspect of the funded research. This strategy requires you to know the possible supervisors in the department and be aware of their research areas. You can acquire this information from their website entries and also by taking note of their teaching areas.

As with all the strategies, there are benefits from this approach and probably some downsides. The main advantage to this strategy is that the tutor will know the research area very well and will be able to guide you quickly and efficiently towards the appropriate literature, method and techniques of analysis. The tutor will also have a personal interest in your research and will be fully motivated to assist you in completing the study.

However, this approach can sometimes feel like a tutor-set assignment, with the topic substantially driven by the tutor, and it is very possible to become demotivated by the apparent lack of personal control.

THE DEVELOPMENT OF EARLIER WORK STRATEGY

This strategy builds on work you have already completed. The topic for the dissertation is a development of earlier work – possibly:

- a development of an undergraduate project or dissertation
- an assignment from either undergraduate work or higher-degree work.

The advantage of this approach is that some of the early tasks – such as reviewing the literature, investigating the method, the collection of some data, and some data analysis – may have taken place. Most of these areas will have to be revisited and improved upon, but the basic groundwork will have been done. Dissertations developed along these lines can sometimes become boring and tedious because the work can seem like mere duplication of what has been done previously.

THE IMPORTANT PROBLEM STRATEGY

The final strategic approach to finding a dissertation topic is to investigate one of the important problems of the time. The notion of 'the important problem' changes quite quickly, and one way to discover what is regarded as important to academics and professionals is to scan the professional journals, such as:

- *People Management*
- *The Economic Journal*
- the *British Journal of Management*
- *The Sociological Review*
- the *British Journal of Sociology*
- *Applied Psychology*
- *Entrepreneurship Theory and Practice.*

Or the websites of such professional societies as:

- the Royal Economic Society (http://www.res.org.uk/)
- the Chartered Institute of Personnel and Development (http://www.cipd.co.uk/ default.cipd)
- the Chartered Institute of Marketing (http://www.cim.co.uk/cim/index.cfm)
- the Institute of Directors (http://www.iod.com/is-bin/INTERSHOP.enfinity/eCS/ Store/ en/-/GBP/IODContentManager-Start;sid=35OpRl4hB5B95Bkytpqj0PbhTePa4A1npD4= ?TemplateName=homePage%2eisml)
- the Chartered Management Institute (http://www.managers.org.uk/)
- the Association of Chartered Certified Accountants (http://www.accaglobal.com/public interest/about/).

You will quickly discover a range of issues that concern each of the groups represented by these journals and websites. The national press business pages also present a selection of important issues of the time.

CASE STUDY

THE IMPORTANT PROBLEM STRATEGY: A WORKED EXAMPLE

Priya was interested in looking at something that was currently important.

She took a look in *People Management* magazine and discovered an article about talent management and what Coca-Cola was doing in its assessment centre in simulating senior roles.

This set her thinking about talent management. Further investigation showed that 'the war for talent' was a very important issue for many companies.

She used Athens™ to search for journal articles relating to talent management, and printed out the eight articles that seemed most important. Having read them, she decided that this was the topic for her dissertation.

Using the eight articles as a literature base she was able to set out the main elements of a dissertation proposal. This she submitted to her supervisor, who approved the topic for her to proceed with.

If you have worked through this section, you should now have a good idea of the type of strategy you will adopt to find your topic. You should also have the area of interest decided. The next section looks at some areas of your emerging dissertation that will be investigated. If the outcomes of these investigations are mostly positive, it will then be time to move on to writing a dissertation proposal – this is covered in Chapter 4.

2.3 CHECKING OUT THE TOPIC AREA

SEARCHING FOR SIMILAR WORK

Regardless of the strategy you have adopted for finding your dissertation topic, you will have to carry out early investigations into work of a similar nature. The following areas should yield useful evidence of whether your research topic will work.

Theory

All research is driven by theory, and at this early stage you have to discover the areas of theory that have been used by other researchers in completing their work. If your topic area is a general one, then the first place to search for theory is in the relevant textbooks. Locate the topic in a general chapter, and then read the chapter noting down the main theories that could apply. A good approach is to do this in different textbooks continuing until three or four of the main textbooks have been consulted.

At the end of each chapter you will find a reference list extending the reading for most parts of the chapter. Study this list and 'follow the academic trail' through the articles you find there. At this stage there should be an increasing volume of literature and theory that relates, or could be related, to your research topic.

Carry on with the investigation of available theory by carrying out a database search using key words – see the 'pets' and 'stress' Reflective Activity at the beginning of this chapter. This search should add a considerable amount of theory that is relevant to your topic area. By this stage, you should have begun to develop an approach to keeping track of the sources and ideas you have read. See Chapter 5 for approaches to recording this reading.

Finally, search the Web for commercial research that relates to your topic. This will reveal the main theoretical drivers of the research. You may also find websites dedicated to your research area, and these may have links to the underlying theory related to your topic.

Empirical research

Most topic areas will have had some research carried out. You can find this research on websites and represented in journal articles. For very important topics, textbooks will have some representation of the main research in the area. The aim in this search is to find maybe three to six research studies relating to your topic, and to make some record of these studies. The detail of the study will give you a general idea of:

- theory relating to the topic
- methods used to study the topic
- types of data the research found
- general conclusions of the research.

These headings would be useful in recording the main details about each study you discover.

WHAT IF I CANNOT FIND ANY OF THESE THINGS?

For most topics, you will be able to find the details of theory and other research. If you cannot find this type of information, it is an indicator that your research area may not be viable. In this case, you will have to rethink your topic and refocus it in such a way that you can find theory and other research relating to it. Some of the strategies outlined above may lead to areas that do not have very much theory or other research. In these circumstances you may have to spend time considering how to relate your proposed study to theory that will support and 'drive' your research.

THE ATTRIBUTES OF A GOOD DISSERTATION TOPIC

The following checklist is designed to answer the question, 'How do I know if my topic area will work?'

A good dissertation topic tends to display the following features:

- [ ] It relates to theory.

- [ ] It is tightly defined and can be expressed as a research problem or hypothesis.

- [ ] It relates to individuals, groups or organisations.

- [ ] It is small enough to be carried out in five to six months.

- [ ] It does not involve many costs.

- [ ] It interests me.

- [ ] It allows for access to participants.

- [ ] It meets university requirements.

If you can tick all of these boxes, you are on the way to a successful dissertation.

CARRYING OUT A RESOURCES AUDIT

At this early stage of developing your dissertation project, you will have to check that you have the resources available to complete the research. The required resources will vary with each project, and the list below sets out only some of those required.

Finance

All research has some costs attached, and these costs can mostly be managed on a student income. They include costs for:

- paper and printing
- postage
- specialist software
- travel and transport
- an interview-recording device and media to store data on
- specialist books and articles.

Time

Research takes time – how much time will depend on the topic area and the method that is adopted. At this stage you will have to calculate how much time you can give over to the project. This will depend on your student circumstances, your family circumstances and your work circumstances. Full-time students have more time to devote to their research than part-time students who must balance the time required for research with the time required for work and family commitments.

Quantitative methods take a lot of time in setting up the questionnaire and much less time in collecting and analysing the data. Qualitative methods take less time in setting up the interview questions, but take considerably longer to conduct the interviews and analyse the data. Qualitative interviews, while being recorded as they take place, may have to be transcribed for analysis. This is a time-consuming process. Some other methods such as 'participant observation' may be unsuited to dissertations because of the huge amount of time involved. At this stage, consider the method you are most likely to use and whether you will be able to find the time to complete the research using that method.

Skills

On the CIPD website there is an opportunity to audit your skill level in relation to a set of skills necessary for carrying out dissertation research. However, there may be an important skill that you do not yet have but that you require to conduct your research. If so, it has to be identified early and provision made so that you are proficient in that skill by the time you need to use it. Such skills are most commonly those of being able to use specific software or statistical measures. If the method you have chosen at this stage requires specialist knowledge, it is wise to check that you can get this training.

IMPORTANT SKILLS: A WORKED EXAMPLE

CASE STUDY

Desmond had carried out quite a lot of projects that required numerical abilities and he was somewhat bored with them, so he determined that he wanted his dissertation to be more involved with people and their views.

He decided that his primary method of data collection would be in-depth interviews, and he realised that he would have a lot of narrative data to analyse. He spoke to his dissertation supervisor, who suggested that a useful software package was NVivo, which was particularly useful when analysing qualitative data. She referred him to the research department, who arranged for him to join a one-day intensive training day on the NVivo software.

The training covered the following areas:

- an overview of the software, its interface and functions
- concepts necessary to handle data
- setting up a new project
- creating or importing sources
- organising and coding data
- using basic queries, models and reports.

After this training, he felt much more confident – and he went on to produce an excellent dissertation on 'Employee perceptions of reward at a major UK bank'.

EARLY ACCESS ISSUES

One of the major problem areas for dissertation research is access to an organisation or to a group of people to carry out the research. Access arrangements must be considered at a very early stage, therefore, and if necessary, negotiations for access will have to be put in hand. An early analysis of the likelihood of gaining access will have to be carried out, and if it suggests that access will not be granted, the topic area may have to be changed or adapted.

Access issues vary depending on the strategy chosen to find and develop the topic area. The Burning Desire, Replication and Important Problem strategies often require a researcher to approach organisations and groups in a 'cold-calling' manner. Cold-calling requires time and persistence for access to be granted. At this stage draw up a list of possible organisations in which the research could be carried out, and make the initial contacts. Many organisations respond best to a well-drafted formal letter on university-headed notepaper and supported by your tutor. Modern organisations generally respond to email contacts and telephone calls, but you will have to discover just who is the right person in the organisation to contact. Whatever form your first contact takes, the following points should be emphasised:

- Provide a clear account of your intended research, the purpose and the type of access you want.
- Clearly state why the research is important, in general, and to the organisation.
- Use language and an approach suitable for the form of the communication and the organisation you are contacting.
- Make replying easy.
- Establish your credibility using only the words of the letter, email or telephone call.
- Your main aim is to get a meeting with a person who can grant access.

EARLY METHODOLOGY ISSUES

The chosen method will make or break most dissertations. It is therefore worth considering and reconsidering your method before you complete a dissertation proposal. All research fits on a continuum between fully qualitative methods and fully quantitative methods.

Figure 1 The research methods continuum

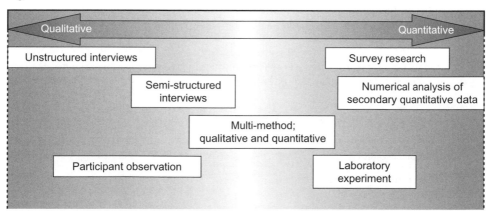

It is worth considering whether your chosen method will fit in with your own abilities and motivations and those of your university department and your supervisor. If you find it difficult interacting with people on a one-to-one basis, it might be best to avoid using in-depth interviews. On the other hand, if you are skilled with manipulating numbers and statistics, a quantitative method may suit you well.

It is worth becoming familiar with your possible research supervisors because that will give you an indication of whether they favour qualitative or quantitative research. Many supervisors are experienced and skilled in both areas, but some will supervise only one or the other.

2.4 CONSIDERING YOUR OWN DESIRES AND MOTIVATIONS

Your performance at university – and in completing a dissertation – is dependent on three things:

- direction (doing the right thing at the right time)
- skills (having the right skills to achieve your goals)
- motivation (having the drive and energy to achieve your goals).

This section looks at two of these things – skills and motivation – in detail. Your ability to organise and plan (direction) is examined in a later chapter.

AUDITING YOUR EXISTING SKILLS

Successful dissertations require a range of skills, some of which you will already have whereas others will need further development. Spend some time filling in the skills audit below. This is a self-audit, so don't exaggerate your skills or underplay them. An accurate assessment of your skills at this stage will enable you to work on the weak areas in a systematic manner. Any area of your skills audit that is rated at 3 or below will require some developmental work – your tutor or skills co-ordinator should be able to help in this respect.

You may also need to develop skills in specific areas related to your dissertation. Many universities have a research methods module that investigates most of the main skills required to complete a dissertation. A university may also arrange for training sessions in the more specific skills of research. Some of the main areas in which training sessions are carried out are:

- interviewing techniques
- quantitative software – SPSS™, snap™
- generating research questions
- qualitative software – Nudist™, NVivo™
- analysing and representing data
- selecting research methods
- academic writing.

SKILLS AUDIT

For each of the skills listed below rate your ability on a scale of 1 to 6, in which a rating of 1 means you have no experience in using this skill, and a rating of 6 means your use of this skill is already excellent.

In the box below each skill rating add some brief evidence of why you have rated your experience as you have.

1 Planning and organising   1   2   3   4   5   6

> *Evidence to support this rating:*

2 Time management   1   2   3   4   5   6

> *Evidence to support this rating:*

3 Reading for different purposes   1   2   3   4   5   6

> *Evidence to support this rating:*

4 Literature retrieval   1   2   3   4   5   6

> *Evidence to support this rating:*

5 Literature organisation   1   2   3   4   5   6

> *Evidence to support this rating:*

6 Numerical skills   1   2   3   4   5   6

> *Evidence to support this rating:*

7 Critically reviewing the literature   1   2   3   4   5   6

> *Evidence to support this rating:*

8 Making academic judgements (evaluation)   1   2   3   4   5   6

> *Evidence to support this rating:*

9 Structuring writing   1   2   3   4   5   6

> *Evidence to support this rating:*

10 Creative problem-solving   1   2   3   4   5   6

> *Evidence to support this rating:*

| 11 Carrying out research | 1 | 2 | 3 | 4 | 5 | 6 |

Evidence to support this rating:

| 12 Analysing data | 1 | 2 | 3 | 4 | 5 | 6 |

Evidence to support this rating:

| 13 Drawing conclusions | 1 | 2 | 3 | 4 | 5 | 6 |

Evidence to support this rating:

INVESTIGATING YOUR MOTIVATION

Motivation is extremely important when it comes to completing a dissertation. There is no external source of motivation – it must come from within you.

Motivation could be defined as:

The internal energy to start and persist towards a goal until that goal is achieved.

Everyone is different in how they motivate themselves to set and achieve goals. One way to avoid disappointment in life is to set no goals or only easily achievable goals. Because you have embarked on completing a dissertation, you have already marked yourself out as someone who sets challenging goals – well done. But how will you motivate yourself to finish the dissertation? No one can answer this for you – but it is possible to investigate the habits of high achievers.

The common habits of high achievers

- *One goal*
  All tasks, no matter how complicated, are achieved one goal at a time. Setting too many goals and goals that are a long way ahead will end up demotivating you. Set one task at a time, and when that is achieved, set another. You will be surprised how quickly you can achieve big things with little goals.
- *Start with a small step*
  Even when you do not feel like doing anything towards your dissertation, start with a very small step. For instance: look in the library at other dissertations.
- *Avoid negativity*
  Negative habits hold us back all the time. You must recognise your negative behaviour for what it is and turn it around to positive behaviour. Perhaps the worst negative behaviour is procrastination. 'Oh, I haven't got enough time to get started on that today!' Whenever you find yourself saying this, stop! Then carry out a very small task towards your goal. In a short time you will stop saying those words and start achieving your goals.

- *Dream about the benefits*
  Higher degrees normally bring huge workplace benefits in the form of new and better-paid jobs. Dream about these new jobs and experiences – they will motivate you.
- *Visualise your goal*
  Your main goal should always be visible to you. Write down your main goal and place a copy of it in all the places you go regularly – your office space, the toilet, your car, the inside of your briefcase or handbag. If a picture can be used to capture your goal, then leave that picture in all the places you go.
- *Be enthusiastic*
  Create enthusiasm for your main goal by talking to others about it. You can also create enthusiasm by reading about your goal and how others achieved the same goal.
- *Find inspiration*
  Finding inspiration to achieve is about finding and understanding how others have been successful. Talk to successful students and read accounts on the Web of successful people. Success breeds inspiration.
- *Think about your main goal daily*
  It is easy to forget what you are aiming for. Avoid this by thinking about your main goal every day. Ask the question, 'What can I do *today* towards achieving that goal?'
- *Create support networks*
  Dissertations can be lonely things to complete. Create support networks from family and friends, and also with other students. These networks will be a source of motivation.
- *Understand your own ebb and flow*
  You need to understand your own ebb and flow for each day, week and month. Everyone works best at some point in the day, week or month. Find the best times for you and plan the major tasks to coincide with your most effective periods of time.

AUDITING YOUR TIME

There are many aspects to time management, but at this point it may be helpful to look at just one theory: the Sweet Jar theory of time management.

Imagine a large sweet jar – the kind you find in old-fashioned sweet shops. They are about 41 centimetres (16 inches) high and about 20 centimetres (8 inches) in diameter. Take the jar and put as many whole chocolate oranges in the jar as will fit (so that you can still get the lid on). Now the jar is full. Correct – nothing else will fit in.

Now take the full jar and put as many chocolate M&Ms into the jar as you can. Really shake the jar and settle those sweets into it until you cannot get another one in. The jar is surely full now.

Or is it?

Take a bag of sugar and tip in as much sugar as you can. You may need a second bag. Fill the jar to the brim. Now it is full.

But now take that full jar and pour as much water into it as you can. Water will still go in. Then the jar is full – so screw on the lid and take a look at that jar.

What does this exercise tell us about time?

Well, the chocolate oranges could represent the important tasks to be completed. We also have a number of other quite important tasks to do each day/week/year – these are represented by the chocolate M&Ms. The sugar represents all the other smaller things that must get done every day/week/year, like buying food and milk. Finally, the water gets everywhere and gums up the works with a sticky sugary mess, and represents all the things that are not our priorities but the priorities of other people. The sugar and the water will combine so that you cannot see the sugar – it is dissolved in the water. So when you are busy on the major tasks (chocolate oranges), you may find there is no food in the fridge or milk for a cup of tea.

None of the items in the jar are bad things, and we will want a balance of things to do – it would be no use having only large, important things to do. But somehow we have to get the large items completed in order to say that we have had a productive and effective day/week/year.

What does this little exercise tell us about time management?

- We only have room for so many whole chocolate oranges – high priority.
- Low-priority work should fit in around the high-priority ones.
- If you don't put the chocolate oranges in first, you won't be able to get them in at all.
- If you start with water in the jar, you will be able to get nothing else in.
- Some items combine and we lose sight of them – the sugar and the water – but they still use time.
- Large goals can be broken down into smaller goals – the chocolate oranges are themselves made up of segments.

If we organise our lives to follow the Sweet Jar theory, we must plan to complete the high-priority items first and then be selective about the other things that we choose to do, and we must never, never let our lives be filled with other people's priorities.

What is your personal time profile?

There are many ways in which we can investigate how we use time, but building a personal time profile will indicate the main areas on which we spend time. The first step in this process is to keep an activity log. For the next week, keep a close track of every activity in every day. You can keep an activity record in any way that works for you, but a common format is shown below.

ACTIVITY LOG

Day	Start time	Finish time	Minutes on task	ACTIVITY
Mon	07.20	07.30	10	Get washed and dressed
Mon	07.30	08.10	40	Eat breakfast and read papers
Mon	08.10	08.35	25	Drive to the university
Mon	08.35	08.55	20	Do some reading in the library
Mon	09.00	10.00	60	Economics lecture
Mon	10.00	10.15	15	Coffee break
Mon	10.15	11.15	60	Economics tutorial

At the end of the week you will have a lot of data about how you spent your time over the previous week. The next step is to put the data in a format by which you can see a graphic representation of your time profile. The companion website for this text contains an Excel file marked 'My Time Profile'. This will help you organise your data and give you a visual readout of your week. But before you can enter the data, you will need a set of categories that reflect the activities you have done in the week you have just 'captured'. You will also have to add up the total number of hours in each category.

Common categories for My Time Profile
- Sleeping
- Studying
- Childcare
- Travel
- Leisure
- Formal lectures
- Eating
- Socialising
- Working
- Exercising
- Family time
- Shopping – essential
- Shopping – pleasure
- Household chores
- No activity undertaken – spare time

Once you have decided on the categories you need to cover your week of activity, you can enter the detail into the 'My Time Profile' spreadsheet that is on the companion website.

STUDENT COMMENT

I was a bit sceptical about the Time Profile idea, but I kept the log, and put the data into the spreadsheet. However, I was really amazed when I saw my profile – 22% of my week was spare time! I was just doing nothing. I was also a bit surprised that I had spent 42% of my time in bed.

After that I really took an interest in what I was doing with my time.

Once you have a pictorial representation of your current time usage, it will be possible to investigate ways to use time differently and find the time to complete a dissertation. 'How long will a dissertation take to complete?' is a question often heard by supervisors, and is almost impossible to answer due to the huge variation in dissertation approaches and the personal motivations that people bring to research. Most dissertations are completed over a period of three to nine months. The fastest completions tend to be by students in full-time study, and the slower completions tend to be from those who combine study with work. The average student who completes a dissertation in a period of six months will have spent approximately 20 to 25 hours per week progressing the work. The final stages of writing up and submitting are likely to absorb more time than this.

SUMMARY

KEY LEARNING POINTS

- Finding a successful dissertation topic may be easier if you adopt one of the following approaches:
  - the Burning Desire strategy
  - the Replication strategy
  - the Career Goals strategy
  - the Practical Problem strategy
  - the Convenient Access strategy
  - the Tutor-Driven strategy
  - the Development of Earlier Work strategy
  - the Important Problem strategy.
- Once you have a topic area, it is worth checking out some aspects of the topic to ensure that it will be successful:
  - the availability of sufficient theory
  - research conducted in the broad area of your topic

- the presence of the attributes of a good dissertation topic
- financial support for producing the dissertation
- the time resources required to complete the work
- your own skills for carrying out research
- early access issues
- early methodology issues.

- At this early stage it is worth investigating your own desires and motivations:
  - auditing your existing skills
  - investigating your motivation
  - understanding the habits of high achievers
  - auditing your time.

EXPLORE FURTHER

Allen, D. (2001) *Getting Things Done*. London: Piatkus Books

Cairo, J. (1998) *Motivation and Goal Setting*. Aldershot: Gower

Levin, P. (2008) *Skilful Time Management*. Milton Keynes: Open University Press
A really useful time management primer

Partington, D. (ed.)(2002) *Essential Skills for Management Research*. London: Sage
A collection of chapters addressing a range of ideas around the philosophy and process of conducting research

Williams, K. and Carrol, J. (2009) *Referencing and Understanding Plagiarism* (Pocket Study Skills). Basingstoke: Palgrave Macmillan

Weblinks

Avoiding plagiarism: http://www.library.dmu. ac.uk/Images/Howto/HowtoAvoidPlagiarism.pdf

Facebook page of help and support for dissertations: http://www.facebook. com/pages/Dissertations-help-and-support/133023343434050

Twitter for Dissertations (Dissertation11): http:// twitter.com/

Get Off Your Butt: 16 ways to get motivated when you're in a slump: http://zenhabits.net/ get-off-your-butt-16-ways-to-get-motivated-when-youre-in-a-slump/

CHAPTER 3

The Key Skills Tested in the Dissertation

What will I learn in this chapter?

- How your work will be assessed: the criteria
- What knowledge and understanding is, and how to display it
- How to use analysis to improve your work
- How to improve your work by using critique
- The role of synthesis and creativity
- How to evaluate sources and your own work

3.1 INTRODUCTION

The submission of your dissertation, although at this stage a long way off, will see the commencement of the process of judging and marking your work. In order to achieve a good mark for the work, you will have to offer evidence of a range of skills. These skills are often laid out and communicated in a document called an assessment criteria grid, or sometimes in a set of written criteria. This chapter aims to explore each of the main skills tested in a dissertation and to offer practical ways to display these skills.

To obtain a good mark for your work, it is essential that you address all the expected areas in the appropriate depth. The best way to use this chapter is to read it fully now, and then return to the various sections as your work progresses. Development of the required skills will have already taken place during the taught phase of the degree. Your aim in the dissertation will be to display those skills in a form that will allow your work to be successful.

3.2 COMMUNICATING ASSESSMENT CRITERIA

Your university or college will issue you with a document that sets out the skills that are tested in a dissertation and the weighting of those skills. These are normally in one of two forms: either as an assessment criteria grid (see the first example below) or as a narrative statement of the skills to be assessed (see the second and third examples below).

EXAMPLE: MASTER'S DISSERTATION, ASSESSMENT CRITERIA GRID

Criterion: Defining and contextualising the research problem	
70+%	Very clear definition of research problem, terms of reference (TORs) and rationale. Thoroughly related to an appropriate academic area of business/management in a wider context. Strategic importance of problem very clearly presented.
60–69%	Clear definition of research problem, TORs and rationale. Well related to an appropriate academic area of business/management in a wider context. Strategic importance of problem clearly presented.
50–59%	Research problem is stated, TORs and rationale are reasonably clear. Related to an appropriate academic area of business/management, and reasonable links are made to the wider overall context. Strategic importance of problem is explicit, although requiring some assumptions by the reader.
40–49%	The student is able to define the research problem, although the terms of reference and rationale lack clarity. Some links are made to an appropriate academic area of business/management, even if contextualisation is limited. Strategic importance of dissertation is stated, but with little substantiation.
Fail	The nature of the research problem is not clear and must be largely assumed. TORs and rationale are absent or ill-defined. Relationship to an appropriate area of business/management is tenuous. Strategic importance of problem reads like a corporate brochure.

Criterion: Evaluation and application of theoretical concepts	
70+%	Material selected from a wide range of appropriate sources; scholarly level of evaluation and critique, many original insights. Excellent use of journal articles. Material follows logically, systematically and persuasively with direct relevance to objectives.
60–69%	Material selected from a good range of sources; level of evaluation and critique is mainly but not consistently high, some original insights. Good use of journal articles. Generally systematic presentation with a high degree of persuasiveness, generally relevant to objectives.
50–59%	Reasonable range of sources consulted, and demonstrates reasonable ability to evaluate and critique complex concepts, with mostly sensible relevance to the argument. Reasonable range of journal articles. A few original insights. Relevance to the objectives is clear, even if not always consistent.
40–49%	Shows evidence of ability to identify assumptions and to evaluate and critique complex concepts, although much of the literature review borders on the descriptive side. The material selected is partially related to the objectives set. Very limited range of sources consulted; few or no journal articles.
Fail	Many key sources are omitted; literature review is largely superficial and descriptive. Material is likely to be drawn mainly from websites. Literature review bears little relation to the objectives set.

Criterion: Design and execution of research methodology	
70+%	Methodology is well explained and entirely justifiable in relation to objectives; high level of reflection on and critique of own approach. Sampling is appropriate and very fit for the purpose. Demonstrates a high level of scholarship in identifying, gathering, analysing and presenting authoritative and relevant data.
60–69%	Methodology is sound and student shows ability to identify limitations and critique own approach. Sampling is appropriate and complete enough for the purpose. Demonstrates good ability to identify, gather, analyse and present authoritative and relevant data.
50–59%	Student is likely to show a range of strengths and weaknesses rather than an overall consistent approach – eg good methodology, evaluation and critique of approach but sampling could be improved. Demonstrates reasonable ability to identify, gather, analyse and present authoritative and relevant data. Shows ability to learn from own mistakes.
40–49%	Demonstrates a problem-solving orientation in the design of methodology even if the execution of it is weak. Offers some critical reflection on research design and execution. The student must have collected both secondary and primary data and made some effort to abstract meaning from it.
Fail	Demonstrates little ability to conduct a major piece of self-managed research. Methodology is ineffective for producing useful findings, or approach taken does not take methodology into account. Scanty primary research data gathered, limited analysis, overall superficial attempt which would not be passed at undergraduate level, let alone Master's.

Criterion: Integration and argument	
70+%	The dissertation is clearly focused and the line of argument consistently and explicitly reflects this focus. Argument displays much originality and is highly persuasive. Each chapter builds logically on the foregoing and drives the argument forward. Theory, secondary and primary data are carefully rigorously integrated. Conclusions and recommendations are logically derived from and fully supported by previous evidence. TORs are fully met.
60–69%	The dissertation is clearly focused and there is a clearly discernible line of argument running through the work. Argument shows some originality and is convincing. Some of the linkages in the argument are more explicit than others. Theory, secondary and primary data show a high level of integration, mainly rigorous. Conclusions and recommendations are logically derived from and mainly supported by previous evidence. TORs are met.
50–59%	The dissertation is mainly focused with a reasonable line of argument, although the reader needs to make a few assumptions as it develops. Theory, secondary and primary evidence are reasonably well integrated, stronger in some areas than others. The conclusions and recommendations are related to the foregoing, but the links between other chapters are less clear. TORs are largely met.

| 40–49% | The dissertation begins with a focus and there are some links back to the original objectives. There is evidence of an intelligible argument, even if patchy and inconsistent. Some clear attempts are made to integrate theoretical ideas and the findings from secondary and primary research. Some of the conclusions and recommendations follow logically from the foregoing. TORs are partially met. |
| Fail | The dissertation lacks focus and comprises several individual elements with little or no integration between them. Conclusions and recommendations are largely unrelated to findings. Organisation of the material and flow of the argument suggest a piecemeal and rushed approach. TORs are not met; scope and nature of the work is shallow and show little evidence of in-depth investigation. Argument lacks rigour. |

Criterion: Written presentation	
70+%	Within word count +/–10%. Sources appropriately cited and referenced. Clearly written English, very well structured and presented.
60–69%	Within word count +/–10%. Sources appropriately cited and referenced. Well written and presented.
50–59%	Within word count +/–10%. Most sources appropriately cited and referenced. Reasonably well written and presented.
40–49%	Some effort to structure appropriately. Meaning can be understood even if use of English is poor. Greatly exceeds wordcount with much largely irrelevant data. Most sources are cited and referenced, although the Harvard system has not been consistently followed.
Fail	Very badly written and presented; 'thrown together' with multiple spelling and grammar errors. Meaning often obscured through poor use of English. Either far too long or far too short. Incorrect citing and referencing of material, several references missing. Ineffective structuring.

EXAMPLE: NARRATIVE CRITERIA STATEMENT (1)

Task definition and methodology   15%

- Subject valid and relevant
- Clear statement of the research problem/question, and associated objectives, with a comprehensive and persuasive rationale
- Appropriate selection of, and justification for, the methodology adopted, indicating a full understanding of its values and limitations.

Literature review and conceptual framework   30%

- Evidence of comprehensive knowledge and a full critical review of the literature relevant to the study

- Development of a coherent and fully justified conceptual framework to underpin the research undertaken.

Data collection, analysis, findings and conclusions | 45% |

- Entirely appropriate selection and implementation of data collection methods that is fully justified and recognises the limitations of the methods adopted

- Clear and extensive evidence of a high level of analysis using appropriate techniques

- Clear presentation of fully justified findings and logical conclusions, based upon the research evidence, which demonstrate the ability to critically evaluate the research results.

Presentation and communication of ideas | 10% |

- Conforms to all the required specifications and has an excellent layout in terms of structure and logical argument

- Clear and correct use of English characterised by a very lucid style of expression, with no imprecise and/or incorrect statements

- Appropriate and innovative use of presentation methods.

EXAMPLE: NARRATIVE ASSESSMENT CRITERIA (2)

	Criteria	Activities to demonstrate criteria
1	Formulate a hypothesis with a view to advancement and contribution to knowledge	Identify a problem and its significance, and develop a proposal illustrating intellectual, analytical and industrial (where appropriate) worth of the research. The proposal should be presented according to the specifications provided in the dissertation guide.
2	Undertake research in the area of business and management	Identify, retrieve, use, and cite (via Harvard system) relevant literature, carefully analysing and arguing in relation to the research.
3	Exhibit knowledge and understanding of various research methodologies and their application	Critically evaluate various research methodologies. Formulate, apply, and justify appropriate research strategies.
4	Demonstrate knowledge and understanding of a business and management issue within the context of today's dynamic business environment.	Identify relevant theories, concepts, principles, models and frameworks.
5	Demonstrate skills of analysis, evaluation, critical thinking, and synthesis.	Critically analyse results, relevant theories, concepts, principles, models and frameworks.

	Criteria	Activities to demonstrate criteria
6	Critically evaluate the results in relation to the objectives and future developments	Critically explore, evaluate, and argue all the main issues, supporting all with the evidence presented, and meeting the project objectives. Further recommendations should also take account of feasibility and practicality of the same.
7	Present the research through a dissertation, and debate with interested parties	(1) Provide a detailed report, presenting the results of the investigation, and communicate in a way that is comprehensible to others, providing evidence (through eg referencing and a bibliography) of effective use of electronic sources. The report should be supported by good written communication skills. (2) Give a professional presentation; demonstrate ability to communicate ideas concisely and effectively, exhibiting knowledge of the work, and the ability to respond to an informed audience.
8	Exhibit personal administration skills and the ability to monitor and control progress	(1) Review learning activities, evaluate critically against criteria, and identify strengths and weaknesses. (2) Set objectives, prioritise, manage tasks, and meet targets. (3) Demonstrate a logical and systematic approach to problem solving. (4) Ensure the originality of the work, using required format. Ensure the clarity and readability of the dissertation together with the standard of written English. Dissertations that do not comply with the required format and standards will not be considered for marking.

You will note from these examples that the main skills being tested are:

- knowledge and understanding
- critique and analysis
- synthesis and creativity
- evaluation.

The titles, layouts, and weightings may differ, but the above headings cover the main areas of all dissertations. There are normally some assessment elements relating to defining the study and presenting the work in the appropriate form.

Take particular note of the following important aspects contained in these assessment criteria statements.

The criteria are normally set out in a form that will be similar to the *structure* of the final dissertation. This is logical but often describes the key skills in different forms, and does not indicate all the possible areas in which a key skill could be displayed.

Some assessment criteria are *not* given weightings – see the first example above (the grid) – whereas the second example above (the statement) does indicate the weightings.

The assessment criteria sometimes introduce new terms or terms that may not be used in your dissertation. For instance, the first example above introduces the acronym TOR, which stands for 'terms of reference' and is one way of describing the aims of the research.

Criteria grids show the performance level required for any given grade. This is useful, but not many students set out to achieve anything but the highest grade, so that in general you need only look at the column marked with the 70+% performance indicators.

In the second example, the narrative sets out the highest performance indicator.

The remainder of this chapter focuses on the main skills and how they can be demonstrated in your dissertation.

STUDENT COMMENT

I had completed my dissertation and handed it in before I even realised that there were published criteria for my work.

It would have been so much easier if I had used the criteria to guide my writing. I think it would have improved my overall grade for the dissertation as well.

3.3 KNOWLEDGE

There is no simple and agreed meaning for the word *knowledge* – philosophy has debated its meaning for centuries. A working definition for the purposes of a dissertation would probably focus on the following aspects:

- the state of knowing something
- familiarity, awareness, or understanding gained through experience or study
- specific information about something
- acquaintance with facts relating to a topic.

Types of knowledge that you will most probably need to display in a dissertation are:

- facts
- theory, concepts, models, typologies
- research data
- approaches to method
- approaches to data-handling
- benchmark and best practice approaches to standard institutional problems.

3.4 UNDERSTANDING

Rather like knowledge, understanding is a concept that is hard to tie down. Most people can recognise it when they see it – but what is it, and how can you demonstrate it in a dissertation? Understanding might be considered to be the ability to think and act flexibly with what one knows. Clearly, this will require knowing something, which is where the previous section comes in useful. But how can we demonstrate understanding?

Using our definition above – 'the ability to think and act flexibly with what one knows' – would lead us to at least the following three ways of demonstrating understanding:

- *offering explanations* – People display their understanding of things by offering explanations. This involves highlighting critical features of a theory or idea, as when someone explains an enthusiasm for doing a task by telling of their desire for the reward that is gained by completing the task. This displays a rudimentary understanding of expectancy theory.
- *displaying relational knowledge* – People express their understanding in explanations constructed of relational knowledge. This is a complex web of cause-and-effect explanation.

A sparse explanation involving only one simple rule would in contrast suggest a sketchy understanding of an idea or theory. The example above would therefore need extension to display multiple motivations and theories.

- *displaying a revisable and extensible explanation* – People demonstrate their understanding by revising and extending their explanations. Explanations must thus be both highly extensible and revisable in fundamental ways. If they are not, we would perceive limitations to the level of understanding.

Demonstrating understanding typically takes place in the following sections of a dissertation:

- the literature review
- methodology
- data analysis
- conclusions and recommendations.

3.5 ANALYSIS

What is analysis, and how can you demonstrate the skill of analysis in your dissertation? This section briefly explores analysis, but it is connected to two other sections. First, it is almost impossible to demonstrate analysis without having an understanding of the relevant knowledge of the area you are analysing, so this section is connected to sections 3.3 and 3.4, and a similar connection will exist in your dissertation. Secondly, analysis on its own will not guarantee that your dissertation is awarded a good grade. Analysis must be connected to critique – see section 3.6 – in order to create a skill and approach called critical analysis. However, it is easier to explain the two skills in separate sections, which is why this section explores analysis and the following section explores critique.

Analysis of data is another key skill, and this type of analysis is dealt with in a separate chapter later in the book.

 STUDENT COMMENT

My supervisor says 'Be more critical! More analysis needed!' That is what he is always saying about my draft chapters. But I don't really know what he means.

I work really hard on my dissertation, and put in lots of work – but it is always the same comment. It was also the same comment I used to get for my assignments.

I don't know what to do, now!

Definitions of analysis tend to focus on these types of approach:

- the study of the constituent parts and the interrelationship of the parts
- the breaking down and separation of the whole into constituent parts
- simplifying the whole into parts to display the logical structure
- an explanation of a process and the parts of that process.

If we explore these approaches in more detail and connect them more directly to dissertations, they may be more useful in guiding us towards greater levels of analysis.

- *The study of the constituent parts and the interrelationship of the parts and the breaking down and separation of the whole into constituent parts*
  A research study looking at reward management might reasonably need to investigate the constituent parts of reward management. In business analysis there is a need to use theory,

ideas, models or typologies to carry out analysis. How can we look at the constituent parts of reward management using theory? Perhaps the simplest theory to demonstrate the approach would be to consider reward as being made up of *extrinsic rewards* and *intrinsic rewards* (Sansone and Harackiewicz, 2000). Using this theory immediately separates the research phenomenon into two parts and allows further analysis of those parts and the relationship between the parts. The analysis might then progress by looking in more detail at the nature of extrinsic rewards using Mahaney and Lederer's ideas (2006) to analyse the practical use of extrinsic rewards in the success of information system projects and the relationship between intrinsic and extrinsic rewards.

- *Simplifying the whole into parts to display the logical structure*
  Reducing a thing, idea or concept to smaller and simpler parts is often an effective form of analysis. Workplace attendance is a complicated organisational problem.

  It is possible to use a theoretical model to simplify the main phenomenon into parts that are easier to research. Steers and Rhodes (1978) present such a model that separates institutional issues from cognitive personal issues. Using this model would allow for more effective research to be carried out on absence management.

- *An explanation of a process and the parts of that process*
  Explaining a process and separating out the parts of that process is another slightly different form of analysis. In business and organisational studies, 'change' is often the subject of research. Descriptive explanation of the change process takes the analysis so far. Introducing a model of the change process and analysing the change against the model reveals more about the nature and extent of the change. Kotter (1996) proposes an eight-step change model for managing change in organisations. By comparing the subject of a research study with the change model it is possible to analyse the changes. Closer inspection of the various parts of the change process should lead to further analysis.

Analysis is a skill that can be demonstrated in various parts of your dissertation and will typically be worth between 30% and 50% of the available marks. In a completed dissertation, analysis would be displayed in several areas:

- the problem statement and aims
- the literature review
- the methodology
- data analysis
- conclusions and recommendations.

- *The problem statement and aims*
  Analysis here will concern your selection of theory and its use to analyse the research problem or aim. Only a very few marks can be achieved in this section due to the brevity of the writing.

- *The literature review*
  This is one of the main sections in which marks are awarded for analysis, but see also the section below on critical analysis. How the theory in the literature review is used to analyse the research problem is the key element here. Most literature reviews introduce competing theory to explain the research problem, applying the theory and carrying out analysis for the three or four competing theoretical positions, moving on to evaluate which is the most appropriate theory to explain the data most effectively.

- *The methodology*
  Analysis in the methodology section offers research methods theory and approaches to address the research question. The analysis will separate out the component parts of the chosen method and explore the interrelationships between methods where a multi-method approach is adopted. The analysis here is trying to explain, and later evaluate, the complete methodology and its relationship to the theory of the literature section.

- *Data analysis*
  This is another main section where analysis can be displayed, and regardless of whether a quantitative or a qualitative data analysis is required, the aim is to turn 'raw' data into meaningful and understandable outputs. There are a number of techniques that can be used to achieve this, and these are covered in the chapter on data analysis.

- *Conclusions and recommendations*
  There is one final, but important, opportunity to accrue marks for analysis – in the conclusions and recommendations section, where the ability to set out the interrelationships of your findings and data and explore the connection to the recommendations is assessed.

 SUPERVISOR COMMENT

Students still find the two skills of analysis and evaluation the most difficult to grasp, develop, and then display.

They try to develop them as they proceed with the dissertation, and this approach partly works. I think a better and more effective approach would be to do specific reading, and practice with these skills, and/or attend one of the university's courses on critical thinking and evaluation.

It is these two skills, and a student's ability in them, that determines the grade the student receives for the dissertation.

The research methods courses run for dissertation students never pay enough attention to this important area.

3.6 CRITIQUE

Critique is the term given to the process of estimating the quality of something. Strictly defined, it is the critical examination of something. In this chapter I have chosen to consider critique and evaluation in two separate sections. The critique element is the close examination of theory, research, writing, ideas and models, and evaluation is the judgement of the worth of those things (and is covered in section 3.7). In explaining these two skills, it is helpful to keep them separate, and whenever you judge work, it is worth regarding the process as having these two separate parts. The review of literature or the whole research process will first involve critique – the close and critical examination of something – and then an evaluative judgement of the worth will be made.

Critique is a very important aspect of academic writing. Our own research claims and argument will be built on the literature that is used. The aim in using critique is to select the strong elements of literature and discard the weak elements.

What is the process of critique when used for theory or journal sources?

First, you will have to paraphrase the ideas contained in the work. Paraphrasing is creating a type of summary that extracts and presents the key elements of the writing. What is the key idea or focus of the writing? What component elements does the writing contain? Strictly speaking, this is termed critical analysis. Next, set out the strengths and weaknesses of the writing. For this section, use other writers' scholarly thoughts, as can be found in textbooks and in journal articles. Most writing that contains theory, research or ideas will make a claim or a series of claims. How well are those claims supported by evidence? When a series of claims are being made, look for the evidence to support each separate claim. You are ultimately trying to assess the support for each claim. Unsupported claims should be detected and disregarded. Also consider if the argument is balanced – does it present counter-evidence or only the evidence that supports the argument? In the final section of the critique, draw together the assessments and report the findings. Try to use a reporting style, as in 'Ford argues that such-and-such is true, and provides some evidence of it, but there are some weakly supported statements …', etc.

CHECKLIST FOR CRITIQUE
- Paraphrase the theory, article or research.
- Draw out the main claim or claims.
- Consider the argument that builds towards the claims.
- Is a balanced or counter-argument presented?
- Review the evidence for each of the claims.
- Bring the thoughts of other scholarly work to bear on the theory, article or research.
- Report the findings of your critique.

The main areas of the dissertation where critique is vital to the success of the work are:

- the literature review
- the methodology
- the claims made in the findings section
- the accuracy of the recommendations
- the claims for the contribution of the research.

3.7 SYNTHESIS AND CREATIVITY

Synthesis can be regarded as the skill of bringing separate components together to form something new. In dissertations, one of the first and most frequently occurring syntheses is the bringing together of theories to form explanations and then possibly new theories. Most 'new' knowledge in business and management occurs by the combining of existing ideas into new explanatory frameworks. Branding, as a concept and as an idea, was developed by marketing into a discipline we now call brand management. Recently this concept has been applied to employers, and we now have the developing area of employer brand management.

When selecting theory to explain research, it would be very unusual if two independent researchers chose the same theoretical ideas to explain a phenomenon that was being researched. It is this diversity of theoretical approach that allows for new insights into well-researched areas. In business and management, theories are often drawn from social science disciplines such as sociology and psychology. A well-researched area of business and management is the experience of women managers, on which narrative study has been combined with Jungian archetypes to investigate the role models guiding female managers (Olsson, 2000). This presents a synthesis of theory to offer new insight into the experiences of women managers.

Synthesis is also commonly displayed in a dissertation's methodology section, where the combination of well-used methods into new approaches often occurs. Synthesis is further evident in the use of new combinations of method and data analysis to create unique approaches to the study of business and management.

Creativity is often linked with synthesis – indeed, it might be argued that synthesis is a type of creativity – but for the purposes of dissertations, a working definition might be 'the ability to bring into existence a new idea or insight'.

Dissertations provide endless opportunity for creativity, but the skill is most frequently displayed in the final sections of data analysis, conclusions and recommendations. The insights from analysing data almost always present – bring into existence – new ways of looking at a problem. The recommendation section is a place for creativity, but it is important that this creativity is grounded in the data you have collected. Recommendations that appear from nowhere are open to criticism. However, strong creative data-grounded ideas for dealing with your research phenomenon are a valuable contribution to knowledge.

3.8 EVALUATION

What is evaluation? How can you display evaluation skills in a dissertation? These are two of the essential questions that this section aims to answer.

Evaluation is the process of judging the worth of something. We make judgements all the time, every day. In the average day, you will make judgements about all sorts of things – breakfast, football matches, handbags, lectures, people, articles, other people's work, our own work, and lots more. If we make judgements (evaluate) all the time, why is it so difficult to be evaluative in our academic work?

REFLECTIVE ACTIVITY

JUDGING

Judging: Do you find it easy to make judgements about everyday things – such as driving behaviour, the quality of dinner, a person's clothes, or a magazine article?

Assuming you answered Yes or Maybe

to the question above, reflect on how you make those judgements. What knowledge or experience do you use?

Could judging academic matters be as easy to do?

In the majority of our everyday judgements, we bring considerable experience to bear on the decisions we make. We have probably eaten hundreds of sandwiches in our life and we have formed a view on what makes a good sandwich. Judging the value of academic theory, research, or methods is not quite so easy because we have much less experience of these things. One way to judge such academic things would be to compare them to a template or set of criteria. Generally, in these academic judgements, no such template or set of criteria exists, so making evaluations has to rely on more creative approaches.

One of the best approaches to evaluating theory and method is to allow other scholars to make the judgement. Using this method would require the finding of journal or textbook sources that critiques theory or method. There are normally some well-reported and well-developed critiques of most management theories, and they can be used to evaluate theory and method in dissertations. Below is an example of academic criticism of the type that can be used to evaluate theory.

EXAMPLE: ACADEMIC CRITIQUE

Herzberg's theory of motivation is often used in discussing both motivation and reward management. But just how effective is it as an explanatory theory? The article below outlines a number of major criticisms of Herzberg's theory by Locke (1976).

Herzberg's view of man's nature implies a split between the psychological and biological processes of the human make-up. The two are of dual nature and function apart, not related to one another. On the contrary, Locke proposes that the mind and body are very closely related. It is through the mind that the human discovers the nature of his/her physical and psychological needs and how they may be satisfied. Locke suggests the proof that the basic need for survival, a biological need, is only reached through the use of the mind.

With regard to Herzberg's correlation between hygiene, motivators, physical and psychological needs, it can be inferred that the first set are unidirectional, and so too are physical and psychological needs. Locke notes there is no justification for this conclusion. Providing the example of the physical need, hunger, he writes that acts like eating can serve not only as aversions of hunger pangs, but also as pleasures for the body.

The third criticism which pertains directly to the previous two, is simply the lack of a parallel relationship between the two groupings of factors and needs. Their relation is hazy and overlapping in several instances. A new company policy (hygiene) may have a significant effect on a worker's interest in the work itself or his/her success with it. The correlation lacks a clear line of distinction.

Source: Tietjen, M. A. and Myers, R. M. (1998) 'Motivation and job satisfaction', *Management Decision*, Vol. 36, No. 4, 226–31.

Academic theory can also be evaluated by how often and how effectively the theory has been used to explain research or to explain practical actions in organisations. By this method, we judge the most often-used theory to be better than the less-used theory. Such an approach can be problematic in that on some occasions inappropriate theory is repeatedly used to explain action. This suggests one further approach to evaluation – judging how well a theory can explain action: good theory tends to have more explanatory power than weak theory. Explanatory power is often judged by the areas of research action that cannot be explained by the chosen theory. If a theory explains most actions and events, it may be judged useful. If it has very little explanatory power, it can be judged less useful.

In a dissertation we can evaluate many things, but there are several areas in which evaluation is critical to achieving a good grade. In most dissertations the following areas require evaluation:

- aims and objectives, and how well they have been met
- theory, and its applicability to this research
- evidence for almost all the claims and statements in the dissertation
- methodology, and how well it has achieved the aims and objectives
- the quality of data and the analysis of that data
- the contribution the dissertation makes to understanding the research area.

- *Aims and objectives, and how well they have been met*
  There are two elements to evaluating the aims and objectives of a dissertation. First, how effective are the objectives in allowing the aim to be achieved? This is likely to be a reflective comment by the author of the dissertation. In the concluding section the evaluation will be of how well the dissertation has achieved the aims and the objectives of the research, and what contribution the research has made to the study of the area.

- *Theory, and its applicability to this research*
  In the main literature section, it is important to evaluate the usefulness of the sources used to guide and explain the research. All theory has strengths and weaknesses. These must be explored and a final evaluative judgement made about each element of theory (see also section 3.6). Journal sources can be judged on a number of factors relating to:
  - How objective has the author been?
  - What is the major claim of the article?
  - How persuasive has the argument been?
  - What evidence has been used to support the argument?
  - What is the rank of the journal in which the article is published?
  - Does the evidence presented support the major claim?

● *Evidence for almost all the claims and statements in the dissertation*
Every statement made in your dissertation should be supported by evidence. The normal approach is thus statement, then evidence source 1, evidence source 2, and so on until the statement is fully supported. This support can be from several sources depending on the type of statement.

The general format for all claims is set out below.

1 the claim

2 evidence that supports the claim

3 a warrant – that is, a general principle, assumption or premise that explains why you think your evidence is relevant to your claim (used when your argument needs to make the connection between claim and evidence)

4 a qualification which makes your claim and evidence more precise, and explains anomalies.

A light-hearted example to show the technique:

1 claim: There must have been a party in the halls of residence last night.

2 evidence: There are balloons and streamers everywhere.

3 warrant: Party debris normally indicates that a party has taken place.

4 qualification: There are occasions when people have dumped their rubbish in the halls of residence.

You are unlikely to need to make claims about parties in your dissertation, unless you are researching the effects of parties on student performance, but the example shows the format that should be adopted in your academic writing. The variation required from the example to the writing in a dissertation is that you will have to provide multiple sources of evidence so that the form becomes, claim, evidence, warrant, evidence, warrant, etc, until you have fully supported the claim, then qualification. The evaluation of the claims and statements will be concerned with the strength of the evidence, the logic of the warrant and the openness of the qualification.

REFLECTIVE ACTIVITY

SUBSTANTIATING CLAIMS

Examine one of your marked assignments and assess how well each of the claims of the assignment was supported by evidence, warrant and qualification.

How strong was the evidence?

Did you make a warrant? If you did, how logical was it?

Did you qualify the warrant? How open was that qualification?

Use these reflections to adjust and improve your claims in the dissertation.

You should present evaluation statements about your own work! There will always be marks awarded for self-evaluation of your own writing – see the assessment criteria published by your university. You should cover at least the following areas of your work:

- *Methodology and how well it will achieve the aims and objectives*
  The evaluation of the methodology involves a judgement on the suitability of the method in achieving the aims and objectives of the research. This evaluation is more fully examined in the chapter devoted to methodology.

- *The quality of data and the analysis of that data*
  The strength of the data and the power of explanation that the analysis provides is a specialised and specific skill and is more fully examined in the data analysis section.

- *The contribution the dissertation makes to understanding the research area*
  The concluding section of the dissertation should reflectively evaluate how well the aim, in whatever form, has been achieved. This reflective evaluation requires an approach different from the evaluation carried out so far – Chapter 11 addresses this skill.

KEY LEARNING POINTS

SUMMARY

The main skills tested in a dissertation are set out below:

Skill tested	Section of dissertation					
	Title, aims and introduction	Literature review	Method-ology	Data analysis	Recom-men-dations	Conclusions
Knowledge	√	√	√			
Understanding	√	√	√			
Analysis	√	√	√	√	√	
Critique		√	√	√	√	
Evaluation		√	√	√	√	√
Reflective evaluation						√
Synthesis		√	√	√	√	√
Creativity			√	√	√	√

- There are, however, further skills required in a successful dissertation, including:

  - argument
  - logic
  - research
  - breadth of reading
  - mathematics
  - reflection
  - integration
  - rigour

  - use of English
  - spreadsheet use
  - data representation
  - presentation
  - communication

  and these are examined in other areas of this book.

EXPLORE FURTHER

Horn, R. (2009) *The Business Skills Handbook*. London: CIPD

Kotter, J. (1996) *Leading Change*. Boston: Harvard Business School Press

Mahaney, R. C. and Lederer, A. L. (2006) 'The effect of intrinsic and extrinsic rewards for developers in information systems' project success', *Project Management Journal*, Vol. 37, No. 4; 42

Moon, J. A. (2007) *Critical Thinking: An exploration of theory and practice*. London: Routledge

Olsson, S. (2000) 'Acknowledging the female archetype: women managers' narratives of gender', *Women in Management Review*, Vol. 15, Nos 5/6; 296

Sansone, C. and Harackiewicz, J. M. (2000) *Intrinsic and Extrinsic Motivation: The search for optimal motivation and performance*. London: Academic Press

Steers, R. M. and Rhodes, S. R. (1978) 'Major influences on employee attendance: a process model', *Journal of Applied Psychology*, Vol. 63, No. 4, August; 391–407

Tietjen, M. and Myers, R. (1998) 'Motivation and job satisfaction', *Management Decision*, Vol. 36. No. 4; 226–31

CHAPTER 4

The Research Proposal

What will I learn in this chapter?

- The purpose of the research proposal
- The importance of the research proposal
- The headline contents of a research proposal
- What should be included in the main sections of a research proposal:
  - Title
  - Background to the research
  - The research problem
  - The objectives of the research
  - Literature
  - Methodology
  - Ethical issues
  - Access issues
  - Timescale
  - Bibliography

4.1 INTRODUCTION

The research proposal is the key 'gateway' document to your dissertation. It sets out the main details of how your research will be conducted. In many universities, the dissertation cannot be progressed until a supervisor has been allocated and the research proposal agreed between student and supervisor. It is also a key document in formulating and crystallising your topic ideas into a do-able dissertation. You should expect to spend around three to four weeks developing the proposal, and typically, your supervisor will review and feedback on three to five occasions. Because the proposal comes at the commencement of the supervision process, you and your tutor will quickly have to develop a relationship that will allow genuine and critical feedback to take place. Critical feedback at this stage is vital but can be uncomfortable for many students. Prepare yourself therefore to have open and critical discussions about your proposal. Even at this early stage of the supervision process you should be prepared to raise issues and have a critical debate with your supervisor.

This chapter covers the main elements expected in a research proposal. The best way to use the chapter is to dip in and out of each topic area as your own proposal progresses. The main aim of the chapter is to assist you in developing a well researched, academically sound and critical research proposal.

4.2 THE PURPOSE OF THE RESEACH PROPOSAL

The research proposal is a critical part of producing successful dissertations. It can often seem to those involved in producing them that they are rather slow to develop and wasteful of time. If you were going to set out on a long journey, you would most likely carry out extensive planning for the trip. You should think of the research proposal as the important planning for a long journey. Unplanned journeys can land up anywhere and often end in chaos and failure – these are not the outcomes you want for your research. The main purposes of the research proposal are set out in the following sections.

ORGANISING AND DEVELOPING YOUR TOPIC IDEAS

Writing can be one of the best ways of 'consolidating' your ideas into some form of research. Thinking about a topic is nearly always the first step in developing a research idea, but thinking can only take you a few steps down the process before your thinking becomes circular. By committing ideas to paper you create something that can be developed in further steps. By writing ideas down you also have a solid object for your own critique and evaluation. At the early stage of a proposal your ideas may be in the form of a mind map or other pictorial approach. At some point these ideas must be turned into words and argument.

TESTING THE SCOPE OF THE RESEARCH

The first version of your proposal will set out the scope of the work. This is a statement of what you intend to complete, where and by when. Initially, the scope is all too often much too wide to enable the work to be successfully completed in the time available.

Problems of scope are often either of two types. First, they attempt to address more than one research problem. Take for example the scope envisaged in this early proposal draft: 'The aim of the dissertation is to investigate women entrepreneurs, by looking into personal characteristics, exploring the reason behind their success and the challenges they are faced with.'

This is a very wide and ill-defined scope statement. The scope of this proposal could be 'tightened' by adjusting it to 'The aim of this dissertation is to investigate the reasons female entrepreneurs start enterprises.'

The proposal is now looking at a more closely defined area – that area being the reasons female entrepreneurs start enterprises.

Secondly, the 'geographical' scope of the proposal may be too wide-ranging and therefore require tightening. This is achieved by specifying the areas in which the research is to be conducted. For example: 'The aim of this research is to investigate employee perceptions of reward management in one retail store.'

Until the aims and objectives are written and discussed with your supervisor, it is very difficult to judge if the scope of the proposal may lead to a successful dissertation.

IDENTIFYING AN APPROPRIATE SUPERVISOR

Once you have developed the main areas of your proposal – see section 4.3 – it is possible to allocate a personal supervisor. The discussion of your proposal is normally the first point of contact between you and your supervisor. The course leader will allocate provisional supervisors to each of the proposals. If discussions between supervisor and student confirm that there is common academic ground, the supervision relationship will become established.

CONVINCING YOUR SUPERVISOR OF THE MERIT IN YOUR IDEAS

Following on from the initial debate, your document should then be able to convince your supervisor of the merit of the research. Normally, once a supervisory relationship is established there is a critical exchange of views about all aspects of the proposal, and normally, a number of versions are developed until the proposal provides a sound 'map' of the way the dissertation will proceed. Don't worry if at this stage of development you are asked to rewrite the proposal several times – this is the standard development process and should result in a successful dissertation.

INITIATING PROGRESS ON THE RESEARCH

Many universities, but not all, use the proposal as a formal progression point. This means that your proposal must be approved before you can carry on with the research. Approval is normally given only after the process described above and your proposal has improved to the point at which it provides a sound basis for the full research project. Even if your university does not use the proposal as a formal progression point, it is worth spending time developing the proposal until it is at a stage where it provides the sound basis needed for the carrying out of the research.

GAINING SUPPORT AND EARLY ACCESS RIGHTS

The proposal is also very useful for gaining financial support from your employer or external sponsor. At this early stage, it is the only document you have that describes and explains the research. If you are attempting to obtain access to an organisation, the proposal – especially if it is approved and endorsed by your supervisor – is the most useful document to do it with. Together with a suitable covering letter the proposal is often successful in gaining access to organisations.

AS A FOUNDATION FOR DEVELOPING YOUR RESEARCH

The proposal is your 'thinking' document and provides the foundation of all the work that follows. Making sure that this foundation is suitable is of vital importance. Time spent adjusting and developing the proposal is normally time well spent.

4.3 THE CONTENTS OF THE RESEACH PROPOSAL

Research proposals can take many forms and can look very different, but a good starting point is to follow the main outline headings given below. If you find that this standard approach does not fully represent your ideas or the approach you wish to take, you should amend and develop the headings and sections yourself. You may also find that some of the headings are not required for your research, so you will have to make some adjustments for your own research proposal anyway.

THE MAIN SECTIONS OF A RESEARCH PROPOSAL

1 Title

2 Background to the research

3 The research problem

4 The objectives of the research

5 Literature

6 Methodology

7 Ethical issues

8 Access issues

9 Time scale

10 Bibliography.

DETAILED SECTIONS OF THE RESEARCH PROPOSAL

Title

A title must be short and snappy and give a good feel for the work to follow, yet titles are often of a two-part nature, such as 'An exploratory study of sex at work: finding love in the workplace'. Note, however, that the second part of the title is not strictly necessary to explain the research. The normal way to proceed with titles is give your proposal a 'working title' and return to the title as the last act before submitting your proposal. Also, don't get too hung up on the title – it will not make or break your proposal.

Background to the research

This is normally a section that explains the context of your proposed research in terms of where the research will be carried out and why you want to carry out this research. You must try to convey your enthusiasm for exploring the area or solving the problem that your proposal presents. This may also be the section in which you introduce the fundamental literature relating to your research – for example: 'The guiding theory that I will use in conducting this research is the Steers and Rhodes (1978) model of employee attendance, from which I develop and explore the area of perceived ability to attend.'

The main literature section is where the theory will be fully described, analysed and evaluated.

The research problem

This is the section in which the research problem is set out and discussed in a formal way. There are three common ways of stating your research problem:

- with an aim statement
- through research questions
- via hypotheses.

It is common for the research problem to be specified in more than one manner, so that (for example) an aim statement is followed by a set of detailed research questions or a set of hypotheses.

Aim statement

An aim statement is a common way to express the research problem. It is – to give an example – normally of the form: 'The aim of this research is to investigate absence at SEDO Ltd.'

Note that this is still a fairly loose statement of aim. This aim can be 'tightened' by further specifying the following:

- the place of research (partly stated above)
- the guiding theory for the research
- the type of study – quantitative or qualitative
- the method – for example, a comparative study, a case study, etc.

The aim above could now become 'A qualitative case investigation of absence at SEDO Ltd, using Steers and Rhodes' (1978) notion of the ability to attend'.

The specified areas are now:

- the place of research – (specified premises of) SEDO Ltd
- the guiding theory for the research – Steers and Rhodes (1978)
- the type of study – qualitative
- the method – a case study.

Using an aim statement to specify a research problem works well when the research is of a broad, exploratory or investigative nature.

Research questions

Using research questions is a more specific way to state the research problem. The normal arrangement is to list a number of questions that the research will answer, such as:

RQ(1) – What are the current attendance levels at SEDO Ltd?

RQ(2) – What is the pattern of absence for individual employees (using the 'Bradford factor' to measure this absence)?

RQ(3) – What aspects of the work design is affecting absence at SEDO Ltd?

RQ(4) – What are the employee issues around ability to attend?

RQ(5) – What aspects are reported that lie outside the Steers and Rhodes (1978) absence model?

Using this method expresses your research problem in a much 'tighter' manner from the start, and is suitable where you have a clear set of issues arising from the literature that addresses the research problem.

Hypotheses

The research problem can also be specified using a set of testable hypotheses – a set of logical, reasonable, tentative explanations of the subject under investigation. It is normal to reject the 'null hypothesis' H_0 before testing alternative hypotheses. The null hypothesis states that the two variables under consideration occurred solely by chance. If the null hypothesis is rejected, alternative hypotheses may be developed. Continuing with our example of absence management, the following hypotheses might be tested (Burton, Lee and Holtom, 2002):

Hypothesis 1: Ability to attend will be positively related to the frequency of absenteeism that is attributed to family issues.

Hypothesis 2: Ability to attend will be positively related to the frequency of absenteeism that is attributed to transportation problems.

Hypothesis 3a): Motivation to attend will be negatively related to the frequency of absenteeism that is attributed to illness.

Hypothesis 3b): Ability to attend will be positively related to the frequency of absenteeism that is attributed to illness.

Hypothesis 4: Motivation to attend will be negatively related to the frequency of absenteeism that results in a failure to notify the organisation.

Note: Hypothesis 3 is split into a) and b), which test the relationship to that factor, a) testing the negative relation, and b) testing the positive relation.

Hypotheses are never proved or disproved. In a research study, it is normal to either support or reject a hypothesis. Once a hypothesis is rejected it is common practice to substitute a new hypothesis that is then either supported or rejected. If a hypothesis is supported by the data in your study, it may later be supported by further research studies. Eventually, a hypothesis that is well supported from multiple sources will be developed into a well-grounded theory. It could be that your research is testing, in a different context, hypotheses from earlier research studies.

The objectives of the research

Once the aim of the research has been clearly stated, the next section in the proposal deals with the detail of how the aim is to be achieved. The objectives are normally expressed as a set of closely specified statements that would enable the aim to be achieved. The objectives are likely to be the milestones of the research as it progresses, and for a typical dissertation may look like this:

Objective 1 – Critically review the literature and the development of one guiding theory.

Objective 2 – Develop and pilot the methodology, consistent with the theoretical framework adopted in objective 1.

Objective 3 – Clarify and define the population for the study, and select the sample.

Objective 4 – Distribute the questionnaires and follow up with a telephone enquiry for maximum response.

Objective 5 – Analyse the data and present the findings.

Objective 6 – Make recommendations to improve management practice.

Literature

At the proposal stage, the literature review is likely to be a list of possible sources related to the research problem. Even at this stage, it is important to be critical and evaluative. The sources must be closely related to the research you intend to carry out. Most literature reviews in a research proposal – but not all – contain the following:

1 A critical explanation of three or four main theories that could guide the research.

2 An overview of two or three professional body websites related to the research topic.

3 10 to 15 journal articles relating to the research. These may serve a number of different purposes:
   – empirical articles related to the research problem
   – articles that critique or extend the main theories
   – explanation and critique of methods and their use
   – articles containing data analysis techniques likely to be used in the research.

4 Secondary data sources related to your research study – for example, ESRC Labour Force Survey.

EXAMPLE: STUDENT LITERATURE ANALYSIS

Employer branding is considered by Sullivan (2003) to be a three-step process which identifies a 'value proposition'. In particular, Sullivan looks at a company's culture and management style, the qualities of its current employees and its employment image. The value proposition is the next step to target potential employees. Then internal marketing is the final step which includes the employment 'promise'.

[Note how the Sullivan article carries out the first step of analysis, separating one notion – 'employer branding' – into its component parts, according to Sullivan.]

At this stage, the level of analysis, critique and evaluation does not have to be high, but it is important to avoid simply providing a list of sources. The major problem at this stage is the mass of information that you can generate very quickly, and you will have to develop a strategy for selecting the most useful and appropriate sources. There are three main elements to the selection of strong, appropriate and critical theory. The most reliable, strongest and critical theory is presented in journals, and these should be the main source of your literature. Secondly, not all journals are of equal value. If you have a choice of using a journal article from a major international journal, a practice journal or a European journal, choose the major international journal – the articles in these journals are thoroughly and critically reviewed before publication. Finally, the authors of articles in the major journals tend to be the leading scholars in the area and therefore represent the clearest and most critical stance on the area of your study.

The list below is of the journals that are generally acknowledged on the international scene to be in the top rank, the best of their fields.

Academy of Management Journal
Academy of Management Review
Accounting Organizations and Society
Accounting Review
Administrative Science Quarterly
American Economic Review
American Journal of International Law
American Journal of Sociology
Cognitive Psychology
Econometrica
Economic Geography
Harvard Law Review
Information Systems Research (Informs)
International Journal of Research in Marketing
Journal of Accounting and Economics
Journal of Accounting Research
Journal of Banking and Finance
Journal of Business
Journal of Consumer Research
Journal of Economic Literature
Journal of Economic Theory
Journal of Finance
Journal of Financial and Quantitative Analysis
Journal of Financial Economics
Journal of International Economic Law

Journal of Law and Economics
Journal of Management Information Systems
Journal of Marketing
Journal of Marketing Research
Journal of Monetary Economics
Journal of Political Economy
Journal of Regional Science
Journal of the American Statistical Association
Journal of the Royal Statistical Society: Series A
Journal of the Royal Statistical Society: Series B
M.I.S. Quarterly
Management Science
Marketing Science
Mathematical Finance
Operations Research
Organization Science
Psychological Bulletin
Psychological Review
Quarterly Journal of Economics
Rand Journal of Economics
Real Estate Economics
Review of Economic Studies
Review of Economics and Statistics
Review of Financial Studies
Strategic Management Journal

Journals are generally ranked in groups according their status. Access the full list to see the ranking of journals in all the categories.

- *Group 0* (rare), as listed above
  A small number of scientific journals unanimously acknowledged on the international scene to be the best in the field. These journals' review committees comprise the cream of current research talent in the relevant field.

- *Group 1*
  Excellent scientific journals of international reputation and circulation, but not among the very top journals in their field. These journals' review committees comprise influential, renowned experts in the relevant field.

- *Group 2*
  Scientific journals with a review committee, publishing articles of a generally lower quality than Group 1 journals. Generally national-circulation journals, or international journals of lesser reputation.

- *Group 3*
  Journals having a high editorial standing and containing articles mainly aimed at a public of expert professionals. Scientific journals, with a very narrow area of circulation are also included in this group. Their editorial boards include well-known academics.

Methodology

The methodology section should set out the main method or methods that will be used to investigate the research question. The level of detail does not have to be high, but sufficient detail should be given to enable your supervisor to guide you as to the suitability of the approach in relation to your research problem. The methodology section in the full dissertation will contain other material relating to the philosophy and grounding of the method in theory, but at this stage it is sufficient to set out the approach in general. If you are able to connect the methodology to the theory in the literature section, and the likely philosophical approach of the research, then include those thoughts at this stage.

EXAMPLE: STUDENT METHODOLOGY

Primary research

The research strategy will consider the existing theoretical knowledge, applied and practical, from the literature review along with the objectives set in the introduction as the framework for the research. A focus on exactly what information is required will help plan the methodology of the approach.

The key objectives are:

- to investigate the existing level of engagement

- to investigate the factors constraining or encouraging discretionary effort, framing the research around the three elements of Bernthal's theory

- to identify the processes, procedures and management styles that could be implemented to encourage engagement across all staff.

The methodology must focus on fully achieving the above objectives and also incorporate in the framework the means of collecting relevant data on:

- individual value

- interpersonal support

- focused work.

Appropriate methods

Interviews, questionnaires and focus groups will provide the main method of primary research. The interviews and focus groups will be conducted in a semi-structured format and will focus on Bernthal's three elements and yet allow freedom for further discussion.

Questionnaires to assess individual value

To address this personal aspect in as much detail as possible without the employees having to voice their feelings in person, the questionnaire provides the most suitable method. Once data received from the wide sample of employees has shown where the majority of frustrations are, further research can then be focused on those areas that are causing disengagement, utilising more evocative research methods such as interviews and focus groups.

Interviews to identify the interpersonal support

The main focus will be on how individuals feel in relation to support from their peers and management. A cross-section of candidates will be invited to take part in the research into how far they feel that interpersonal support exists. The interview will provide a more detailed perspective of the environment and culture.

Focus groups to identify procedures in place for focused work

Each focus group will consist of a group of employees who will discuss the interpersonal support they receive. Not only will such a focus group give the employees flexibility in terms of what they perceive as focused work schedules, but it will also allow the researcher to observe how they interact as a group. Each focus group will ideally consist of four employees.

To ensure that all the selected participants can be present at a focus group while also avoiding any disruption to the service or function, a convenient time will have to be arranged with the line manager's consent.

The example above is the work as submitted by a student and as an example is fairly typical. The first section should explain how the theory you will be using leads to the methods you have chosen to use. The method(s) should then be described and applied to your particular study – some detail is required as to how all methods will be applied and where you intend to use them, and the likely population of participants. The next section of the proposal should offer some critique of the method(s): well-developed critique of methods is to be found in any number of journals. These same journals also contain good examples of how the method has been applied in research situations. Finally, an attempt should be made at making evaluation statements concerning your application of the method(s) to answer your stated aims and objectives.

The second part of the methodology section should give an overview of the type of data that is to be collected. This will give preliminary details of how much data will be collected, the population to be sampled, the sampling method, and any essential details of how the data is to be stored. A later section should set out the possible ways in which the data may be analysed and indicate any special requirements for software or equipment.

Ethical issues

All research has ethical implications and in this section some thought should be given to the ethical issues of your research. In some areas of research – such as research involving children, medical research and/or psychological research – there are formal procedures to be followed, and ethical approval is required from your university ethics committee. If you think your research will address one of these areas or will include any human or animal research data that may cause harm, you must indicate this clearly in the research proposal. You should also refer to the ethics section in Chapter 7.

If your research does not require formal approval, your proposal should address the following questions:

- How will the research be designed and undertaken to ensure integrity and quality?
- How will research participants be informed about the purpose, methods and intended possible uses of the research?
- How will possible risks of participating in the research be considered?
- How will you ensure the confidentiality of the information supplied by participants, and how will you assess the need for anonymity?
- How will you ensure that participants engage with your research voluntarily and without coercion?
- How will you record the participants' 'informed consent'?
- How will you indicate that the research is independent and free from conflicts of interest?

(If your research requires ethical committee approval, obtaining it will take at least three to four weeks and maybe longer, so you will have to prepare and present your ethics application as early as possible – see section 7.8 for full details.)

Access issues

The research proposal requires some detail around the access you have to participants for the research study. Typically, where you have access at your place of work, at a former place of work or at a family member's place of work, the following details should be supplied:

- List all the places where you have access to participants for this study.
- Give the name and title of the key authority who is granting this access.
- Describe the characteristics of the participants, and clarify how many subjects will be in the full population, and in the sample.

If you do not currently have access arrangements in place, you should set out your strategy for gaining access to participants.

Timescale

Planning and managing the phases of a dissertation are key skills of a successful dissertation. Putting together the research proposal is as good a time as any to start that planning process. At this stage the timescale element should be in broad terms, representing the phases of the research set out in the proposal. A narrative approach has the advantage of being quick to produce and requires no specialised knowledge.

For dissertations that commence at the beginning of the academic year in September and aim to complete some six or seven months later, the following timescale is often appropriate.

October   Exploratory reading
               Preparation of the proposal

November   Further exploratory reading
               Finalise proposal
               SUBMIT PROPOSAL
               Progress the critical literature review
               Finalise access arrangements
               Consider methodology

December   Further in-depth reading
               Complete the critical literature review
               Complete the methodology section
               SUBMIT EXTENDED SYNOPSIS (if this is a required stage)
               Check access arrangements again

January   Pilot the research survey or interview questions
               Adjust method from the pilot study findings
               Commence data-gathering

February   Continue data-gathering
               Make an early start on the data analysis, if any data has been collected
               Enter data on spreadsheet or database as it is collected
               Continue refining the written sections of the dissertation as time permits

March   Complete data-gathering
               Carry out data analysis
               Continue refining the written sections of the dissertation as time permits

April   Finalise all sections of the dissertation
               Arrange for two or three people (including the supervisor) to read the work to
               expose errors of logic, clarity, English usage
               SUBMIT DISSERTATION AND RELAX

Gantt charts are also a popular visual method for communicating the same information. Whereas in the example above the calendar month is the main divider of the work, in a Gantt chart it is normally the task that is the main divider of the work, each task being allocated a start and a finish date. There are various software packages that will assist with scheduling the tasks in your dissertation. It is worth making a decision about whether to spend time learning to use new software or developing your skills with existing packages, or spending the time progressing the research and using a simple narrative representation of the time-scale. 'Tom's planner'™ is free web-based software for producing Gantt charts. If you visit this book's companion website and follow the links to Blogs, I have set out the whole dissertation process in six blogs: connected to them is a detailed Gantt chart that covers all the stages of the dissertation. You may download the chart and use it in relation to your own dissertation if you wish.

Figure 2 A Gantt chart

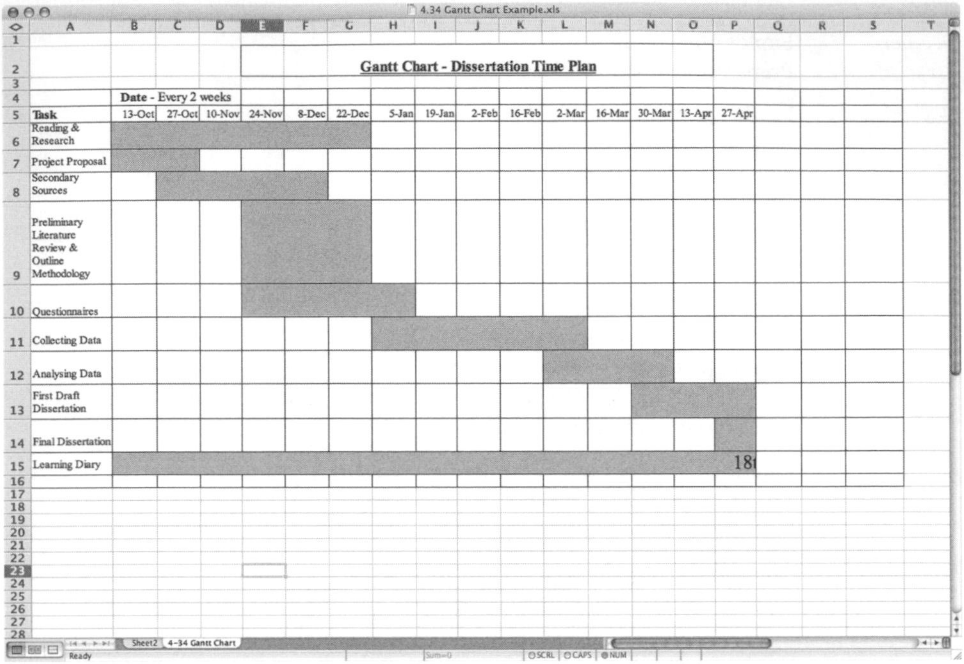

	A	B	C	D	E	F	G	H	I	J	K	L	M	N	O	P	Q	R	S	T
2							**Gantt Chart - Dissertation Time Plan**													
4		Date - Every 2 weeks																		
5	Task	13-Oct	27-Oct	10-Nov	24-Nov	8-Dec	22-Dec	5-Jan	19-Jan	2-Feb	16-Feb	2-Mar	16-Mar	30-Mar	13-Apr	27-Apr				
6	Reading & Research																			
7	Project Proposal																			
8	Secondary Sources																			
9	Preliminary Literature Review & Outline Methodology																			
10	Questionnaires																			
11	Collecting Data																			
12	Analysing Data																			
13	First Draft Dissertation																			
14	Final Dissertation																			
15	Learning Diary															18				

Bibliography

The bibliography section of the proposal traditionally appears at the end and lists all the sources you have used and consulted in preparing your work. This normally does not differentiate the different sources by sections – it lists all sources alphabetically. One referencing system should be used. If there are no other instructions from your university to use a named system, the most often used format is the Harvard system (author, date, title, publication).

You will have to be familiar with one complete referencing system by the time you complete your dissertation, but at this point it is sufficient to understand the basic principles and the format of the two most commonly-cited sources. The basic principle for the Harvard author-date system is that the reference point in the main body of your written work is short and succinct – for example: (Horn, 2009) – and does not impair the flow of reading by requiring the reader to look at footnotes. It also has one major advantage in that the references do not need to be synchronised into a numbered list and the reference in the text stays with the correct sentence even when the document is edited. These advantages make it ideal for extended work like dissertations which normally have several versions and extensive revisions.

There are two main forms of referencing the author in the main text.

When the author's name is cited directly in the text, use this form:

Applying this argument to Griffeth's (2004) forces, we suggest that the lack of trust, communication, and other benefits for subordinates in low-quality relationships lead to negative feelings …

Note that the author's name is used here as part of the sentence, and only the date is in brackets.

When the author's name is not cited directly in the text, use this form:

The quality of the relationship between supervisors and subordinates has often been studied via LMX theory. With its roots in role theory (Kahn, 1964) …

Note that the author and the date are both within the brackets.

The bibliography at the end of the work should then contain a detailed reference, with all references listed in alphabetical order:

> Griffeth, W. (2004) 'Eight motivational forces and voluntary turnover: a theoretical synthesis with implications for research', *Journal of Management*, Vol.30: 667–83.

This is a journal reference and so follows the format: author, initial(s), (year), title of article, full title of journal, volume number, issue or part number, page numbers. This example has no issue or part number so this is omitted.

> Kahn, R. (1964) *Organizational Stress: Studies in role conflict and ambiguity*. New York: Wiley.

This is a book reference and so follows the format: author, initials, (year), title of book, edition. Place of publication: publisher.

The rules for formatting references are very precise and the examples above are intended to assist in the research proposal. You will have to understand and apply the normal rules of referencing to your work. Most university libraries have a guide to referencing and there are numerous sources on the Web. The rules may seem quite difficult to master in that there are different requirements for referencing all the different sources used in a dissertation, but normal academic referencing is a mark of the professional standard of your work.

There is a full reference guide in Chapter 10.

SUMMARY

KEY LEARNING POINTS

The purposes of the proposal are:

- to organise and develop your topic ideas

- to test the scope of the research

- to help identify an appropriate supervisor for your work

- to convince your supervisor of the merit of your ideas

- to fulfil a university requirement to progress the research

- to obtain support and early access rights

- to constitute a foundation for developing your research.

- The main sections of a research proposal are:

  - title

  - background to the research

  - the research problem

  - the objectives of the research

  - literature

  - methodology

  - ethical issues

  - access issues

  - timescale

  - bibliography.

EXPLORE FURTHER

Bernthal, P. R. and Wellins, R. S. (2001) *Retaining Talent: A benchmarking study*. Pittsburgh: Development Dimensions International

Burton, J., Lee, T. and Holtom, B. (2002) 'The influence of motivation to attend, ability to attend, and organizational commitment on different types of absence behaviours', *Journal of Managerial Issues*, Vol. 14, No. 2: 181–97

Easterby-Smith, M., Thorpe, R. and Lowe, A. (2008) *Management Research: Theory and Practice*. London: Sage

Horn, R. (2009) *Researching and Writing Dissertations*. London: CIPD

Steers, R. M. and Rhodes, S. R. (1978) 'Major influences on employee attendance: a process model', *Journal of Applied Psychology*, Vol. 63, No. 4: 391

Punch, K. (ed.) (2006) *Developing Effective Research Proposals*, 2nd edition. London: Sage
A useful text looking at the detail of developing research proposals.

Roberts, B. (2007) *Getting the Most Out of the Research Experience*. London: Sage
Investigates research from a researcher's perspective, by answering the practical questions that all researchers face.

Sullivan, J. (2003) 'Measuring employment brand', *Strategic HR Review*, Vol. 2, No. 6

Weblinks

Ranking academic journals: the Association of Business Schools, *Academic Journal Quality Guide*, Version 4, March 2010: http://www.associationofbusinessschools.org/sites/default/files/ABSalpha_intro_latest.pdf

Tom's Planner Gantt chart software: http://www.tomsplanner.com/

Dissertation blogs and prepared Gantt Chart: http://www.tomsplanner-blog.com/2011/08/toms-planners-dissertation-wizard.html

Fully prepared dissertation plan: https://tomsplanner.com/?template=dissertation

CHAPTER 5

How Can I Manage My Time and Complete On Time?

What will I learn in this chapter?

- How long your dissertation will take to complete
- How the project life cycle can help you to be successful
- What work breakdown structures are, and how you can use them to manage the dissertation
- How to develop and use Gantt charts
- How to use time effectively
- How to manage bibliographical data
- How to manage the supervisor relationship
- How to get help from computer software
- What the main barriers are to completing on time

5.1 INTRODUCTION

Successfully completing a dissertation is a major task. Planning, organising and the effective use of time should make the difference between a major challenge that can be accomplished successfully and a failure to complete. Many of the ideas and suggestions in this chapter are most effective if they are adopted early and used throughout the life of the dissertation.

The best way to use this chapter is to read it fully and slowly, completing each of the exercises as you work through the chapter. It would be ideal if you were able to use this chapter very early in the dissertation process – or even before you start putting your dissertation together.

5.2 DISSERTATION TIMELINE

Most universities are moving towards a timescale that encourages completion of the taught and dissertation phases of master's-level awards within a period of 12 months from commencement of the course. A significant number of universities have a recommended timescale that extends to 18 months from the commencement of the course. It is now unusual, although not impossible, to have timescales that extend beyond 18 months, but it is important to check the particular circumstances with your university. Dissertation handbooks often contain this information, and if you are unsure, contact your course leader and clarify the exact deadlines for submission of the dissertation. The timescale for master's-level awards is therefore 12–18 months.

If your award is an undergraduate award, the timescale will be shorter. Most universities commence undergraduate dissertations in the September of the third year of study and require completion by March or April of the following year. The timescale for undergraduate dissertations is therefore 7–8 months. One immediate complication of this is that you will not be able to focus solely on the dissertation because there will be teaching, learning and assessment tasks to be completed at the same time. In relation to these multiple activities, managing your time and completing on time becomes a significant challenge.

 SUPERVISOR COMMENT

In my experience, no one realises at the beginning of a dissertation just how much time the task will take. To be successful, rigorous planning needs to be done and smart working habits have to be adopted early in the process.

One vital skill is the ability to multi-task so that the dissertation is never 'frozen out' by other tasks related to the taught elements of the course.

How much time does the typical dissertation take to complete? There is no such thing as an 'average' dissertation, but the chart below sets out some indicative figures for the 'typical' dissertation that gathers primary data using either quantitative or qualitative methods. In this example, the total numbers of hours to complete the dissertation falls in the range 260–400 and the total duration in weeks falls in the range 40–70, assuming in relation to both measures that no ethics approval is required and the transcription of data is outsourced. Dissertations that follow the pattern of the example and use the minimum duration figures should thus be completed in 40 weeks using 260 study hours.

Duration of a 'typical' master's-level dissertation

Activity	Study hours	Duration in weeks
General research to find a suitable topic	18–24	3–4
Prepare research proposal	8–12	1–2
Gain ethics approval (if required)	6–10	5–10
Research and develop a critical literature review (1st iteration)	30–40	4–6
Research and develop an appropriate methodology (1st iteration)	15–22	2–4
Further develop the literature review (2nd iteration)	15–25	3–5
Further develop the methodology (2nd iteration)	10–15	2–3
Pilot the research instrument, questionnaire or qualitative method	8–16	2–3
Gather data using a questionnaire[a]	18–30	3–6
Gather data using a qualitative process[b]	30–40	4–8
Transcription of qualitative data[c] (if required)	40–60	3–5
Analysis of data (1st iteration)	18–24	3–5
Further development of the literature review in the light of data	16–22	2–4
Final development of data analysis (2nd iteration)	12–24	2–4
Developing conclusions and recommendations	8–16	3–4

Writing up the full dissertation (1st draft)	25–40	3–6
Writing up the full dissertation (2nd draft)	15–30	2–4
Proofreading and final development	8–10	2–4

[a] Assuming the questionnaire is self-administered: 200 questionnaires sent out and 60–80 returned for data entry
[b] Assuming 20 in-depth interviews of 30 minutes' duration each
[c] 20 30-minute interviews transcribed word for word

This overall 'typical' pattern takes no account of a number of important issues – including the following.

EFFECTIVE DISSERTATION START DATE

Many university courses start in late September or early February, but in the early stages of the taught element of the course it is impossible to start work on the dissertation. The earliest effective start date is likely to be mid- to late October for courses that commence in autumn, and early March for courses that start in the New Year. Following the minimum figures in the example should lead to completion at the end of 12 months. If the longer duration proves to be the reality, the dissertation will be complete in 17 months. This is very likely to be towards the end of the allowed period of 18 months.

Undergraduate degrees normally commence in September. Some preliminary teaching is required before any meaningful work can be done so the effective start date will be the middle to end of October. If the completion point is around Easter, the total duration of the undergraduate dissertation work will be only six months.

OTHER LIFE AND STUDY COMMITMENTS

The timescale example sets out only the work required for the dissertation, but there will be quite a few commitments related to the taught modules of the course, such as assignments, examinations, learning and group work. Many people completing dissertations will also have family, social, sporting or work commitments which will limit the time available to spend on developing and completing the dissertation.

UNFORESEEN EVENTS

Even in the best-planned research, there will be any number of unforeseen events that stall or slow the progress of the work. Most research will experience some delay due to:

- access problems
- illness
- unavailability of resources
- slow ethics approval
- difficult academic areas that need intensive study or thought to solve
- a family or work crisis
- rewriting of sections of the work that are not effective
- redundancy, or more encouraging re-employment or promotion.

Completing a dissertation on time is an effective measure of success, but successful completions require organisation, planning and control. The sections below investigate ways of organising, planning and controlling the dissertation process.

STUDENT COMMENT

I nearly had a dissertation disaster on my hands as my life was so full of non-academic stuff: sport, work, shopping and hanging out with my friends. I didn't really make any progress until well after Christmas – then it was all a big rush. I am pretty certain I would have got a first if I had carved out some more time in the Autumn term.

My advice to new dissertation students is to start early and make sure you spend 15–20 hours every week on your dissertation.

5.3 THE PROJECT LIFE CYCLE

Dissertations have considerable emotional and personal baggage associated with them, but it is possible to view the dissertation process as a project, and to apply project management techniques to ensure successful on-time completion.

Figure 3 The dissertation life cycle

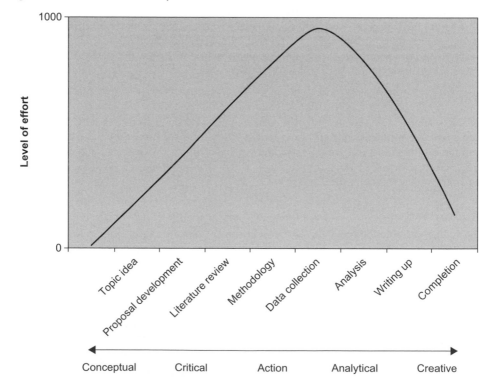

Figure 4 Dissertation phases

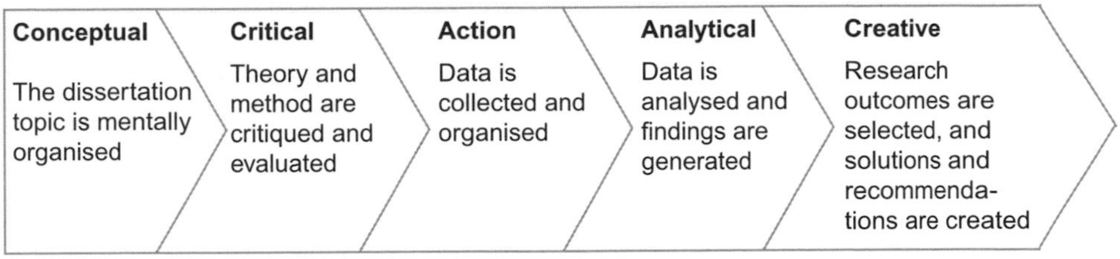

Conceptual	Critical	Action	Analytical	Creative
The dissertation topic is mentally organised	Theory and method are critiqued and evaluated	Data is collected and organised	Data is analysed and findings are generated	Research outcomes are selected, and solutions and recommendations are created

5.4 TASK PLANNING

Like most projects, dissertations are made up of tasks, and when all the tasks are complete, the project or dissertation is complete. There are many good reasons for investing time in the planning of the dissertation. Your dissertation proposal would normally contain an estimate of the time required to complete. The old saying about planning is that 'failing to plan is planning to fail'. The main advantages of carefully planning your dissertation are:

- Planning creates a proactive approach that can replace the more common reactive approach.
- It allows you to initiate and influence outcomes in your favour.
- It enables you to meet deadlines.
- It lowers academic stress.
- It encourages the adoption of a systematic approach.
- It improves your control of the project.
- It permits the setting of 'milestones' to assist in controlling the project.
- It highlights the areas in the dissertation where planned assistance will be needed, such as data-gathering and proofreading.

The most commonly-used approach to planning dissertations is to create a 'work breakdown structure' and then represent this with a Gantt chart. The work breakdown structure (WBS) or chart (WBC) sets out all the tasks needed to complete the dissertation. It incorporates an estimate of the amount of time likely to be taken on each task, a note about who will be doing the task, and a note about resources or about general comments. Below is an example of an excerpt from a WBS showing the detail of these entries.

 SUPERVISOR COMMENT

I always encourage my tutees to create their work breakdown structures in a spreadsheet, because then it becomes really easy to produce the Gantt charts.

EXAMPLE: EXCERPT FROM A WORK BREAKDOWN STRUCTURE

WBS No.	Task description	Estim. hours	Who	Resources/comments
3.1	Develop pilot questionnaire	12	Me	
3.2	Arrange for supervisor to check the pilot questionnaire	1	Supervisor	Arrange meeting for Thur 20 Feb
3.3	Arrange three focus groups meeting for 4, 5, 6 March	3	Me	Invitation letter in the main work file
3.4	Carry out the focus groups and record responses	6	Me and Ano	Ano needs payment for assisting
3.5	Send thank you letters	1½	Secretary	
3.6	Carry out analysis of the records, looking for improvements to the questionnaire	6	Me	Remember to keep a reflective journal exploring the thoughts behind the changes
3.7	Send improved questionnaire to supervisor for comment and feedback	½	Me	Check for feedback after five days

Lately, I point them at the online Gantt chart source of Tom's Planner.

The WBS or WBC is a living, dynamic document and will change over time for a number of reasons. Most first attempts at creating a WBS do not list all the necessary tasks to complete the work. It typically takes about three or four iterations before the WBS covers all the necessary points. As the dissertation progresses, changes may have to be made to the task list to reflect changes that have to be made to complete the work. The WBS can have a further column added – commonly when the work is well under way – to indicate the completion or partial completion of each task. If the WBS is kept up to date, it can be a useful tool to communicate progress with your supervisor.

 ## SUPERVISOR COMMENT

Some of the students I supervise come from a project management background and often display high levels of planning and organisation. They often send me their work-scheduling spreadsheet with updates on progress included. This is a very fast, easy way for them to keep in touch and let me know what is happening.

A SHORT NOTE ON ESTIMATING THE TIME A TASK WILL TAKE

At the beginning of a dissertation, it is very hard to accurately estimate the time any task will take. There is very little help available from either research or practice about how to accurately estimate the time required to complete ill-defined tasks. This probably means that it is a good topic for a dissertation. It is known that different motivational beliefs affect the accuracy of estimating the time required to complete tasks. If you are well-organised, motivated and a good time manager, you are likely to underestimate how long any task will take. If you are not, you may well overestimate it. Personal historical experience can be useful in that if you have completed many academic tasks beforehand, you can use your experience of these tasks to estimate better the time required for dissertation tasks. Most dissertation students have previously carried out a review of literature for an assignment.

The literature section of a dissertation is typically 4,000 to 5,000 words in length and has to be critical and evaluative. If an assignment task of 2,500 words has, for example, taken 18–20 hours to complete, then the longer and more involved dissertation literature review is likely to take three times as long: 54–60 hours. As the dissertation progresses, you will become much better at estimating the time that tasks take to complete. The table in section 5.2 above may be useful to give you some typical figures for some of the tasks involved in a dissertation, but they are typical only of general activities. For the planning to be successful, time estimation must be as accurate as possible.

If the WBS is completed on a spreadsheet, the production of the Gantt chart becomes much easier. The most commonly-used spreadsheet program is Microsoft Excel, but this program in standard format will not produce Gantt charts. There are, however, many free programs that can be downloaded as an add-on to Excel that allow for automatic creation of Gantt charts – see the web-link section at the end of the chapter.

REFLECTIVE ACTIVITY

A WBS WITH PROGRESS REPORT

It is never too early to start planning the progress of your dissertation. This exercise should provide you with a useful WBS that incorporates provision for displaying your progress. This will be useful for your dissertation proposal and for communicating your progress to your supervisor.

Open a new spreadsheet.

In cell a1 add a title – maybe 'Dissertation work breakdown structure with progress reporting'.

In cells a3 to e3 add the headings from the example of a WBS sheet – these are:

WBS No.	Task description	Estim. hours	Who	Resources/ Comments

In cell f3 add the heading 'Progress %'.

Highlight the columns f to q, in the header – the whole column should highlight.

Then 'Format' 'Column' 'Width', then enter '2' 'OK'.

The next instructions follow the same format for ten cells – for each one go 'Format', 'Conditional formatting', then in the box, click 'Formula Is' and in the box to the right cut and paste the following:

g6 = AND($F8>0)
h6 = AND($F8>10)
i6 = AND($F8>20)
j6 = AND($F8>30)
k6 = AND($F8>40)
l6 – AND($F8>50)

```
m6 = AND($F8>60)
n6 = AND($F8>70)
o6 = AND($F8>80)
p6 = AND($F8>90)
q6 = AND($F85100)
```

You now need to enter each individual task that will allow you to complete your dissertation. Allocate an identification number in the first cell, then fill in the task description, estimate the time to complete it, who is to do it, and add any comments or necessary resources. A typical set of dissertation tasks can be found at the Tom's Planner website: https://tomsplanner.com/?template=dissertation.

Highlight the cells g6 to q6, then 'Copy'. Highlight the cells going down the sheet until the end of your tasks list, and then 'Paste'.

You now have the basics of a WBS with a progress-reporting bar.

To display the progress add a percentage completion between 1 and 100 into the progress cell for each task.

You can finish the formatting of the sheet by bordering cells, and using colours of your own choosing.

When you have created a WBS chart in this way it is an easy task to update it once a week with progress and any extra tasks that are required. You can then use the chart to communicate progress with your supervisor. Using a WBS chart keeps you in control of the various individual elements of your dissertation and assists with its on-time completion.

There are many online resources to help with planning a dissertation. I have created a set of six blogs and a typical Gantt chart for all the stages of a dissertation. You can see these resources on the site 'Tom's Planner'™ : Link http://www.tomsplanner.com/, then click: Blogs.

5.5 SPECIALISED AREAS TO BE MANAGED

There are three specialised areas that must be managed in the majority of dissertations. That is not to say that any individual dissertation will not have some particular specialised tasks that are not represented in this book. First, successful dissertations generally manage the recording of bibliographical data in a quick, precise and efficient manner. Secondly, successful dissertations generally manage the supervision relationship in a precise and controlled manner. Finally, successful dissertations always require the meticulous reading and recording of notes.

BIBLIOGRAPHICAL DATA

Bibliographical data starts to accumulate in a dissertation from the very first moment of a topic's birth. Realising this and planning a method to trap, record, access and display this data is essential, or a very large and difficult-to-solve problem will become apparent later in the dissertation – when the average student is already very busy with the tasks of analysing data and writing up the research. Early planning will avoid this problem. There are only two approaches that can be adopted and your chosen approach may well depend on how much money you can spend, and whether you are likely to require the more sophisticated elements of bibliographical software. In my experience most students now manage their bibliography using the facilities of Word 2007 or later variants. Your awarding university will indicate which form of referencing you should use: it is very important that you conform to this requirement.

Using a Word document

In writing a dissertation you are creating an academic argument. Your argument will need extensive support from the work of other authors. Managing these sources can be difficult but Word can help in this respect. To create references and a bibliography in your dissertation you need to use the Citation and Bibliography commands of Word. Once you are familiar with how this works, you will be amazed how easy it is to keep track of your references.

You create a reference and bibliography (in Word 2007) in the following way:

At the point where you want to add the reference in your writing,

- on the **References** tab,
- click the reference style that you want: use **GOST – Name Sort**;
- click on the **Insert Citation** button;
- click on the **Add New Source** button.

In the new task pane that appears,

- choose **Type of Source – Book**;
- add the author name, title, year, city (place of publication), publisher, volume, if any;
- click on **OK**.

A reference will be entered at the text insertion point. A note of warning: **GOST – Name Sort** is as close as Microsoft can get to Harvard referencing. Later, when you produce the bibliography, you will need to change the style – but this is easy to do and is fully explained below. It does not, however, conform to the British Standard for referencing using the Harvard format. Most universities accept that the system is sound and accurate, if not totally correct, but do check with your tutor. There are now some downloadable 'plugins' that will create completely accurate Harvard referencing.

Figure 5 The Word Create Source box

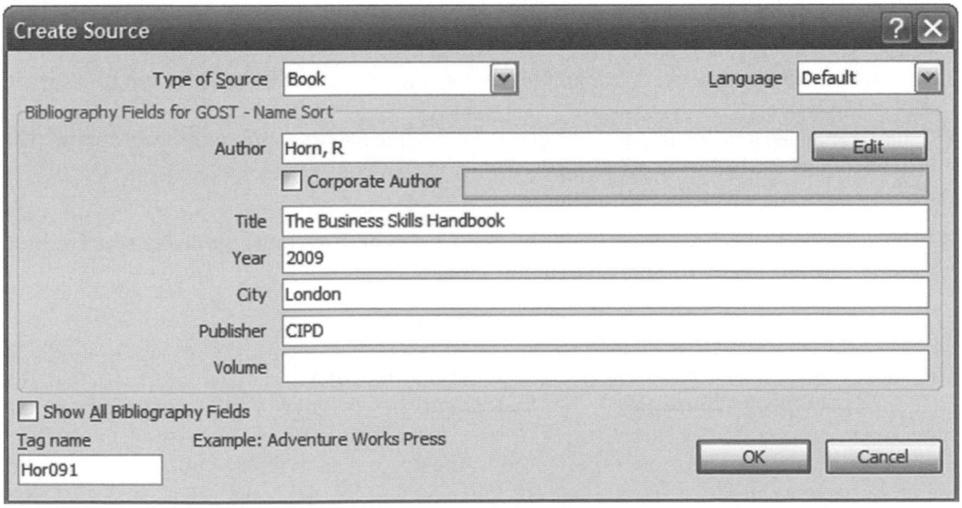

It is quicker in normal working to add a reference or citation by using the Access Key shortcuts, **Alt, S, C, S**. (Note: shortcuts are quick and accurate and mean that you do not have to take your fingers off the keyboard when you are typing.)

Once you have entered a citation or reference it will be available to use again from a list of citations once you press the **Insert Citation** command.

When your dissertation is complete, it is easy to add the bibliography at the end in the following way:

- on the **References** tab,
- change the **Style** to **APA**;
- click **Bibliography**;
- insert Bibliography.

Your bibliography is added at the insertion point in the correct alphabetical order. If you make a mistake in a reference or just want to add more and then build a new bibliography, just delete the old one and insert it again. There is one added advantage to this method. You can make your references or selected references in one document available in another document. This saves a lot of time and stress. You would do this in the following way:

- on the **References** tab,
- click **Manage Sources**;
- in the **Master List** pane copy the references you want into the **Current List** pane;
- and click **Close**.

When you add a citation in the new document the copied citations will appear in the select citation list. Referencing has never been easier. If you are looking for just one or two sources within a long list, there is a search facility at the top of the **Manage Sources** pane.

Specialist bibliography software

Specialist software to manage references, citations and bibliographies is available and has a tremendously useful range of functions. Such programs store the information in very usable forms, but can also 'collect' reference data from various sources. Most importantly, the reference data can be imported from Athens and other database search engines, and if you have existing bibliographical data in Word or Excel, these can be imported. One publisher owns three of the most familiar software packages: Endnote, Reference Manager and Procite. These all cost in excess of £100 – student versions are cheaper. Bibliographix has a very simple version that is free, and a full-function version for about £75. Refworks and Biblioscape are about £100. There are free versions of bibliographical software available – check out:

- WIKINDX, which is a free bibliographical and quotations/notes management and article authoring system
- Bibliography Writer, by Impact Software LLC: a free bibliography-writing program that makes it quick and easy to source work
- EasyBib, a web-based reference manager.

Whatever method you choose to manage this aspect of your dissertation, it makes sense to start recording this data as early in the dissertation process as possible.

MANAGING THE SUPERVISION PROCESS

The supervision process can be positive and very productive, but it is important that the relationship is effectively managed. The first essential is to know what to expect from the supervision process. In the initial stages of supervision the rules of the relationship will be negotiated. Most supervisors are experienced in the process and will have successfully helped many students to produce interesting, engaging and successful work. It is vital that you understand the context for your supervisor. The parameters within which they work are likely to be similar but not identical. Supervisors have a number of academic tasks to carry out, of which your supervision is one among a list of teaching, course administration, research, consultancy work, seeking external funding, book-writing and attending all manner of external events. Within this context the role of the supervisor generally covers the following points:

- helping to decide on an appropriate topic
- guidance as to the appropriate academic literature

- discussion and agreement of the aims and objectives of the research
- discussion and guidance on the appropriate methodology
- reviewing your draft work and providing developmental feedback
- guidance on the structure of the work
- guidance in relation to the analysis of the data
- reviewing the complete work as it nears completion.

It is important to remember that the dissertation is your work. Most supervisors give advice on your progress and on specific and general matters. It is your responsibility to weigh this advice and make your own decisions on how to proceed. The motivation and commitment to succeed must all come from you. Most supervisors view their role as that of a guide and facilitator – the journey is yours and you are responsible for its successful conclusion.

 SUPERVISOR COMMENT

I view the dissertation as the student's academic journey and my role is as the spirit guide. I am always very careful about not turning this into my idea of their journey. So the role is to make their chosen journey possible, by helping to avoid some of the potholes and get them over the hurdles.

Dissertation supervision habits of successful students

- Keep in regular contact with your supervisor. This need not be through meetings – a regular, short update by email, memo or note works well.
- Be open and reflective about feedback – not defensive.
- Send written work regularly and always before meetings.
- Ask specific questions about process and structure.
- Ensure that the written work you send is well developed and with as few spelling and grammatical errors as possible.
- Attend meetings punctually and try to avoid cancelling at short notice.
- Review any research methods materials before asking questions that have already been covered.

READING AND RECORDING SOURCE NOTES

From the moment you start reading about a possible dissertation topic you will need to record information. If you are being analytical and evaluative, as you should be, you will need to record this as well. The third strand to your note-taking must be reflective of your reading, your actions, your skills and the process of your research. This can be done in the normal manner of keeping notes in a file, but there are also more efficient electronic methods to record your notes and thinking. This section focuses on one Microsoft solution called OneNote™. OneNote looks just like a normal paper file but has all the practicalities of computer-based systems such as: sorting, mixed media content, searching, drag-and-drop organisation and electronic connection to other devices. There is a smart phone/iPad app that allows you to take notes on the move with your phone or iPad™ and integrate them into your main OneNote file.

I am not a salesman for Microsoft products but it is an accepted fact that at university and at work Microsoft's is the most frequently-found office software. Microsoft Office comes in quite a few different packages containing different combinations of software. A typical full application contains:

- Word: a word processing package
- Excel: a spreadsheet application
- PowerPoint: a presentation program

- Outlook: an organisation package
- Access: a database application.

Premium software packs also come with other less well-known software, typically:

- InfoPath 2007: data management software
- Groove 2007: team information-sharing package
- OneNote 2007: information organisation software
- Publisher 2007: software to create publications and marketing literature.

At any point in time Microsoft has a discounted version of Office that is available to students and educators for under £40.

But the one package that I believe is most valuable to dissertation writers yet also not very well known is Microsoft OneNote. The rest of this section outlines some of the features of OneNote and how you can use it to organise your university notes and learning.

At the basic level OneNote is just like a ringbinder for keeping all your notes and reflections together. But it is very hard to lose anything, and searching the mass of information is very quick and easy. In fact it is not like a ringbinder so much as like ten ringbinders. It is a large program that can easily store three years' worth of lecture, seminar data and dissertation information in a searchable form. Of course, though, when you first open OneNote it may take a short while to become acquainted with the layout.

Figure 6 The general layout of OneNote

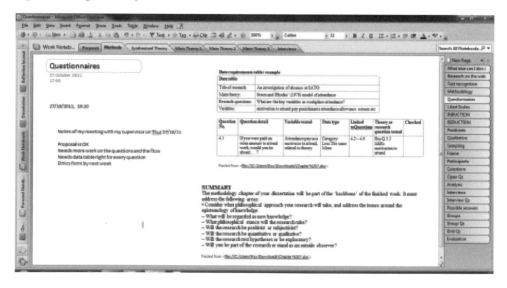

1 Separate notebooks are shown on the left-hand side. In this example the first two are called Reflective Journal and Dissertation. Each of these can be likened to a separate ringbinder.

2 Within each notebook there are tabs along the top of the window that can be likened to the dividers in a ringbinder. The figure shows the tabs What else can I do with OneNote? (this is the current page we are viewing), Proposal, Methods, Synthesised Theory, Main Theories, Interviews, and so on.

3 There are the pages under each tab (shown on the right of the window) which can be likened to the pages in each section of a ringbinder. In this example they are What else can I do with OneNote?, Research on the Web, Text recognition, and so on. There are about 23 pages on the right of the screen.

4 Any unfiled pages are placed in a special unfiled notebook section and can be filed later. This is the small pages symbol in the bottom left corner of the screen.

So the basic structure is to have notebooks listed on the left, section tabs listed across the top, and pages listed on the right. You can add a new page, section tab or notebook by right-clicking in the appropriate space and then clicking **New**. This will allow you to create one large organised set of notes and other learning-related things. OneNote saves all the changes automatically, so you do not have to think about that aspect. OneNote will also save a backup copy of your notes. By default OneNote saves the most recent copy and the one before last. You can set the number of backup copies on the **Tools** menu by clicking on **Options**, then in the **Category** table clicking **Backup** and changing the default of 2 to another number. (I would advise either 4 or 5.) But remember: these are backup copies on the same computer, so they are still vulnerable to loss.

Your notebooks are so important that you cannot rely on this backup method alone. If your computer is lost or stolen, all your notes will be lost as well. This is such an important point that I advise the following strategy.

You can access the OneNote files in the following way. Right-click the **Start** button, then **Explore All Users**, then **My Documents**, and you will find a file called **OneNote Notebooks**. Right-click this, and **Copy**. You can then **Paste** this onto a flash drive/memory stick. You now have a copy of your notebooks on a mobile memory stick. This is a backup copy – but memory sticks are easily lost or damaged, so as soon as you can, copy this file in turn to your storage area on the university computer system. Such areas are very secure and should ensure that you can easily get your Notebooks back if they are lost. You will need to do this regularly – I strongly suggest at least once per week. You would then have three copies of your Notebooks: one on your computer, one on a memory stick, and one on the university server. As an alternative, you could use Skydrive™ in conjunction with a hotmail account. This will provide guaranteed backup storage of your Microsoft files.

If you want to be totally secure, every month or so copy the OneNote folders to a CD/DVD along with any other important documents, pictures or files, and take the disc or send it home or to another address. This will provide an archive of files that you can return to in the event of any major crisis. It is unlikely that you will lose your computer, the university will burn down and you will sit on and crush your flash drive all in the same day – but you never know! Remember: you have a lot to lose.

STUDENT COMMENT: ONENOTE

This is awesome. I've had OneNote on my computer since I got it and never even once opened it, but after looking at it just now, this might be my saviour this semester where I have a whole bunch of dissertation notes and don't know what to do with them. The dissertation generates masses of information and data that is hard to control and then find the bits I need. Looks like this will beat opening Word documents and saving all of them to a folder.

Creating simple written notes

This could not be easier with OneNote. Open with a new tab and OneNote page: the cursor will be blinking in the title to this new page. Type in your title – let's say, 'Dissertation'. Then type away, recording your notes. When the topic needs to change, right-click in the page area and add new page, and continue.

For typed notes, click anywhere in the page and start typing, and a text box will open and you can record your notes. You can tab lines to show hierarchy and add bullets. You can scan lecturer's notes into the page or add e-learning resources. In this way you can use OneNote as a traditional set of typed notes. Because OneNote enables you to move things around after you have typed them, it is not difficult to alter the order of points or change the emphasis of points. You can drag and drop and format the shape of a text box.

You will need to be able to carry out a few extra commands to function effectively in OneNote.

To make the page larger so that you can add more material, use **Insert**, **Extra Writing Space**, then, when the arrow and line appear, draw it down the page to create more space.

As you add notes you can place Smart Tags that will make it easy to return to the point. The most common tags and their shortcut keys are:

- To Do: **Ctrl** +1
- Important: **Ctrl** +2
- Question: **Ctrl** +3
- Remember for later: **Ctrl** +4
- Definition: **Ctrl** +5
- Highlight: **Ctrl** +6
- Contact: **Ctrl** +7
- Address: **Ctrl** +8
- Phone number: **Ctrl** +9

The main command is **Insert**, **Tag**, then select the required Tag. A logo is added to the page related to the tag used, so you might for instance use a ? for a question, and a * for 'important'.

My general advice is to have a page for each significant source and one extra page at the beginning for the overall summary for the sources. You might like to consider using a clock index on which it might be easier to remember the main sources you are using as 'driving theory'.

To use a clock index for sources, you would have a small text box for each source that covers the title, source type, bibliography data, a short intro, the main points made and a short summary. These are placed around the points of a clock. There will be a corresponding detailed notes page for each week; you can insert hyperlinks to connect the summary in the clock index to the main page.

Searching

As your notes build up you will find the search function to be increasingly useful. So if you know that there is a reference to the work of Horn (2009) in a number of the pages, using **Search** will reveal all the incidences of this author. The search box is just above the page listing on the right of the OneNote screen. It can even find words and phrases in pictures.

Other objects in OneNote

It is not just text that you can add to OneNote. You can create fully interactive notes by incorporating some of the following:

- images and screenshots
- tables and data from other Office software
- numbered lists
- simple drawings and shapes
- audio recordings
- video recordings
- scanned documents
- handwriting, if you have a Tablet PC.

Reflective diaries

OneNote is an excellent vehicle for recording learning and reflection. You can keep a notebook that is solely focused on trapping and reflecting – in Figure 6 it is a separate notebook called Reflective Diary. As you move to the world of work it can be used to record your personal development planning and other work-related learning.

Optical character recognition

OneNote has built-in Optical Character Recognition so that pictures, web sources and video can be searched for specific items. If you have a Tablet PC or iPhone/iPad, it will also recognise handwriting.

Sharing and emailing

You can share a OneNote notebook with other students or a work team. It is also very easy to email a page of notes to other students who are also using a theory or method.

In summary, OneNote is an excellent way to organise and communicate your dissertation notes.

5.6 THE EFFECTIVE USE OF TIME

There are 168 hours in every week. No one gets any more than anyone else, and yet some people get more done than others. This section investigates some of the ideas and practices that can help you complete your dissertation. You will, if you have completed the time audit in Chapter 2, know how you spend your time at the moment, but you may have to make some adjustments to your time usage to enable you to complete a dissertation.

PROCRASTINATION

Procrastination is a common problem. We might say it is part of being human. Procrastination is normal – we all put things off, we cannot do all the things we need to do immediately, and yet after a while it does dawn on us that we are deliberately leaving things before we do them, or possibly (for the chronic procrastinator) we never do them. Dissertations can have this effect on people: people just put off doing anything until it becomes too late to complete in the time available. Perhaps if we investigate why we procrastinate, we will be able to control it better.

We don't like the process of writing. The process of writing is a slow, precise and often difficult task. Developing the skill to enjoy any task is often the key to enjoying doing that task. Take some time to analyse the skills you need to write successfully, such as generating ideas, planning writing, using sentences and phrases, reviewing the work, and condensing or expanding the writing. If you feel that for you any of these areas are not as strong as you would like, seek help from your university skills unit.

We don't like the quality of our writing work. No one who ever wrote a word actually liked what they wrote. This seems to be a truism of writing, so you need a strategy to overcome the feeling. The perfectionists among us suffer most with this problem. But ultimately the only way to overcome these feelings is to adopt the saying 'It is as good as I can get it in the time available,' implying that you will come back and improve it at a later point. You may come back and work on it again – most writers do – but this little saying allows you to write with some freedom from the feeling that the words are not good enough.

Practical concerns distract us. There are commonly two camps relating to this problem. Either clear all the distractions and then start writing, or ignore distractions as not as important as getting this chapter of the work complete. I personally fall into the former camp. I have to deal with all the little chores, emails and other stuff, and only then do I feel I have a long period to write without worrying about any other thing.

We are looking for perfection. If you are someone who wants everything to be absolutely right, perfect, you might think about these seven steps to achieving *or avoiding* perfection.

- Step 1 – First, acknowledge your real goals. Is perfection necessary and appropriate?
- Step 2 – What is the cost of perfection? Getting one thing perfect invariably means that lots of other things are done very poorly or not at all.
- Step 3 – Next, substitute a more realistic, more attainable goal, such as creating good-quality academic work, a B grade rather than an A grade.
- Step 4 – Use 'to do' lists and set priorities, but also set maximum allowable times.
- Step 5 – Review the to do list daily and adjust the time you are willing to spend on a task. Don't be afraid to say 'That is enough time spent on that task – it is good enough.' It will then drop off the to do list.
- Step 6 – Every week consider the regular tasks you have to do. Is it really necessary to do all these tasks this often? Could cleaning the kitchen (for example) be done every two weeks rather than every week?
- Step 7 – Learn to delegate a task, and accept the quality of the outcome. For instance, if you have a number of interviews to transcribe and one of your family offers to help, let them do the transcript and only comment to say how grateful you are for their help.

We are lazy – we are human, and unless you are some sort of super-person, we are all lazy to lesser and greater degrees. Sometimes we need to stop and do nothing, go for a walk, sit in front of the television, go for a drink. If you have followed the other sections looking at time, motivation, and effective working, you may have lazy periods, but they will not last very long. The reward of completing the work, and having all the time you are currently spending on the dissertation available for other enjoyments is quite a strong motivator.

We are fearful of something.

STUDENT COMMENT

I find it so easy not to do any university work. I can go for weeks without once opening my books or doing any dissertation stuff. There is always something else to do! As I found, you cannot go on like that. Unfortunately, it took a very nasty experience to snap me out of my procrastination.

I was called into university and issued with a major warning about missed deadlines and not attending lectures. The ultimatum was 'shape up' or you will be 'sent down' – thrown out, in normal language. My tutor, as part of the 'survival' actions, did put me on a university skills course for procrastination called DO IT NOW STUPID! – Right Now!

Fear of failure – if we fear that our work isn't going to be good enough this can stop us starting it. Universities are very good at the development of skills and people, so be assured that if your work isn't quite good enough at the draft stage, there will be help and advice to improve it. Success is often about sticking at a task rather than being successful immediately.

Fear of success – success brings with it expectations, and if we are once successful, the bar will be raised forever and we may not be able to reach such heights again. We may also fear that success will become addictive, that once we have tasted it we will become workaholics to taste it again.

Fear of being alone – the procrastinator who fears being alone does nothing so that someone or maybe even several people will come and help them. So doing nothing ensures that help will arrive.

Fear of attachment – some procrastinators fear being reliant on others. They fail to progress any work so that their chaotic lack of progress puts other people off from helping.

Finally, there can be major problems if you believe that you can do only one thing at a time. Everyone has many things to do in a day, week, month or year, and the ability to carry out these tasks in a planned and sequenced manner is vital to successfully completing a dissertation. Even the one task of completing a dissertation has many elements that must be carried out in some sort of sequence. This area is dealt with later under the heading 'The myth of multi-tasking'.

How to avoid procrastination

Work out when it is that you tend to procrastinate. We do not all avoid the same things. If you keep a diary, note down in the diary when you think you really should be getting on with a task and what task you are avoiding. I imagine that cleaning the student kitchen may be high on most people's agenda for procrastination, but I mean the avoidance of academic tasks. A lot of people start to feel that they have other more important things to do when they have to start writing – all academics dread the blank sheet of paper. However, by the time I have written a hundred words I am enjoying the writing, and those hundred words don't matter. I often end up deleting them. I know some colleagues who also start by typing the same, or roughly the same, 100–200 words. It becomes like an easy warm-up.

After the writing process has started, the procrastination is gone, and often many hours of work are completed. Once you know the pattern of your procrastination and the tasks you are avoiding, you will be in a better position to control it. If the problem is at certain times, it could well be that you are not doing the quality tasks at your 'prime time' – everyone has a prime time in a day, week or month. Learn when these times are and use them to do the most demanding work. If the problem is task-related, you need a strategy to encourage you to start:

- a small reward when you get started
- a light warm-up technique – as above
- kid yourself by saying, 'I will just review what I wrote yesterday'. Invariably, when you have done this, you carry on writing
- the promise of a reward at the end of the task
- ensure that you are intending to work in your prime time
- create a pleasant and welcoming environment.

Other techniques to help avoid procrastination

Use reminders so that a task cannot be forgotten. Set your phone or computer to remind you. Leave notes in prominent places. Post electronic sticky notes on your desktop. Create priority lists so that the important academic tasks feature at the top of the list – Microsoft Outlook or a personal digital assistant (PDA) can help with this. Try to underestimate the amount of time any task will take: it is the idea that maybe you do not have time to complete the task that stops you from starting it. Many 'effective' people significantly underestimate how long a task will take, but once started, it does not matter.

Make an outline plan of what you will write, then add the headings to a document so that when you do start it is easy to make progress. This is another 'delusion' strategy, in that once the plan and the headings are produced you will often continue on to do some writing.

Avoid the 'distraction' problem, where the tasks you procrastinate about are left because you carry on doing a task you like. The most common academic 'distraction' task is researching going on and on when there is no need for more information, while the task of writing is avoided.

The myth of multi-tasking

You often hear people say, in a triumphant sort of way, that they can multi-task. It is true that human rather than computer multi-tasking can be done. Many people can iron and watch the television at the same time, read and talk at the same time, walk and think at the same time. However, academic multi-tasking requiring your full attention and thinking is not possible. Yet in a student life there are many academic things that must be completed. If you can only work on one task until it is completed and then move on to the next task, your ability to use your time effectively is very limited. Why is this so?

Task-fatigue sometimes becomes a problem after several hours' doing the same thing. We require a varied diet of activity to stop this happening. So if you are only working on one aspect of your university work, when task-fatigue occurs, stop your academic work and do a non-academic task (maybe clean that kitchen).

Creativity works to a cycle of preparation, incubation, illumination and verification. Once the cycle has been completed, fatigue sets in and the ideas become poorer.

Personal motivation to continue lessens as we spend time on the task, so after a while we just choose to stop – often described as being bored with it.

If multi-tasking is not possible for academic work, how could we organise our use of time to relieve some of the negative effects attributed to time on the task. In trying to explain this to my

Figure 7 Intermittent parallel tasking

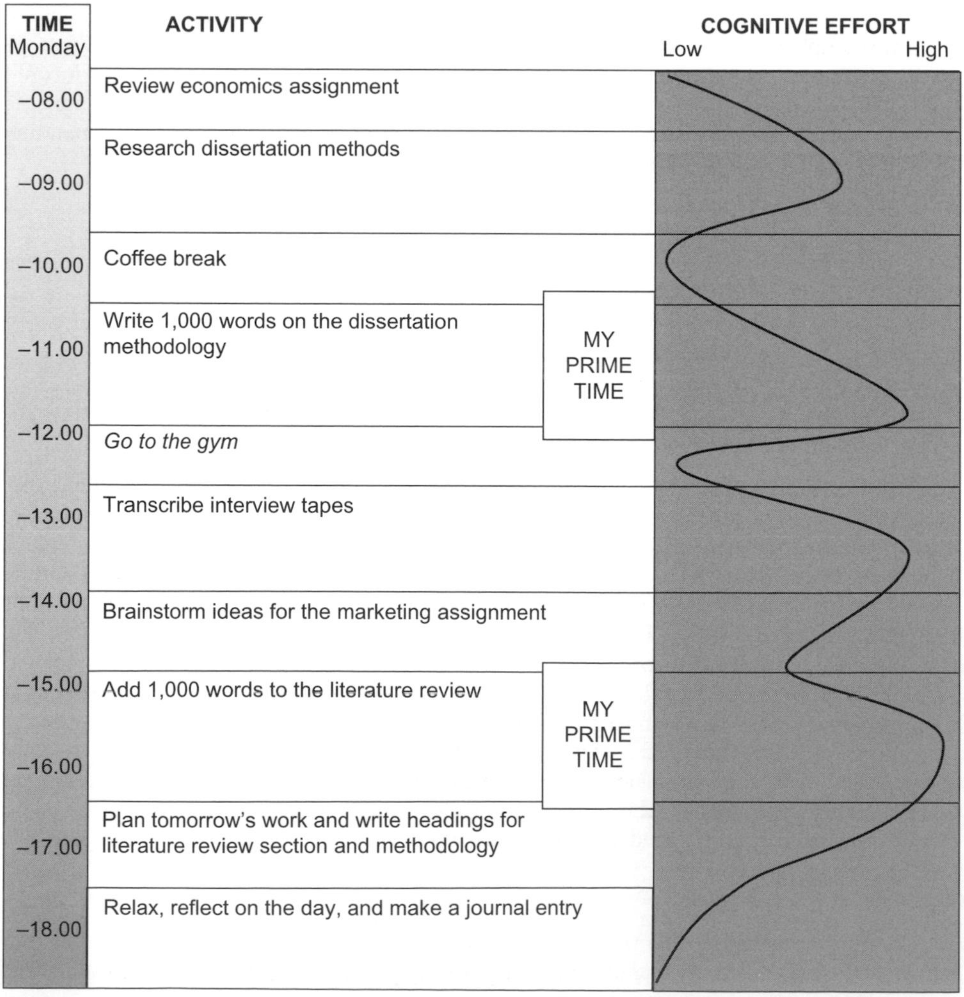

TIME Monday	ACTIVITY	COGNITIVE EFFORT Low — High
–08.00	Review economics assignment	
–09.00	Research dissertation methods	
–10.00	Coffee break	
–11.00	Write 1,000 words on the dissertation methodology	MY PRIME TIME
–12.00	Go to the gym	
–13.00	Transcribe interview tapes	
–14.00	Brainstorm ideas for the marketing assignment	
–15.00	Add 1,000 words to the literature review	MY PRIME TIME
–16.00		
–17.00	Plan tomorrow's work and write headings for literature review section and methodology	
–18.00	Relax, reflect on the day, and make a journal entry	

own students I have started to call the approach 'intermittent parallel tasking'. It is founded on the two major principles that we can only do one academic task at a time, and that task-fatigue has to be avoided.

Figure 7 uses Monday as an example. The basic principles are:

- Only one task can be carried out at a time.
- The cognitive effort has to vary throughout the day to avoid fatigue.
- The tasks requiring the highest cognitive effort must be carried out during your 'prime time'.
- Plan the next cycle of activity (days, in this case) during the previous cycle.
- Create structures for writing in the previous cycle so that when you resume work you can progress immediately.

When you look at the cognitive effort chart in Figure 7 you can see why the process is described as 'intermittent' – the more difficult cognitive tasks are well spread out throughout the day. If you analyse any procrastination that you feel, and try to adopt techniques for avoiding it, you will be able to generate and use more productive time. The next section considers ways to use the small spaces of time between the major activities of a day.

Making use of small passages of time

Dissertations are made up of a number of major tasks and a lot of smaller, less time-consuming tasks. One way to effectively use the time available to you is to become proficient at completing the smaller tasks in the short passages of time between more major activities. You will need a strategy to facilitate this approach. Because most of our academic work is completed on

Figure 8 Screen shot of five task notes for completion

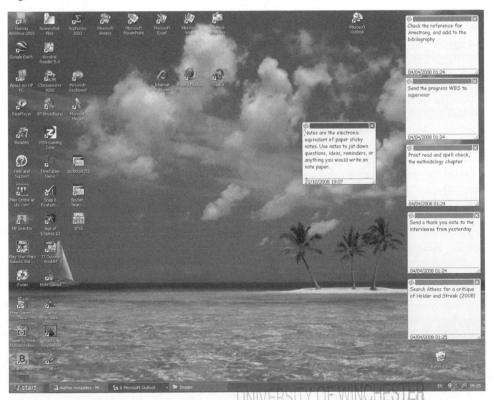

computers, the computer is the interface where we should facilitate the effective use of these small packages of time. In Microsoft Outlook you can post notes onto your desktop.

At the beginning of each day, then, post notes for five small dissertation tasks onto your desktop. During the day when you have a few spare minutes, complete one of the small tasks and remove the note. If any tasks remain at the end of the day, you should judge their urgency and either complete them or carry them over to the next day. As you become more familiar with this technique you can increase the number of small tasks to 10 per day. A variation on this technique is to split up more major tasks into 10 small tasks so that you will be able to complete some larger tasks using time that would otherwise be wasted.

5.7 USING ELECTRONIC MEANS TO SUBMIT ON TIME

There are many electronic devices to help you successfully organise the tasks required to complete a dissertation. The most important point to stress is that arranging some sort of system to ensure that tasks are completed on time will go a long way towards completing successfully and on time. Broadly, there are three mediums to organise the work required to complete a dissertation. Some people are comfortable and effective using pen-and-paper methods. If this is your preferred approach, you will have to create a WBS chart on paper, listing the tasks needed to complete the dissertation, and keep track of progress manually.

Probably the most frequently-used organising software is Microsoft Outlook, and the information that follows refers to this software. If your preferred software is different from this, the information should nonetheless transfer for use with any organising software. Controlling your diary, contacts, setting tasks and dealing with email are all possible with Outlook, and this section sets out ways to use these facilities as tools to assist with on-time completion.

In the main window of Outlook there is a menu bar that contains **Inbox**, **Calendar**, **Contacts**, **Task**, **Journal**, **Notes** and a **Waste** bin. Because versions of Microsoft Outlook differ in the detail of how they operate and how you set up various processing for each of those sections, you may need to refer to the assistance in the **Help** menu.

When you start using Outlook, set up a 'Personal Folder File': use these words in the **Help** menu and follow the instructions.

Then set up the 'Remote Mail' setting to access your email account. This will allow you to use the data in Outlook, such as **Contacts**, to speed your email processes. Again, use **Help** and follow the instructions.

You may be using a PDA or phone. Most PDAs, iPads, and phones come with software that allows you to link to Outlook. You'll have to load that software, and synchronise the **Calendar** in Outlook to the calendar on the device. You will be working on your computer for long periods while you complete your dissertation, so it will make you more efficient if you use the Outlook program as the hub of your activity. If you are not using a phone, PDA or Tablet, enter the contacts from your diary into the **Calendar** function of Outlook, and then work from this going forward.

If you want to develop Outlook as your main dissertation hub separately from your personal organisation, then only add contacts from your address book that relate to the dissertation. If you are using a device, you will be able to upload the contacts data into Outlook.

After maybe an hour of setting up work, you will have Outlook functioning in a reasonably practical manner relating to your contacts, email and diary. The sections below look in more detail at setting and using tasks, the journal, and sticky notes.

Controlling tasks, as this chapter has been explaining, is the main issue for on-time completion. You will probably have developed a WBS chart in one of the earlier activities – now is the time to convert that into a more interactive and controlled set of tasks in Outlook. If you developed your WBS in Excel, open it now so that you can transfer the data into Outlook. Click on the task shortcut on the menu bar. In the top left corner click on **New Task** – a window will open. Add a short title name to the box. Set the start date and then the due date from the data in the WBS chart. Set the status, priority and progress made. Set a reminder date and time. Finally, cut and paste the detail of the task and the comments into the main window. The first task is now complete: click **Save**, and close.

Now enter each of the other WBS chart entries into an Outlook task. You may find as you enter the data that you want to refine a task or split a task into smaller components, or discover that there are tasks you omitted from the WBS chart. When the data is entered, you should have a well-structured set of tasks with built-in monitoring. The tasks will need further refining as the dissertation progresses, but this should take less than one hour a week.

Figure 9 Screenshot of Outlook task

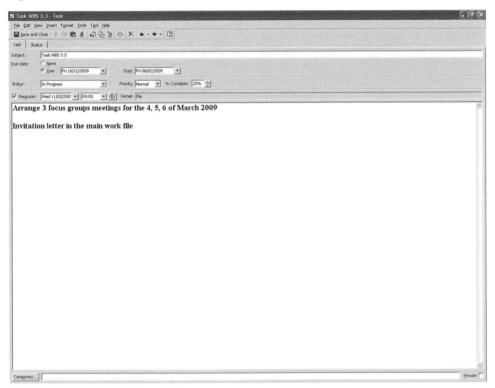

As a researcher, keeping a journal is a valuable technique to record successes, difficulties, thoughts, details of activities and ideas for improvements. Outlook or other devices can help with this aspect of your research. The first very useful function in Outlook Journal is the automatic recording of events in the journal. All the following information, duties and programs can be automatically recorded in the journal.

- email message
- meeting request
- meeting response
- task request
- task response
- Microsoft Access
- Microsoft Excel
- Microsoft Office Binder
- Microsoft PowerPoint
- Microsoft Word.

You can set each of these options in the **Tools, Options, Journal** menu.

It is important to consider what type of entry you are adding to the journal, as the main access to your entries is by the type of document. The following can be added:

- all Office documents, Word, etc
- emails
- conversations
- tasks
- notes
- phonecalls
- letters
- fax.

You must be consistent in your use of journal entry types to enable efficient retrieval of the data.

Finally, the posting of notes in prominent positions was covered in section 5.6 under the heading of using small passages of time. The simple Post-It note can be a very efficient motivator and organiser. Following the non-procrastination techniques described earlier in the chapter, the final task of one day might well be to plan the next day's activities. Using Outlook and posting notes on the desktop for each activity that has to be completed is very motivational and somewhat addictive. First, having the activities organised the day before assists with an effective start to the following day. It is very motivational as the notes disappear consecutively during the day, until at last the final task is complete and you can relax.

5.8 THE MAIN BARRIERS TO ON-TIME COMPLETION

There is remarkably very little research concerning the barriers to completing dissertations on time and the overall rates of completion of UK university dissertations. An American survey (Rivera, Levine and Wright, 2005) of 138 medicine 'residents' (medical students) successfully completing projects on time discovered the following themes for success:

- Start early.
- Set aside adequate time.
- Adhere to a timeline.
- Work with a strong mentor (or supervisor, in the UK system).
- Choose a research topic that genuinely interests you.
- Keep the project simple yet innovative.

Residents' suggestions about how their programmes could more effectively facilitate scholarly activity were:

- Provide adequate amounts of protected time.
- Improve the technical resources available to residents.
- Enhance or establish a research curriculum.
- Match trainees with appropriate mentors.
- Make funding available to those who need it.
- Provide encouragement.

SAM AND ALEX

CASE STUDY

Sam and Alex had known each other for some time, but Sam had never been to Alex's flat. On that day, however, Sam met Alex in the coffee shop and they chatted about 'stuff'. To Sam, Alex seemed a bit depressed.

Sam: 'You look a bit down.'

Alex: 'I'm OK. I am having trouble with my dissertation.'

Sam: 'What's the trouble?'

Alex: 'It's a mess. I can't do any more of it. I am finished. I am going to drop out and go and do something more enjoyable.'

Sam: 'Wow! That's a big step. That course cost you £36,000, didn't it?'

Alex: 'Yes, it did. That's true.'

> (A slight moistening comes to Alex's eye.)

Sam: 'Can I help?'

Alex: 'I doubt it.'

Sam: 'Go on! I'd like to help!'

Alex: 'Well, come back to the flat and take a look at it.'

On entering the flat Sam was a bit surprised. The kitchen was covered in dirty dishes and old food. Using the loo it was impossible not to notice the mountain of empty toilet-roll centres made into a pyramid – maybe 60 or 70 of them altogether. In the little office that Alex used there were piles of papers on the desk. Some sheets had evidently fallen off their piles and lay wherever they had slipped to on the floor. Picking up one of them up, Sam noticed that it was a printout of a journal article. Then Sam realised that all the papers on desk and floor were the same – full text printouts of journal articles. 'A thorough literature search', thought Sam. On the corner of the desk was a card index,

each card representing a book or journal that Alex had read. There were probably 500 cards.

Sam: 'What's with the cards?'

Alex: 'My dad said that was the way he kept his bibliography.'

Sam: 'Wow! How much of the dissertation have you done?'

Alex: 'I haven't written a thing since the proposal.'

Sam: 'Nothing at all?'

Alex: 'No, nothing. I've just read a lot of stuff.'

Sam: 'When will you be getting some data?'

Alex: (shrugging) 'I dunno!'

Sam: 'How long have you got to finish?'

Alex: 'Three months.'

Sam: 'Hey – that's do-able! Just get on with it and get organised.'

Alex: (laughing) 'That may be the problem!'

Sam: 'No! It can be done – and you have all the basic reading done ...'

Alex: 'I haven't even spoken to my tutor for four months. She probably thinks I've left already.'

Sam: 'No! No! You just need to get organised! I can help you with that.'

To think about ...

Take on the role of Sam and help Alex finish in the three months he has left.

1   Prepare an action plan that addresses all the necessary tasks.

2   Set out the personal issues that Alex must address.

3   What areas of the dissertation can helpful friends or family tackle?

SUMMARY

Developing effective dissertation habits early in your dissertation process will largely determine how successful you will be.

- Consider how long your dissertation will take to complete by thinking about:
    - how much time you can set aside for the dissertation each week
    - the likely tasks to be completed
    - how long each task will take
    - whether you can get help to complete some of the tasks
    - creating a detailed WBS chart
    - contingencies for unforeseen distractions and delays.
- Early organisation of some of the key components will lead to success:
    - bibliographical data
    - the supervision process
    - adopting the habits of successful people
    - managing and monitoring the completion of tasks.
- Develop effective habits for using time:
    - avoid procrastination
    - learn to use your best study times for the most challenging work
    - plan and organise
    - try out the idea of intermittent parallel tasking
    - learn to use small passages of time.
- Using software to assist in the dissertation process will help you towards on-time completion:
    - Microsoft Outlook
    - convert your WBS chart to Outlook with reminders
    - make effective use of posting notes
    - make use of a journal.
- Know the key elements for on-time completion:
    - start early
    - set aside adequate time
    - adhere to a timeline
    - work with a strong supervisor/ mentor
    - choose a research topic that genuinely interests you
    - keep the project simple yet innovative.

KEY LEARNING POINTS

EXPLORE FURTHER

Applegarth, M. and Posner, K. (2008) *The Project Management Pocketbook*, revised edition. Alresford: Management Pocketbooks

Neville, C. and Broome, M. R. (2007) *The Complete Guide to Referencing and Avoiding Plagiarism*. Milton Keynes: Open University Press

Rivera, J., Levine, R. and Wright, S. (2005) 'Completing a scholarly project during residency training: perspectives of residents who have been successful', *Journal of General Internal Medicine*, Vol. 20, No. 4: 366–69

Weblinks

Tom's Planner – excellent easy-to-use Gantt chart software: http://www.tomsplanner.com/

A brief tutorial on Gantt charts: http://www.me.umn.edu/courses/me4054/

Details of bibliography production: http://office.microsoft.com/en-us/word/

Free download of Gantt chartbuilder for Excel at PC World: http://www.pcworld.com/downloads/ file_download/fid,62196-order,2-page,1-c,spreadsheet/download.html#

Gantt chart Excel template from Microsoft: http://office.microsoft.com/en-us/templates/TC300003501033.aspx

CHAPTER 6

Theory and Literature

What will I learn in this chapter?

- The importance of the literature review
- How your own exploration of the literature fits into the sea of knowledge
- Sources of literature and theory
- How to evaluate sources
- The role of critique and evaluation
- Strategies for controlling the literature review
- The links from literature to method and analysis

6.1 INTRODUCTION

In any dissertation there is a set of chapters that might be described as the 'backbone' of the work. I regard the backbone of a dissertation to be the literature, the method and the data analysis. Chapters 6, 7 and 8 deal with this 'backbone'. The analogy with a backbone is useful in a number of ways. All the other sections hang from these important chapters. Without a strong backbone it is difficult for the dissertation to be successful. Many dissertations carry out some primary research and use either a quantitative survey approach or a qualitative approach often involving interviews. This chapter is mainly channelled to this approach, but also recognises the diversity of dissertation research including secondary research, experiments, observation, critical reviews and analysis of large data sets.

The aim of this chapter is to explore the processes, procedures and outputs of a typical literature review. If your research has adopted a unique or unusual stance, you will have to modify the ideas presented here, but a substantial and critical link to a body of literature is always required. The early part of the chapter investigates the importance of the literature review and the possible sources of literature. Developing a critical and evaluative stance is a very important part of literature reviews and is explored and expanded on throughout the chapter. A section looks at the practical issues around reading, recording and writing such a large body of knowledge. Finally, the important links from the literature to the method and the data analysis are explored.

The best way to use this chapter is to read the sections on the importance of the literature review and the section on sources before you complete the research proposal. As the literature review develops, use the sections relating to the academic funnel, critique, evaluation and the relationship of the literature to methodology.

6.2 THE IMPORTANCE OF THE LITERATURE REVIEW

As noted above, the literature review may be regarded as part of the 'backbone' of the dissertation, and just as most mammals would not function without a backbone, so dissertations cannot be successful without strong and critical literature reviews. There are other important aspects to reviewing the literature, and these are explored below.

SUPPORTING AND EMBEDDING YOUR DISSERTATION WITH KNOWN THEORY AND RESEARCH

Any approach or knowledge you bring to your research will have been discovered in the process of your reading and learning. The literature review must revisit this learning and test the accuracy of what is known, explore it critically, and evaluate its worth. Your topic area will have been developed from what you know or what you have read. This reading may not have been critical and evaluative, but a literature review must be both of these things. As your reading, recording and thinking about known theory develops, the place of your research will be embedded in that reading and knowledge. The knowledge as represented by theory, research and the critical writing of others will also support your research. It is possible thus to think of your research as a pearl, slowly growing in an oyster – a small rock pool protects the oyster, and the rock pool is a small extension of a large ocean. Your research as a pearl needs protection and support from a large and violent ocean of knowledge and activity: without protection it will be swept away.

PROVING YOU KNOW THE RESEARCH AREA

Your literature review will display to your tutors and other readers of your work that you know the theory and knowledge that applies to an area of research. Even a cursory investigation of a topic should reveal the 'common' ways in which any phenomenon is analysed or grounded.

REFLECTIVE ACTIVITY

PRACTICE IN ANALYSING

Choose one of the following topics:

- Motivation
- Diversity
- The glass ceiling
- Leadership

Spend exactly 60 minutes investigating your chosen topic, using 20 minutes to read textbooks, 20 minutes searching websites, and 20 minutes reading journal sources. As you read, summarise using a mind map, so that at the end of the 60-minute period you have an outline of the theory, knowledge and approaches used in the study of the chosen topic. It is important to only skim-read and record the headline theory, research and ideas.

The knowledge you must display in the literature review will have to be more extensive than any you pick up when doing the *Practice in analysing* Reflective Activity, but the activity is designed to show how every topic is located in a body of knowledge. Your knowledge of the area you are researching will be assessed when your dissertation is submitted, and the literature review is the ideal place to display that you are familiar with the body of knowledge related to your dissertation.

PROVIDING AN OPPORTUNITY TO DISPLAY THE SKILLS OF ANALYSIS, CRITIQUE AND EVALUATION

As noted in Chapter 3, your dissertation will be assessed against a set of criteria that includes analysis, critique and evaluation. The literature review provides an opportunity to display those skills and accrue marks for doing so. Quickly review Chapter 3 so that you are familiar with each of the skills. You will have to check the assessment criteria for dissertations in your university, but typically, critique, analysis and evaluation should take up about half the words in a literature review.

REFLECTIVE ACTIVITY

SKILLS MARK-UP

Once you have written a section of the literature review, print out the section and lay the work in sheets on a large table. Using three different-coloured highlighters mark up the areas that you consider are:

- critical

- analytical

- evaluative.

When you have finished the *Skills mark-up* Reflective Activity, according to the general rubric, half your work should be highlighted. If more than half of the text is highlighted, well done – you are consistently displaying the right level of critique, analysis and evaluation. If less than half your work is highlighted, you need to investigate which areas are not being displayed. It is relatively common for the evaluative areas to be quite low, but the critique areas should be high, and the analysis area should represent at least 15% of your writing. If a low proportion of your writing is highlighted, you must revisit the work and look at ways to be more critical, analytical and evaluative. There is some help and guidance on this in Chapter 3 and later in this chapter. This Reflective Activity can be usefully employed a number of times as your literature review develops. It then acts as a useful diagnostic and eventually as a summative indicator.

PROVIDING THE BUILDING BLOCKS OF METHOD, METHODOLOGY AND DATA ANALYSIS

As your literature review progresses, you will discover theory and other research that can lead directly or indirectly to important areas of your dissertation. The dominant philosophical approach will quickly become apparent in any study of literature around a topic. For instance, if your topic is absence management, the associated knowledge and research that you investigate will have a predominantly deductive stance. A deductive approach assumes and uses known facts and properties to form an argument or statement. Such an argument might be that lots of short-term absence corresponds to malingering. From the literature review the predominant approach will surface, but this approach does not have to be accepted. It is possible to adopt the normal approach, or to reject it and argue that important new insights will arise if the opposite inductive approach is adopted for your study. The important element is to be able to argue what the predominant approach is and why your work will adopt it or reject it.

In any research area there will have been studies that have developed a common method. This common method can be accepted and used by your own research, or you can develop a new or hybrid method. In some areas there will be a well-developed research instrument – maybe a questionnaire or interview schedule. (We often use the word 'instrument' for the detailed method of research.) If your research were to investigate stress at work, for instance, you would soon discover that there are a number of competing questionnaires to measure stress at work. Using a well-developed instrument can have a lot of advantages. It often saves time because the instrument is already in existence and there will already be sets of data and analysis from other research. Your literature review should seek out these commonly-used methods – it shows that you are up to date with the area and it may also provide more reliable data and save time. The most likely source of this type of information is journal articles, but many of the professional websites such as those of the Chartered Institute of Personnel and Development (the CIPD) and the Health and Safety Executive (the HSE) have reports of commissioned research. These have a lot of information about method and data analysis as well as the data results of the research.

The literature will feature a range of ways in which data from research in an area has been analysed. Quantitative data obtained from research and the analysis of that data involving some commonly-used statistical tools are to be found in any journal article that represents quantitative research. The analysis of qualitative data is a lot more varied. A literature review will discover a vast array of different methods, and therefore of data forms derived from qualitative research. These varied data-gathering techniques also give rise to a vast array of techniques of data analysis, which are dealt with specifically in the next chapter.

OFFERING A PERSPECTIVE ON YOUR RESEARCH

For the majority of research on business, human resources and personal topics there is more literature than you will be able to read. The literature review also reveals to the reader a lot about your thinking around a subject or topic. For every source of information you come across you will make a decision about how useful the source is in developing both the research and your eventual argument. You must select the sources you represent in the literature review carefully in order to display a wide range of approaches to your topic, a representative set of methods and data analysis, and a coherent and broad set of philosophical underpinnings. Through this selection process a reader of your work will be able – easily – to read your stance on the topic area. They will also read things into the literature you have included and those sources you have not included. Take the example of absence management that was used before: there are lots of studies on this topic. If you include and comment and critique a number of quantitative studies, the reader of your work will assume you are a numerate person, comfortable with interpreting and analysing quantitative data. If, on the other hand, you do not represent any of the quantitative studies in your literature – even if you then argue that they do not assist the research – the reader will assume you are not numerate. Your literature review will allow readers of your work to form an opinion about you as a researcher, and also allow your tutors to judge your work.

PROVIDING KNOWLEDGE OF SECONDARY SOURCES

The literature review is the place to include any secondary sources that you will use in the research study. You may be planning a comparative study of stress in one organisation – an approach to this would be to compare the organisation with a known group of people.

Secondary sources can also be used to support your argument, or in a reflective stance, to provide evidence of competing or different positions. On the HSE website referred to in *The HSE and stress* Reflective Activity there are a set of Management Standards – these suggest the use of the Indicator Tool. If your research recommendations suggest some form of organisational monitoring, the point is supported by the HSE Management Standards. In business, HR and human research there is often extensive secondary research from reliable sources which can be used to inform the process of your own research.

THE HSE AND STRESS

The following Web address is the Health and Safety Executive's stress data page: http://www.hse.gov.uk/statistics/causdis/stress/age.htm .
Click on the link to Occupation and industry. Click on the link to STROCC2_3YR.
You will now have a table of data from 2007–2010 showing stress by occupation.

See if you can answer these questions:

- Who are the most stressed employees in this group?

- What does the abbreviation C.I. stand for?

- If you were carrying out research on workplace stress, how could you use these figures in your own research?

PROVIDING A SYNTHESIS OF LITERATURE THAT CAN BRING NEW INSIGHTS TO AN AREA OF RESEARCH

When you bring together the efforts of a literature review, it often provides a new insight or view of a research area. The most potent elements for providing new insights are where ideas and approaches from one subject or research area are brought into another. For instance, some researchers have brought in the concept of spirituality as a dimension of stress control and regulation. Brian Luke Seaward investigates this idea in his book *Essentials of Managing Stress*. If in your literature review you became aware of this book, you would possibly include elements of spirituality and soul in a research study on workplace stress. In any literature review it is these unforeseen connections of ideas that create new ways of seeing a problem. My illustrative example is meant to be dramatic – the synthesis you display in a dissertation need not be dramatic, but you should look out for new ways of combining ideas.

6.3 THE LITERATURE REVIEW PROCESS

Most dissertation researchers will not have produced a large critical review of literature before starting on the dissertation literature review. However, they will have completed smaller reviews of literature, and the experience of this will be useful, but their methods of working on that will require adaptation to serve the needs of a dissertation.

STRENGTHS AND WEAKNESSES

Spend 15–20 minutes reflecting on the literature review process you have followed for assignments, and examinations. Consider the following areas and indicate whether you feel each is a strength or a weakness:

- finding information

- knowing what is important and what to include

- controlling the amount of information

- recording what has been read and what is important

- understanding the information you have found

- being critical of the theories, research, ideas

- evaluating the literature.

PRIMARY AND SECONDARY SOURCES

Primary sources are those that contain data collected for the purposes of the published research. Secondary sources are those that contain data from another research study. It is the principal source of data that determines the category. If a study collects data from respondents, it is a primary source, even if it also has some secondary sources reported in the findings. If research does not collect any data from respondents, it is a secondary source. Avoid using these terms in relation to literature. The characteristics of primary and secondary relate to research and the reports of research, not to literature.

THE ACADEMIC FUNNEL

The literature review can usefully be thought of as an academic funnel – see Figure 10 – in which a lot of information goes in at the top and one consistent stream of literature comes out at the bottom. What is likely to go in at the top of the funnel? Theories – for most literature reviews there is some established theory relating to the topic. Often, there are competing theories. These are all added to the academic funnel to display your breadth of knowledge. Research studies should also be added to the funnel. Any research directly related to your topic should likewise be added. If there is a lot of research that has been conducted in your topic area, it may be better to add a meta-analysis of the research rather than the original sources. Add journal articles that relate to your topic – these can be in any of three main forms: articles reporting new research findings, critical reviews of literature, and articles relating to management practice. Data sets from previous research can also be included in the academic funnel, and in well-researched areas there will be meta-data-sets. Most research will have all of the things listed put within the academic funnel, but specific research will also put in some of the other sources discussed later in the chapter.

Figure 10 The academic funnel

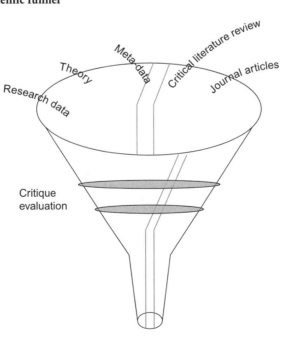

Synthesised theory

The funnel can also have filters added, such as critique and evaluation. In this way the funnel takes in a lot of diverse information, filters it through a screen of critique and evaluation so that only the best and most appropriate theory, ideas and research comes out of the funnel, and weaker or inappropriate material is caught in the filter. Your literature review will thus start with a wide range of sources, data and documents and produce 'synthesised theory' that can be used to guide your research, drive the method, and provide a framework for the data analysis.

The attributes of synthesised theory are:

- It is relevant to the aims and objectives and the study.
- It has been critically considered and regarded as good research, theory or data.
- It is selective – it only includes work directly related to the research.
- It is concise, from evaluation, using the best theory for the research study.
- It identifies and addresses gaps in the literature.
- It is comprehensive – it covers the important literature, while also being concise.
- It is well-written and well-argued.
- It is up to date in that it reviews the latest literature.

HOW TO PROCEED

Many readers will have an established way of carrying out a literature review – but for those who have not, the following section deals with the basic mechanics of the process.

Assuming you have established your dissertation title and completed the proposal, you will have a small section of the literature review already written. At this stage, it is worth putting that aside and working from the beginning. Your topic title, the aims and the objectives must be constantly in your mind during this process.

REFLECTIVE ACTIVITY

EVER BEFORE YOU

Search your dissertation proposal and find the aim, the objectives, the research questions and the hypotheses where they are listed.

Cut and paste them all onto a new document together.

Adjust the page orientation to landscape, and increase the font size until the page is full.

Print out four copies, and place one in each of the following positions:

- on the bottom edge of the computer screen
- in your bathroom
- in your office space
- in your briefcase or bag.

This is not quite as trivial as it may seem at first. You will be amazed at the focusing and motivating effect of this simple idea.

According to Rowley and Slack (2004) there are five steps in the creation of a literature review:

1 scanning the document sources
2 making notes
3 structuring the literature review
4 writing the literature review
5 building the bibliography.

These steps are a sound way to proceed. The next sections explore the detailed process of carrying out the literature review.

SCANNING THE LITERATURE

First, investigating a topic area can seem a very daunting task. It may look as if you will never be able to find enough information on your dissertation area – and then it soon becomes apparent, at least with most topics, that there is too much information. You will have to come up with a strategy that takes account of the important literature and ignores the less important work. Because the literature review is a time-consuming, involved and iterative process, you will also need a strategy that will see the work accomplished in about 6–10 weeks of, perhaps, 16–24 hours per week.

Figure 11 A strategy for searching the literature

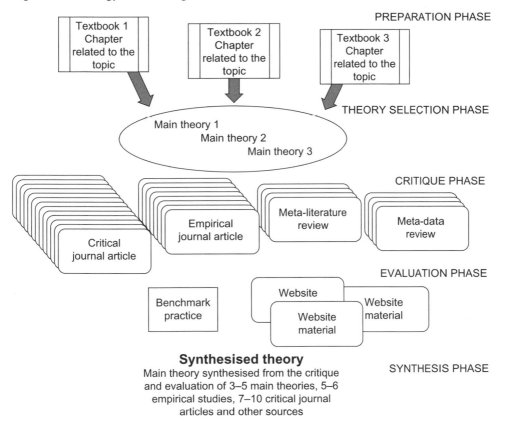

The preparation phase involves reading around your topic from textbooks. Only the specific chapters of the textbooks need be read. As a general approach, read the complete chapter, then focus on the areas that directly address your dissertation research – read this carefully and critically. Then make notes on the main theories involved and any reference to empirical work. If there is a critique of any theory or research, note that down as a separate box related to the theory it is critiquing.

Then work systematically through the other sources making notes and recording thoughts and criticisms of the source.

6.4 SOURCES OF THEORY AND LITERATURE

This section considers the possible sources of theory and literature, examines the role of the sources, and suggests making an evaluation of how useful these sources will be in dissertations. To make this process as clear and understandable as possible, the first part deals with the two most frequently-used sources in business dissertations: textbooks and journal sources. The second part investigates other possible but less often-used sources of theory, literature and data. This approach is best for dissertations that collect primary data. If your dissertation is a secondary-data investigation or meta-analysis, you will have to adapt your use of the section.

TEXTBOOKS

As indicated in Figure 11, textbooks are the first sources to investigate, reading two or three times over those chapters that relate to your research. You must be aware of the attributes of standard textbooks, in that they are a personal account of the author's synthesis of the available ideas around any topic. They often do not represent the most current thinking in an area because they take time to be published, and although the version you are reading may be only a year or so old, the ideas, theory or models may be based on earlier editions from years before. Many textbooks represent empirical research – that is, they represent research data – but it is often in a partial and sterilised form. Textbooks are designed to be easily read by people not always familiar with a subject area, so this limitation has to be remembered.

Textbooks do have an important role to play in dissertation literature, because they facilitate the understanding of the background theory to a subject area. They normally alert the reader to the key writers in an area. They also provide pointers to original empirical research and other more detailed books on the subject.

Their value in a literature review is in providing a fast learning-curve in a set subject area.

REFLECTIVE ACTIVITY

THE USEFULNESS OF TEXTBOOKS

Using your university library or a copy that you may own, consult Linstead, Fulop and Lilley (2004). You may be able to use a later edition.

Consult Chapter 2, Gender and management. This chapter is 36 pages long and may be your first introduction to gender in organisations. If it is not, you may wish to use a chapter on a different unfamiliar subject for this activity.

'Process' the chapter in the following way:

- Quickly skim-read the chapter and jot down the main thrust of its content.

- Selectively read the chapter and note down all the theoretical perspectives that are offered.

- Selectively read the chapter and note down all the empirical research that is referenced.

- Compile a list of 10 writers who are active in this research area. The references list may be very useful here.

- Make a list of five journals that have published work in this area.

- Make a list of five other books that relate to this subject area.

- Finally, write down some reflective thoughts about whether you have learned anything about gender in organisations, how effective this approach is in getting you up to speed with a topic area, and where your literature investigation would go next.

The estimated time for completing this exercise is 75–90 minutes.

If you have carried out *The usefulness of textbooks* Reflective Activity, you should have a much clearer view of the theory, approaches, writers and researchers, and the sources to consult next, related to gender in management. The main value of textbooks in a literature review lies in being able to quickly establish the base knowledge for a topic area, including the detail of theory, active authors and empirical studies. If your research has a less well-defined or multiple-theory approach, you may well have to consult several chapters. This initial work on a subject area using textbooks should always include between three and five textbooks – one book is not normally sufficient to display the full range of ideas, theory and data concerning a topic.

JOURNAL SOURCES

As *The usefulness of textbooks* Reflective Activity should have shown, there are a lot of journals published that relate to business and management. In recent years access to journal sources has become much easier with the common use of academic portals. The most common of these is Athens, and your university probably subscribes to a number of electronic sources through the Athens portal. Not all universities subscribe to the same information sources, however, and not all databases deliver full text articles either. To obtain full text articles electronically whenever possible is a major advance in the speed of researching other writers' work and offers many advantages over hardcopy journals. Articles can be sent to you by email for further study, a citation can be sent to you to add to your bibliography, bibliographical software can add these automatically, and you can send articles on to other students or colleagues.

Prior to the advances in electronic access, researchers used a bibliographical service (most universities used BIDS) to identify a useful article in a journal, then the researcher would visit their library service for the journal, and either read it and make notes or photocopy the article and study it elsewhere. Whereas it is very much the practice to access journals using electronic databases, there are some reasons for using the hardcopy sources as well. The most up-to-date journals cannot be accessed by electronic means – abstracts are available, but you will have to use a copy of the journal for full text access.

Your university librarian can generally advise you about the availability of books and journals. Most university libraries are also able to acquire articles and books that they do not have access to by using the inter-library loan system – which also includes the British Library that has access to all printed material published. Its headline banner notes that 'We hold around 14 million books, 920,000 journal and newspaper titles, 58 million patents, 3 million sound recordings, and so much more.'

There is another reason for not being completely reliant on electronic journal sources. If you visit your library on a regular basis and consult the journals, you can develop the habit of skimming all the relevant journals. This provides a wider perspective on your area than the rather narrow database searches can provide, and often sparks new insights into your research. An early indication of research being published can be obtained by looking directly at a journal's website. Once you are familiar with the journals that publish work in your area, bookmark their pages and visit them once every few months.

VIEWING JOURNAL WEBSITES

Visit the British Journal of Management website at: http://www.blackwellpublishing.com/ journal.asp?ref51045-3172&site51
Towards the bottom of this opening page you will find links to groupings of journal articles, such as:

- Featured article

- Highly accessed articles
- Special issues.
Investigate these articles.
For the journal's most up-to-date output, see the section 'Articles published online ahead of print'. You will be able to browse the abstracts but not the full text.

There are several reasons for using journal articles in your literature review: they are more up to date, they are normally more specific, and they have been through a process called 'peer review'. Peer review means that other academics within the area of study have critically reviewed each article, maybe several times, before it is printed. Because of this you can be reasonably sure of its soundness and academic standing. Journal articles can take many forms and it is important to use articles for the correct reasons. Three commonly-occurring types of articles are empirical reports, critical accounts, and best practice accounts meta-analysis and data sets. The following sections introduce these forms and their possible uses, followed by an abstract of an example to display the attributes of the form. To understand what an article might contribute to a literature review it is advisable to retrieve the full text article and investigate the areas it presents.

Empirical reports report the findings of research and normally include theory, method, data and data analysis, and implications for practice. Their primary use in a literature review would be in bringing comparative data into the research. But they could make a secondary contribution to theory, method, or contributions for practice. Soltani (2003, p.347) provides the following abstract that reports the study of 150 organisations:

> Reports findings from a research designed to investigate the main issues of the current human resource (HR) performance evaluation systems in over 150 UK-based quality-focused organisations. The study identifies the main characteristics of HR performance evaluation systems currently conducting in total quality management (TQM)-based organisations. The research approach consisted of a questionnaire survey in a sample of cross-section organisations in different economic sectors with enough experience of quality management to reflect the widest possible range of characteristics in the HR performance evaluation practices. The survey results provide the most recent details of the performance appraisal systems currently conducting in TQM organisations and their effectiveness in improving and achieving TQM objectives. Also discusses implications of these findings for HR performance evaluation system in general, and a quality-driven HR performance evaluation in particular.

Critical accounts bring known and often competing theory to play on a problem. The primary contribution of articles such as Wilson (2007, p.609) is as a critical foil to a known theory, in this case constitutional economics:

> The paper *Constitutional Economics and its Policy Agenda* develops a Thorstein Veblen-inspired critique of the foundations of constitutional economics. The paper also discusses a key aspect of its policy agenda. In recent years, that agenda has focused on tax and

expenditure limitations, which are often promoted as voter initiatives. It is argued that this tradition in economic thought involves a fundamental misunderstanding of classical political economy. From a Veblenian perspective, rent seeking is only one among numerous lines of leisure-class pursuits. From the standpoint of scientific interest, it is beside the point whether some such pursuits really are justified, whereas others are not. Veblen would not have been quick to endeavour to persuade the world to change its maxims of behaviour. Nevertheless, had he extended his theory in the direction of public finance, he would have been keen to identify existing maxims of behaviour, which govern the conduct of public finance and that might facilitate or constrain the use of public budgets in the solution of economic problems.

It is vital that a critical stance is adopted in the literature review, and journal articles of this kind often bring well-rehearsed and peer reviewed critique into your argument.

Best practice accounts offer theory and empirically grounded accounts of improvement in practice. The primary use of these articles in a literature review is to enable new insights into the synthesis of recommendations and outcomes from the dissertation research. Secondary outcomes can be in relation to theory, method or data for comparison with the dissertation data. Thus, for instance, Khanna and New (2005, p.37):

> To assist leaders and planners, the researchers provide a new human resource planning model and suggest best practices for planning and implementing an outsourcing engagement. Based on dynamic HR planning theory, and research into current outsourcing cases and approaches, the researchers provide a roadmap to confront the challenges of outsourcing. The researchers also suggest directions for further research on the contemporary outsourcing issues. First and foremost, HR planning should not be outsourced during the outsourcing process. Companies rushing into outsourcing sometimes depend so much on consultants and potential vendors for advice that the critical job of determining the new organisation is left to these third parties. Letting go of this analysis is like letting go of your strategy – the human resources strategy. The proposed model recognises the important stages of an outsourcing engagement and describes the role that HR planners need to play during each stage of this organisational change: evaluation, contract negotiation, transition, and stabilisation.

Meta-analysis reinterprets the data from earlier studies to display new analysis. In the example below (Zacharatos, Hershcovis, Turner and Barling, 2007, p.231) the authors looked at 14 earlier studies relating to the effects of HRM practices in the automotive industry:

> This article aims to provide a quantitative review of the range and effects of human resource management (HRM) practices in the North American automotive industry. A total of 14 studies provided data for an employee-level meta-analysis of the relationships comprising high-performance work systems in the automotive manufacturing sector. As an extension of research in this context, the authors hypothesised that three clusters of organisational practices (work systems, HR policies, and leadership) would be associated with two clusters of employee-level psychosocial outcomes (person-focused, organisational-focused) which, in turn, would be related to employee performance. It was found that work systems and HR policies related to both person-focused (comprising individual job satisfaction, health, self-esteem, and social support) and organisation-focused (comprising organisational commitment and perceptions of organisational justice) outcomes. The leadership cluster had a strong association with the person-focused outcomes. Organisational- but not personal-focused outcomes were associated with employee performance comprising employee effectiveness, self-ratings of performance, turnover, and absenteeism.

Meta-analysis could be regarded as a summary of data, and as such should offer a more grounded set of research outcomes. The primary use in a dissertation is as a large and well-analysed data set that can compare with the data collected from the dissertation study. Secondary outcomes could be related to theory, method and analysis.

Textbooks and journals should provide most of the literature sources, but there are other important sources of literature.

BEST PRACTICE WEBSITES

In any discipline area there are a range of professional associations many of which are the repository of research data and best practice policies. They form another important source of literature for dissertations. The Chartered Institute of Personnel and Development, for example, is an organisation devoted to the research and study of human resources.

The following is not an exhaustive list but includes many of the important organisations related to business:

Association of Accounting Technicians
Association of Chartered Certified Accountants
Association of Publishing Agencies
Association for Project Management
British Banking Association
British Computer Society (BCS)
British Psychological Society (BPS)
British Web Design and Marketing Association (BWDMA)
Business Application Software Developers Association (BASDA)
Chartered Institute of Arbitrators (CIArb)
Chartered Institute of Logistics and Transport (CILT)
Chartered Institute of Management Accountants (CIMA)
Chartered Institute of Marketing (CIM)
Chartered Institute of Personnel and Development (CIPD)
Chartered Institute of Public Finance and Accountancy (CIPA)
Chartered Institute of Purchasing and Supply (CIPS)
Chartered Institute of Taxation (CIOT)
Chartered Management Institute
Chartered Quality Institute
Confederation of British Industry
Direct Marketing Association
Institute of Business Consulting
Institute of Chartered Accountants in England and Wales (ICAEW)
Institute of Chartered Accountants in Ireland
Institute of Chartered Accountants in Scotland (ICAS)
Institute of Direct Marketing
Institute of Directors (IOD)
Institute for the Management of Information Systems (IMIS)
Institute of Management Consultants
Institute of Operations Management (IOM)
Institute of Professional Sales
Institute of Quality Assurance
Management Consultants Association
the Market Research Society
the Mathematical Association
National Association of Data Protection Officers (NADPO)
the Society of Information Technology Management [in local government] (SOCITM)
Strategic Planning Society
UK Academy for Information Systems (UKAIS)

USING PROFESSIONAL ASSOCIATION WEBSITES

Visit the Chartered Institute of Personnel and Development's website at: http://www.cipd.co.uk/default.cipd. Navigate to the Professional Standards page.

● What are the core competencies of human resources management?

● How would these core competencies match up with the core competencies for the successful completion of a dissertation?

Investigate the site further:

● Look for applicable research using your own research questions.

SOCIAL DATA SETS

If you intend to carry out research using secondary data, you will need access to what are called the 'social data sets'. These are most frequently accessed through the Economic and Social Data Service (ESDS).

Figure 12 Screenshot of the ESDS website front page

The main government surveys are:

Annual Population Survey
British Crime Survey/Scottish Crime Survey
British Social Attitudes Survey/Northern Ireland Social Attitudes Survey/Scottish Social Attitudes Survey/Northern Ireland Life and Times Survey/Young People's Social Attitudes
Expenditure and Food Survey
Family Expenditure Survey/Northern Ireland Family Expenditure Survey
Family Resources Survey
General Household Survey/Continuous Household Survey (Northern Ireland)
Health Survey For England/Welsh Health Survey/Scottish Health Survey
Households Below Average Income
Labour Force Survey/Northern Ireland Labour Force Survey
National Food Survey
National Travel Survey
ONS Omnibus Survey
Survey of English Housing
United Kingdom Time Use Survey
Vital Statistics for England and Wales

There are many thousands of data sets held by numerous organisations – even a cursory Internet search can reveal them.

CASE STUDY

 CHRIS'S LITERATURE REVIEW

Chris, a friend from university, has asked you to read her literature review and give her some feedback. The following is a typical excerpt from her review:

Books

Reid, M.A. and Barrington, H. (2003) *Training Interventions: Promoting learning opportunities*, 6th edition. London: CIPD This literature identifies a range of definitions of training and outlines a general perspective of what training involves. Additionally, Reid and Barrington identify the need for training in relation to the success of the company.

Simmonds, D. (2003) *Designing and Delivering Training*. London: CIPD In this book, Simmonds identifies numerous theories and models related to the need for training and critically analyses each one. In addition to this, Simmonds evaluates various training methods and programmes giving both the advantages and disadvantages of each method.

Truelove, S. (1996) *The Handbook of Training and Development*, 2nd edition. Cambridge: Blackwell Publishers In this book, Truelove analyses the need for training within various organisations and presents numerous tables regarding training standards, needs and strategies.

Journal articles

Essery, E. (2006) 'Learn the value of training', *Works Management*, Volume 59, Issue 8, p.14 In this journal article, Elaine Essery focuses on how training can maximise an individual's potential, emphasising the need for effective training in the workplace. The article shows numerous examples of how companies have benefited hugely from investing in effective training programmes.

Anonymous (2006) 'UK business ignores employment development need', *E-Learning Age*, July/August Issue, p.4 This section of the journal illustrates how businesses ignore the need for training. The journal includes figures of training budgets, training culture and the percentage of businesses who overlook training.

Anonymous (2005) 'Education and training linked to profitability', *Graphic Arts Monthly*, February Issue, p.59 The article from this journal analyses the relation between training and profitability. The article illustrates that there is a clear correlation between the two, therefore demonstrating that effective training is key to success.

Press articles

Davies, H. (2006) 'How to get the most from the training budget', *Sunday Times*, 13 September This article focuses on how businesses are starting to increase their training budgets in order for employees to maximise their full potential. The article illustrates with an example how an employee can be unsuccessful if not given the correct training.

O'Connell, S. (2006) 'Staff training pays off in the long run', *Sunday Times*, 6 August In this article Sandra O'Connell illustrates using examples how companies who have

invested in training are rewarded with higher productivity and an increase in profits. Despite this, the article also portrays the idea that not all businesses perceive training as essential.

To think about ...

1 Provide Chris with feedback under the following headings:

  – Layout of the review

  – Estimate of how critical the review is

  – How well the review synthesises theory

  – Evaluation of the strength of the 'storyline' in the review

2 Make a five-point list of things Chris should do to improve the approach she has taken in the literature review.

3 Suggest ways that Chris can get help in the future on this aspect of her dissertation.

KEY LEARNING POINTS

SUMMARY

Developing a successful literature review requires the bringing together of a range of skills. The following sections focus on those skills and attempt to develop a critical and evaluative approach to reviewing and using literature.

- Try to address the areas in your writing of the literature review that tutors will regard as important:

  – supporting and embedding your dissertation with known theory and research

  – proving you know the research area

  – providing an opportunity to display the skills of analysis, critique and evaluation

  – providing the building blocks of method, methodology and data analysis

  – offering a perspective on your research

  – providing knowledge of secondary sources.

- Reflect on and develop a sound literature review process:

  – use the academic funnel

  – know the attributes of synthesised theory

  – follow Rowley and Slack's (2004) five steps in the creation of a literature review.

- Use a wide range of literature sources to fully develop and evidence your academic argument:

  – textbooks

  – journals

- professional association websites
- social data sets.
- Develop a critical and evaluative stance to the literature.

- Recognise and develop the links from theory to methodology.

EXPLORE FURTHER

Bath Information and Data Services. Available: http://www.bids.ac.uk/info/fs_aboutbids.htm

British Journal of Management. Available: http://www.blackwellpublishing.com/journal.asp?ref51045-3172&site51

British Library. Available: http://www.bl.uk/

Khanna, S. and New, R. (2005) 'An HR planning model for outsourcing HR', *Human Resource Planning*, Vol. 28, No. 4: 37

Linstead, S., Fulop, L. and Lilley, S. (2004) *Management and Organization*. London: Palgrave Macmillan

Rowley, J. and Slack, F. (2004) 'Conducting a literature review', *Management Research News*, Vol. 27, No. 6: 31–9

Seaward, B. L. (2006) *Essentials of Managing Stress*. Sudbury: Jones & Bartlett

Soltani, E. (2003) 'Towards a TQM-driven HR performance evaluation: an empirical study', *Employee Relations*, Vol. 25, No. 4: 347–70

Wilson, M. (2007) 'Constitutional economics and its policy agenda: a Veblen-inspired critique', *Journal of Economic Issues*, Vol. 41, No. 2: 609

Zacharatos, A., Hershcovis, M., Turner, M. and Barling, J. (2007) 'Human resource management in the North American automotive industry: a meta-analytic review', *Personnel Review*, Vol. 36, No. 2: 231

Weblinks

Short and explicit Loughborough University guide to writing a literature review: http://www.lboro.ac.uk/library/skills/Advice/ Literature%20review.pdf

Palgrave postgraduate guide to writing a literature review: http://www.palgrave.com/skills4study/studentlife/postgraduate/carrying.asp

Literature review example (American), with annotated commentary of what each section accomplishes: http://owl.english.purdue.edu/media/pdf/20070515025950_667.pdf

Literature review – example on the topic of sustainable tourism: http://www.macaulay.ac.uk/ruralsustainability/LiteratureReview.pdf

CHAPTER 7

Methodology

What will I learn in this chapter?

- The importance of explaining methodology, and its connection with epistemology
- How to critically evaluate methods in research
- The appropriate use of questionnaires and interviews
- A range of wider methods
- The usefulness of combining methods
- The role of sampling in research
- Ethical considerations in research

7.1 INTRODUCTION

This chapter considers two main areas: methodology, and a range of commonly-used research methods. Methodology is an important, but often neglected, area of dissertations. It refers to the way that knowledge is created and is closely related to epistemology, which is the philosophical theory of knowledge. Dissertations must address both these two areas, and this would normally be covered in the methodology chapter.

There are myriad possible methods that can be used in a dissertation. Many researchers develop new methods to solve organisational and research problems, and there are many journals devoted to research methods. How might this chapter unravel this very complicated area? The chapter uses a graduated approach to investigating the possible methods that can be used in a dissertation. Two of the most commonly-used methods for investigating problems and issues in business and management are the questionnaire and the interview. These methods are examined and evaluated thoroughly. There is then a variety of methods that are rather less frequently used, and these are also covered in detail. The final section introduces a range of methods encountered relatively rarely in research but very useful in certain research circumstances. Samplings of populations to create valid predictions and generalisations are investigated and related to research methods and specific research questions.

The best way to use this chapter is to read the sections on methodology and epistemology as an introduction before preparing your dissertation proposal. Then skim-read the two first layers of methods as an introduction to methods to enable you to write with confidence about methods in the proposal document. As the dissertation develops, return and study in detail the methods you are using. It is highly likely that you will have to investigate methods in greater detail than this text can cover: some suggested sources and publications are listed in the *Explore further* section. It is particularly important that you form a critical and evaluative argument about your choice and use of particular methods.

7.2 METHODOLOGY AND EPISTEMOLOGY

Methodology can be usefully thought of as an organised critical discussion of the principles and methods of a subject area. Principles can be regarded as the underlying philosophy of the research. Methods and practices of a discipline must be discussed, critiqued and evaluated. All dissertations should have a section that sets out these underlying philosophical principles and should develop a critical discussion of appropriate methods. Many disciplines of business have a distinct approach to the creation of new knowledge – your dissertation will create new knowledge. Epistemology is the study of the creation and dissemination of knowledge in a subject area. The types of question you should address in this section are: What will we regard as knowledge? What is the source of the knowledge? What are the limits of the knowledge? These are not easy questions to grapple with but a structured attempt should be made to think about and discuss these issues. Plato's formulation of knowledge is as a 'justified true belief', so you may have to explain how you will justify what is a true belief. For some the creation of reliable knowledge lies in the methods and rigour of the inquiry, so our methodology section must discuss and justify the nature, rigour, and justification of the methods that are chosen to answer the research question or to test the hypotheses. A mark of a first-class dissertation is the extensive and justified critique of the methodology.

INDUCTION AND DEDUCTION

One philosophical starting point might be to consider inductive or deductive reasoning, and which is guiding your research. In inductive approaches generalisations are made from individual instances, often known as 'bottom-up' reasoning. In research terms, this involves observing instances of something, looking for a pattern in the instances, building a tentative theory, and then testing that general theory to provide generalisations about behaviour. Deductive reasoning works the other way around, from the general to the specific, often known as 'top-down' reasoning. Deduction starts with a theory, focuses down to a hypothesis about specific matters, then makes observations to test the hypothesis, finally confirming or refuting the hypothesis. It is important to decide, argue and justify the approach you will be taking in the methodology. One small word of warning: often both types of reasoning are called for in a research study, so it may be necessary to explain where in the research inductive approaches are being used and where deductive approaches are used.

POSITIVIST AND SUBJECTIVIST

Another dimension that you may wish to discuss in a methodology is the positivist–subjectivist dimension. Positivists believe that in the world we live in there are universal truths, and that research goals should discover the laws of the universe relating to these universal truths. Subjectivists believe there is no universal truth but a reality that we all contribute to making. From this stance the research goals are to discover the methods by which this reality is made or constructed, or to explore the agreed reality. There are many variations between the two ends of this continuum. The detailed positions you can research yourself. In explaining your research approach you will have to consider how you and your research will see the world. Adopting a positivist approach implies certain methods and reasoning, whereas the subjectivist approach requires different methods and reasoning.

QUANTITATIVE AND QUALITATIVE

The qualitative–quantitative dimension must be discussed and related to your proposed method of inquiry. Some methods use one approach whereas others adopt a strategy of both approaches.

Quantitative methods, as the name suggests, refers to a group of methods in which the main focus is on quantities. Thus the main task is counting the number of times things occur or the amounts of items (like money). Using quantitative methods the main data will be numbers, and these are normally analysed with statistical measures. In order to have confidence in the results, the chosen sample and other statistical measures must be well thought out and discussed critically.

Qualitative research starts from the stance that people understand and relate to things cognitively – from within the mind. Qualitative methods relate to people in ways that allow them to express their beliefs, assumptions, desires and understandings. A qualitative method seeks to provide contexts, like one-to-one interviewing, that allow a participant to express such things. Analysis of qualitative data seeks to place these beliefs, assumptions and understandings in a wider social context. The main data will be words, but in modern studies can also be video or audio material.

TESTING AND EXPLORING

Research can be defined on the dimension of testing or exploring. Where theory and research is well developed, it would be possible to test a hypothesis about some behaviour or action. When investigating areas that are not well researched, or areas that have little justified theory, an exploratory approach may be preferable. Your methodology section will have to explain and justify the approach you are taking. Exploratory research is useful when your aim is to fully describe and understand a unique research situation. But it can also be useful in well-researched areas so that new insights are developed from jaded or heavily researched topics or areas. As a research area becomes well studied there is a tendency for the approaches to converge, become similar – adopting an exploratory research design can reverse this trend.

PARTICIPANT AND OBJECTIVE

The participant or objective dimension is less often considered in dissertation research because time is always limited and participant techniques are often time-consuming. When a researcher stands aside from the research and observes what takes place, the study may be classified as objective. But note that the word 'objective' is itself burdened with a number of different meanings.

7.3 SAMPLING

CONCEPTS

Choosing the participants to be involved in a study is called sampling. All dissertations must have a section that relates how the participants were chosen. There are several important concepts related to sampling.

Census

A research census is a study of all the possible cases of a particular type. For instance, if your study is of a particular organisation and you survey or interview all the people in that organisation, then you have taken a census. If you include all the possible cases in your research, there is no need for sampling. The difficulty with a census occurs when deciding who is included and who is excluded. Close definition of the criteria for inclusion in a study should ensure accurate representation of the cases that should be legitimately included in a study. Because dissertation research is often completed in small-scale settings, using a census will avoid the need for sampling. But in all other cases your research must explain and justify how the participants were chosen.

Population

A population may be defined as the set of individuals, items or data from which a sample is taken. Defining a research population for business research frequently centres on being a member of a particular group, such as:

- staff in an organisation
- users of a product
- members of a group
- those with a condition – for example, stress.

It is important to set criteria that make it clear who or what is included in a population. Even defining something as apparently simple as being a member of an organisation can raise problems. Would part-time members of staff be included in a population of staff? Would outsourced staff be included? Would members of staff who have recently joined be included? Should members of staff who have recently left be included? Would staff on long-term sick leave or those suspended from work be included? I hope you can see that defining the population is important and should be included in all dissertations where sampling is required.

Sampling frame

Even in well-defined populations not every member is accessible. A sampling frame is the list of accessible members of a population. The alumni of a university are all those who have attended the university in the past. The population would be all those who had attended the university. The sampling frame would be all those who had attended and for whom there was sufficient data for them to be contacted. Some reasons why they cannot be contacted might include lost contact details, death, and determined privacy.

Sample

Once a population is well defined and a sampling frame of the population is produced, it may be necessary to research only a proportion of the population. The research sample is the list of people or items that you choose to be in your study. Note that this is not the list of people or items that finally are in the study.

METHODS OF SAMPLING

There are two possible sampling methods: probability sampling and non-probability sampling.
　　Probability sampling uses some form of random selection of cases from the sampling frame. This is a commonly-used method when inductive reasoning drives the methodology.
　　Non-probability sampling does not involve the random selection of cases from a sampling frame. This method is commonly used when deductive reasoning drives the methodology.
　　The need for sampling occurs because of:

- the increasing costs of conducting a census of large populations. As the size of the population grows it becomes uneconomic to study all the cases. A representative sample will provide accurate analysis of the general population. In dissertation research, surveys of up to 500 participants are normally regarded as economic – beyond this size sampling would be necessary. The dissertation research economic limit for interview samples is around 30 participants.
- restrictions on the amount of time available to conduct the research. Dissertations have a limited amount of time in which they must be completed and the economic limits above would apply again here.
- inaccessibility of some of the sampling frame. Some populations are not all accessible. We may have a sampling frame that details all the possible members or items but some them may not be accessible. For instance, we may want to interview all the staff that left an

organisation in the last year, and we may have the details of all these people, but some of them may not want to participate. In this case we will have to use the sample available and make allowance for the non-participants.

- potential destruction, when a full study would involve unavoidable damage. Destruction of a whole population may be inappropriate. If our research study is looking at the quality of the micro-components in a laptop computer, for example, studying this might involve damaging or destroying the components. It would be inappropriate to damage too many items from the production process, so a sample of the produced items would be used.

PROBABILITY SAMPLING

Simple random sampling

Simple random sampling is easy to understand and provides a reasonable representation of a population. If you have a list of 100 staff members in an organisation and you only have the time and money to interview 20 members of staff in relation to some aspect of your research, you can randomly select 20 names by placing all the names in a hat and drawing out 20. An Excel spreadsheet would accomplish this in just a few minutes – and would provide an evidence trail of these actions.

REFLECTIVE ACTIVITY

GENERATING A SAMPLE OF 20 FROM A POPULATION OF 100

Open an Excel spreadsheet.

Add the formula =INT(RAND()*100) to the first cell.

Copy the cell above and paste to the next 19 cells.

You now have a list of 20 numbers representing a random sample from a total of 100 names.

The simple random sample can look like a very sound way to draw a sample, and yet by pure chance it may generate a sample that does not represent subgroups in your population very accurately. For instance, your sampling frame of 100 may contain 50 women and 50 men but the sample of 20 may draw all women. Where subgroups are important to the nature of the research, they should be defined in a stratified sample.

Stratified random sampling

Stratified random sampling ensures an accurate representation of the population and any important subgroups within that population. In sampling 20 members of staff from a workforce of 100, we may want to study the different perceptions of managers, technical workers, administrative workers, and sales staff. Using a random sample we would expect to select five from each group – but when the selection has taken place we may find that only three sales staff have been included. This example assumes there are equal proportions of the four staff groups – ie 25 managers, 25 sales personnel, etc. If there are different proportions of staff, a decision will have to be made about the sampling rate for each stratum. To obtain a representative sample it is often necessary to increase the sampling rate for smaller groups.

Cluster random sampling

Cluster random sampling or area random sampling is used when populations spread over a large geographical area are to be studied because it can reduce the costs and the time involved. The population is grouped for sampling – let's say, by the counties in England. There are 48 counties in England. First we randomly select a representative sample of these – a 10% sample would mean the sample was five counties. Then either we study all the cases in the five counties, or if this is too large, we randomly select cases to study from within each of the five counties.

Multi-stage sampling

Multi-stage sampling involves combining simple, stratified and cluster sampling in stages to develop a representative sample of large and diverse populations. Applied social research frequently uses this technique, but it is required less in dissertation research.

NON-PROBABILITY SAMPLING

Opportunity sampling

Opportunity sampling, also called accidental, haphazard or convenience sampling, is used when random methods are not required to answer your research questions, or when it is impossible to construct a sampling frame. In this method, the selection of cases to be studied is purely related to accessibility or by chance meeting. If you conduct your research by stopping people on campus and asking them questions, you will not be able to make many claims about the people you questioned and their relation to a larger population. All you may be able to determine is that although opportunity sampling is quick and convenient, it also weakens the research and does not allow for the findings to be reliably extended to larger groups.

Purposeful sampling

Purposeful sampling is a non-probability method in which the selected cases are related to the purpose of the study. A recent study involved the users of e-learning, and the sample was of those people who had used the e-learning suite in the previous month. This is a quick and easy way to find cases to study, but cannot be regarded as representing any well-defined population. The basis of the purposeful sample might be:

- modal – cases from the most common group
- expertise – those displaying certain knowledge of expertise
- quotas – a set number of cases from pre-defined groups
- diversity – selecting the widest range of cases possible
- snowball – one participant recommends the next participant, and so on
- critical incidents – studying important events that occur
- self-selection – samples of cases that present themselves to be studied.

7.4 QUESTIONNAIRES

Questionnaires are commonly used in dissertation research for gathering data. This section examines a number of important aspects of using questionnaires effectively. The first consideration is how questionnaires can contribute to a sound methodology. Then various aspects of questionnaires are considered, including types of data, methods of administration, how to devise individual questions, and piloting a questionnaire.

THE APPROPRIATE USE OF QUESTIONNAIRES

In dissertation research there always comes a point when you wonder whether to use a questionnaire. It is important to consider other methods and actively choose to use a questionnaire because it is the best method to gather the data you need to achieve your research aims. Questionnaires are effective when the research is well defined in theory and the research questions or hypotheses are clear and specific.

PRELIMINARY POINTS TO CONSIDER

The following sections investigate early considerations when using a questionnaire. Often, these preliminaries require decisions to be made that will affect the conduct of the questionnaire and the research. Later sections deal with the detail of many of these preliminary points.

How will the questionnaire be administered? Will the questionnaire be given to groups that are well known to you, such as colleagues, or to a general group that is not well known? There are several options in how to administer the questionnaire, such as by post or online, and to groups or individuals.

What is the main synthesised theory, from the literature review, that will 'drive' the survey and provide the framework for analysis? What type of data is required? This is determined by the link to theory and the research questions. It is important that all the questions relate directly to the synthesised theory and the research aims.

How will you persuade people to respond to the questionnaire? If you have access to a work environment or if access was obtained through a top management decision, this can be implied in the questionnaire and may well provide good response rates. Will you offer some sort of reward – entry into a draw for a prize, a voucher for something, cash for completion? It is quite normal to report back the findings to the respondents – and this suggestion to respondents can act as a motivator to complete the questionnaire. Emotional blackmail, in its gentlest form, can work well, by explaining that you are a student carrying out the research on a shoestring and as part of an award. Perhaps the easiest approach to finding participants is to use the social networking sites. Any day on Twitter you will see posted many links to online surveys. These can yield a lot of responses but extra care must be taken to ensure that the respondents are appropriate to your study.

Is the questionnaire to be answered anonymously? If so, the procedures to ensure anonymity must be put in place early and the questions will have to reflect it. You will need statements of anonymity that assure possible participants that the anonymity arrangements are robust.

When will the questionnaire be administered? Timing is very important in obtaining valid data relating to organisational events. If your survey is investigating change in an organisation, a survey given during the change will elicit different responses from one administered some months after the change is completed. This is further complicated by the changing nature of the population. Consider the example of an organisation undergoing change. It is very typical for staff to leave an organisation during or soon after major change, and the staff that leave probably have a distinctive view of the organisation and the change. If the survey occurs three months after the change, these possible respondents will have left the organisation and the views that you get will be from the 'survivors'. When using data you should reflect on the aspects of its collection that may restrict what can be said about the data. For instance, it would be correct in the situation above to describe the data as from those people who remained in the organisation, or who joined after the change and have no knowledge of the change. It would not be correct to describe the data as from all those people in the organisation during the change. By asking the right biographical questions and being critically reflective about the sample and the timing of data collection, it is possible to make accurate statements about the representative nature of the data.

What research studies have previously been conducted? Could any of the questions used in these studies also be used in your own? There is an advantage to using questions that have already been used in a study or studies – they have been piloted and evaluated, have a data set, and some analysis has been carried out on the questions. Using selected questions or complete survey instruments from published research is regarded as normal practice in the research community, and generally considered sound practice too.

What arrangements will be made for piloting the questionnaire? Several pilots may have to be involved before you and your supervisor are confident that the questionnaire will gather appropriate and valid data.

What arrangements will be made for analysing the data? Using survey software normally determines the data analysis techniques that can be used. If you are using survey software, the possible statistical analysis may be limited when compared to statistical software such as SPSS. Your research questions will be a major guide in this respect. If your research question or hypothesis requires making a casual connection between two or more variables, the greater statistical functionality of SPSS may be more useful than survey software such as Snap.

METHOD OF ADMINISTRATION

Questionnaires are often given out to participants or posted to them for them to complete the questionnaire and return it to the researcher. One of two major drawbacks with this system is that the number returned is often comparatively small – the reduction in number is called the attrition rate. The average postal or self-administered questionnaire has an attrition rate of 66% to 75%, and individual rates can be even greater. You will have to develop a strategy to cope with this high attrition rate and link it to the sampling system you use. The main way to cope with the problem is to increase the number of questionnaires sent out. If 300 questionnaires are sent out in a postal survey and 100 are returned, you can regard this as a very good rate of return. However, if your sample was carefully selected in four categories (a, b, c, d), it will be important to check that all categories remain appropriately represented when the questionnaires are returned. The other main disadvantage in self-administered questionnaires is that a respondent cannot get any personal guidance on what a question means in relation to the study, and may therefore provide inappropriate or invalid answers. Respondents must also be willing to reveal the answers to the questions you are asking. You should consider the sensitivity of the questions in your survey. Clearly, most respondents would be willing to reveal which chocolate bar they prefer, or whether they prefer tea or coffee. But they may be more reluctant to reveal their sexual preferences, or their true feelings about their manager. The problem of respondents' finding questions too sensitive is revealed in two ways: either the response rate is very low, or the answers are not a true reflection of the respondents' views. It is often possible to ask more sensitive questions in a self-administered questionnaire than when the interviewer is present.

Respondents finding the questions too sensitive to answer truthfully can be partly overcome by the promise and practice of anonymity. The promise is easy to give, but the practice can sometimes be difficult to achieve. One main way is to have no identification sections in the questionnaires – although there will still have to be biographical data if the data analysis is likely to depend on biographical differences in the sample. To give absolute confidence to respondents, a 'confidence moat' must be provided such that the questionnaires are returned to an independent returning officer, who ensures anonymity of the questionnaires and then passes on the data to the researcher.

Web-based questionnaires are another but distinct form of self-administered questionnaire. The common use of questionnaire software such as Survey monkey or Google docs means that placing your questionnaire in a web environment is relatively easy. The difficulty with web-based questionnaires is that it is relatively hard to control the sampling of respondents. In using web-based questionnaires it is normal to investigate the sampling once the data has been collected and then to make allowances in the data analysis. It is normal to create a preferred sample from the population, the collected data is then compared to the preferred sample, and if necessary the analysis and the outcomes are qualified by this comparison.

Questionnaires can also be administered by researchers *in situ*. Most people have experience of this type of questionnaire administration by being stopped in the street and asked for their opinions on this or that. The two major problems with self-administered questionnaires are immediately removed by using this method. Attrition rates are normally low. If respondents say they are willing to help, it would be rare to find them refusing to complete the questionnaire, unless it is excessively long. This produces very low attrition rates, and should ensure a good representation of the preferred sample. If a respondent is unsure of what a question is asking, he or she can ask for clarity, ensuring that a valid answer is given. Sampling for self-administered questionnaires is achieved by using 'screening' questions before the main questionnaire is used. If your sample is stratified by age – so that, say, 10 respondents are required in five age categories – then the screening questionnaire is used first and a running quota is kept so that the survey is complete when 10 respondents have answered the questionnaire from the five age categories. One major disadvantage of researcher-administered questionnaires is that the process is very time-consuming. There is also a problem known as the 'researcher effect', where the interaction of the researcher – say, in answering the 'I don't quite understand' questions from the respondent – may affect the response. Most respondents like to give answers they think the researcher wants. For example, there may be a question that relates to the packaging of a chocolate bar. The respondent may not care about this aspect of the product, but because saying 'I don't care' may seem a little anti-environment, the respondent may give an answer that indicates that he or she does care, simply to come up with what he/she thinks is the right thing to say.

A variation of researcher-administered questionnaires is group-administered questionnaires. This removes one of the main drawbacks to researcher-administered questionnaires in that it reduces the amount of time it takes to gather the data. Typically, the screening questionnaire is used to identify appropriate and willing participants, who then meet at a pre-arranged time, and the researcher guides the group through the filling in of the questionnaire. Controlling group questionnaire events requires a bit of practice and it is advisable to try out the technique with a friendly group before tackling a 'live' group.

DATA TYPES

Data can be categorised in either of two types. Some data – such as time, salaries, or the amount spent on training in a year – is *continuous* in that it can take values between whole numbers. It will then mean something to say (for example) that a respondent is 23.66 years old, or that someone earns £87,343.22 a year. The other type of data is described as *discrete*, in that it can only be meaningful as whole numbers, so that (for example) the number of cars a person has access to can be two or three, but not 2.3.

It is important at an early stage to understand what types of data will be generated from the questions you use. Subsequent analysis of the data will be limited by the type of data you have collected.

Data types

Level of measurement	Discrete examples	Continuous examples
Nominal or category	Company name Gender Subjects studied	–
Ordinal or ranked	Subject grades Finishing position in a test Job level	–
Interval	Examination scores	Temperature
Ratio	Number of people employed Number of exam passes	Salary Age

Nominal or category data records only the name of the category to which something belongs. This data is very useful for description purposes but cannot be used to create inferences or connections to other things.

Ordinal or ranked data reveals a name but also where the named thing lies in relation to others in a list. But note that the gaps between items in a ranking list will not be consistent and so can give no indication about the distance between one item and another. If we had a list of employees ranked by age, we might know that Fred was the oldest employee, and that Freda was the second-oldest employee, but we would not know the age difference between them. If sales staff were ranked by their sales performance, we might know that Freda was the top performer and that Fred was the second-best performer, but we would not know how much more Freda sold than Fred. Rating scales – such as 'essential', 'very important', 'important', 'not very important', 'unimportant' – produce ordinal data. From a rating scale you may know that respondent a) thinks something is more important than respondent b), but you will not know by how much. Questionnaires are often designed to collect ordinal data using rating scales, and this limits the amount of analysis that can be done on the data. Ordinal data is effective when it is intended to carry out descriptive analysis, but not very effective when inferential analysis is the intention.

Interval data can be used to calculate how far apart one data item is from another. Interval data is obtained by asking respondents to rate something on a scale with equal intervals. Interval data has no absolute zero point. Even scales that have a zero in them are not absolute zeros – in an examination in which one student scores 30% and another scores 60%, it would not be possible to say that the student scoring 60% is twice as good as the student scoring 30%. Interval data allows you to specify the distance between two data points but not their worth in relation to each other. Thus if respondent a) indicates that he/she rates a chocolate bar as a 10 on a scale of 1 to 10 and respondent b) rates the chocolate bar as a 5, it is not possible to say that respondent a) likes the chocolate twice as much as respondent b). It is possible to say that respondent a) likes the chocolate bar more than respondent b), and more than any other respondent answering with a rating of 6, 7, 8 or 9.

Ratio data allows conclusions to be drawn about the relative size or worth of the data. For example, we can accurately say that someone with a salary of £80,000 per annum has twice as much as someone with £40,000 per annum.

When designing your questionnaire, ensure that you are aware of the type of data that any question will generate. Also, reflect on the type of data your research question or hypothesis requires and ensure that the questions will generate that type of data.

DEVISING QUESTIONS

The questions used in a questionnaire may be either of two types: biographical questions related to the characteristics of the participants, and investigative questions that focus on the research questions of the study. Biographical questions must be selected carefully so those characteristics of the participants can be used to explain the outcomes of the study. For instance, if your research was investigating the frequency and success of using e-learning and your theory and literature indicated that this might be related to age, it would be useful to collect data on the age of participants. The biographical detail collected will be important in allowing explanations of the data to be made. Commonly-used variables will be represented in the literature, but you may also need variables selected by 'hunch'. A frivolous example might be that you have a hunch that e-learning is linked to height. If you do not collect data about height, you will not be able to explain the usage by this factor. But do not ask for too much unnecessary data – it is time-consuming to code and often irritates participants if they think you are being 'too nosy'.

The investigative questions must relate to the synthesised theory and the research question or one of the hypotheses of the research. The questions must adequately investigate each aspect of the theory and each hypothesis. Research questions will be quite broad and will need further refinement until it is possible to ask specific questions. A data requirements table is the standard technique for controlling the generation of questions in a questionnaire.

Data requirements table: example

Data table	
Title of research:	An investigation of absence at SATO
Main theory:	Steers and Rhodes' (1978) model of attendance
Research questions:	What are the key variables in workplace attendance?
Variables:	motivation to attend pay punishments attendance allowance esteem etc

Question No.	Question detail	Variable tested	Data type	Linked to Questions	Theory or research question tested	Checked
4.1	If you were paid an extra amount to attend work, would you be absent ...?	Attendance pay as a motivator to attend, related to theory	Category: Less The same More	4.2–4.6	Res Q 5.2 S&Rs motivation to attend	

DESIGN

Designing questionnaires is a skilled task that rewards experience, but this is probably the one thing dissertation researchers do not have. There is a large range of opinions on how to design a questionnaire, and the following is presented not as a definitive or prescriptive list but as a collection of experience to help you get started.

Introduction

Questionnaires should contain a short introduction to the survey that states what is being researched and why the respondent's help is being requested. At the end of the survey a short thank you note and the researcher's contact details should be included. If the questionnaire is being administered by post, a covering letter will be required that sets out:

- the purpose of the research
- the timescale for completion
- the approximate time required to complete it
- why the respondent is regarded as a useful source of information

- information on confidentiality or anonymity
- how the results are to be used
- the researcher's contact details.

The wording of questions

Short, simple sentences are generally less confusing and ambiguous than long, complex ones. As a rule of thumb, most sentences should contain one or two clauses. Ask for only one piece of information at a time. Avoid asking negative questions. Ask precise questions – this requires closely specified questions with clear time frames. (So you might ask: 'In the last week, how many times have you used an e-learning package that lasted more than 15 minutes?') Ask questions that do not assume the participant knows anything specific about the researched area. Do not ask questions like this: 'Do you think Kirkpatrick's model represents your view of e-learning?' (If you wanted to know this information, you would have to specify the part of Kirkpatrick's model you wanted an opinion about.) Be careful in specifying the level of detail required – too little and you cannot answer your research question, too much and respondents will get bored and answer flippantly or not complete the question. Be especially careful with the wording of sensitive questions. If you ask someone whether they have ever stolen something, you are likely to get a non-response or a negative answer. Work the sensitive questions into a list of items and you may get an honest response. Avoid indicating a socially preferred answer by using neutral wording in questions.

Types of question

At the first level, questions can be open or closed. Closed questions provide the possible answers to the question. For example, 'I find this book to be: brilliant/excellent/marvellous'. One drawback with closed questions is that the available responses are limited. This is sometimes overcome by adding the category 'Other' and 'Please specify'. Open questions ask the question but do not specify a response. For example, 'How do you find this book?' The data analysis of closed questions is considerably easier than analysing the data from open questions.

Closed questions can be constructed in various forms offering responses that present:

- a list of items from which one item is to be chosen
- a set of categories from which any number may be chosen
- a rating scale – say, 1 to 10, or a descriptive scale
- a list to be ranked in order
- a box, in which to enter an amount, a number, a salary, etc
- a grid, referred to as a matrix, which allows for answering more than one question, as for instance invited by: 'Please rank the following seven items on a scale of 1 to 10'.

Likert scales

Rensis Likert provided a way of measuring a respondent's agreement or disagreement to a question. The question is commonly framed as a proposition, such as, 'I feel my university tutor listens to me', then an even or uneven scale is provide for the respondent's agreement or disagreement with the proposition. Note that this is framed as a positive proposition. It could alternatively be framed as a negative proposition. It would then become: 'I feel my university tutor never listens to me'.

EXAMPLE: LIKERT SCALE ANSWERS

Try responding to the following proposition in the four different forms. This may help you to see the effect of positive/negative questions and even and uneven Likert scales.

Q1

Indicate on the scale the answer that matches your view most closely.

I feel the assignment grades I receive are directly within my control.

Agree	Tend to agree	Neither agree nor disagree	Tend to disagree	Disagree
☐	☐	☐	☐	☐

Positive statement, uneven scale

Q2

Indicate on the scale the answer that matches your view most closely.

I feel the assignment grades I receive are directly within my control.

Strongly agree	Agree	Tend to agree	Tend to disagree	Disagree	Strongly disagree
☐	☐	☐	☐	☐	☐

Positive statement, even scale

Q3

Indicate on the scale the answer that matches your view most closely.

I feel the assignment grades I receive are outside my control.

Agree	Tend to agree	Neither agree nor disagree	Tend to disagree	Disagree
☐	☐	☐	☐	☐

Negative statement, uneven scale

Q4

Indicate on the scale the answer that matches your view most closely.

I feel the assignment grades I receive are outside my control.

Strongly agree	Agree	Tend to agree	Tend to disagree	Disagree	Strongly disagree
☐	☐	☐	☐	☐	☐

Negative statement, even scale

The ideal length of a questionnaire

There is no universal agreement about the optimum length of a questionnaire. It probably depends on the type of respondents and the subject of the research. However, short simple questionnaires usually attract higher response rates than long complex ones. In dissertation research there is also the data entry and analysis to be considered – the longer the questionnaire, the more data that has to be entered and analysed. Both these tasks are time-consuming, although the data entry can be either automated or carried out by a willing friend.

Because dissertation research is likely to have quite focused research aims, questions or hypotheses, questionnaires are unlikely to comprise more than 40 simple questions.

The order of the questions is also important. Try to follow these simple rules:

- Go from general to particular.
- Go from easy to difficult.
- Go from factual to abstract.
- Start with closed-format questions.
- Start with questions relevant to the main subject.
- Do not start with demographic and personal questions – place these at the end.

Maintain the interest of the respondent by using a variety of questions. When it is necessary to use a number of scale questions, try to ensure that the scales work in different directions – this may reduce a respondent's tendency to just tick down a list using the same response.

The questionnaire will have to be piloted with a group of people who have characteristics similar to the research population's. This process involves a small group of 6–10 people completing the questionnaire and providing feedback on:

- the clarity of each question
- the appropriateness of each question
- the language used in each question
- whether some questions are too sensitive
- the layout and format of the questionnaire
- whether it is too long or too short
- the helpfulness and clarity of the introduction and ending
- their feelings on whether they would willingly complete the questionnaire.

Depending on the first reaction to the questionnaire, another piloting meeting or meetings may be needed. It is normal to revise a questionnaire in the light of feedback and then to pilot it again. The majority of newly designed questionnaires go through this iterative process between one and six times.

In the piloting phase, judgements must be sought from academic peers about the likely validity of each question. Validity corresponds to how well the question measures what it sets out to measure. There will also have to be a judgement made about the coverage of the questionnaire in answering the research questions or covering all aspects of a guiding theory. In dissertation research, there is less need than in commercial research to worry about reliability, because a questionnaire is often only used once.

One final area to consider is how easy it will be to code and enter the data that the questionnaire produces. The ease of entry and coding will be in part related to the number of questions asked, the number of surveys likely to be returned, and the number of open questions used. At the piloting stage, the data entry and coding can be planned and the data from the pilot survey can be entered. From this experience changes can be made to the questionnaire related to the ease of data entry and coding. If you are using an online survey such as Google docs, the data is entered automatically.

CREATING A GOOGLE DOC SURVEY

Google docs provides a suite of software, free to students, containing a word processor, spreadsheet, presentation, database and, most importantly for us, a survey tool called Form. This section guides you through the process of creating a basic survey that you can easily expand and use in your own research.

First, you will need an iGoogle account, if you don't have one already.
- Find the Google search engine on the web.
- Search for and navigate to the iGoogle page.
- Sign up for an iGoogle account – you will create an account based on username@gmail.com.
- Search for and click on **Google docs for students**.
- Then click **Start using Google docs**.
- In the topline menu you will now see **Documents**.

Now let's get on with that survey. Follow these steps:
- Hit the topline menu **Documents**.
- Then, top left, **Create**, and choose **Form**.
- In the box with **Untitled Form** add the name of your survey.
- The first question box is waiting to be complete – so add the first question (it is a good idea also to have a numerical label like Q1, Q2, amd so on).
- Add some help text in the next box down.
- Choose the question type from this list:
  - **Text**: a simple text question
  - **Text paragraph**: for a longer answer
  - **Multiple choice**: select from a list of answers
  - **Check boxes**: answer by ticking one or more tick boxes
  - **Choose from a list**: present a list of possible answers
  - **Scale**: Likert scale answers
  - **Grid**: present a set of column headings for answers and ask questions in the rows
- Fill in the answers required by your particular question selection.
- If the question is compulsory then check the tick box at the bottom.
- Then 'Done' to finish that question.

Question 2 then appears: click on the pen image on the right to edit.

After Question 2 you will need to use the **Add item** button at the top of the page.

Carry on adding questions until you have approximately six to ten questions.

Figure 13 Google doc survey form (1)

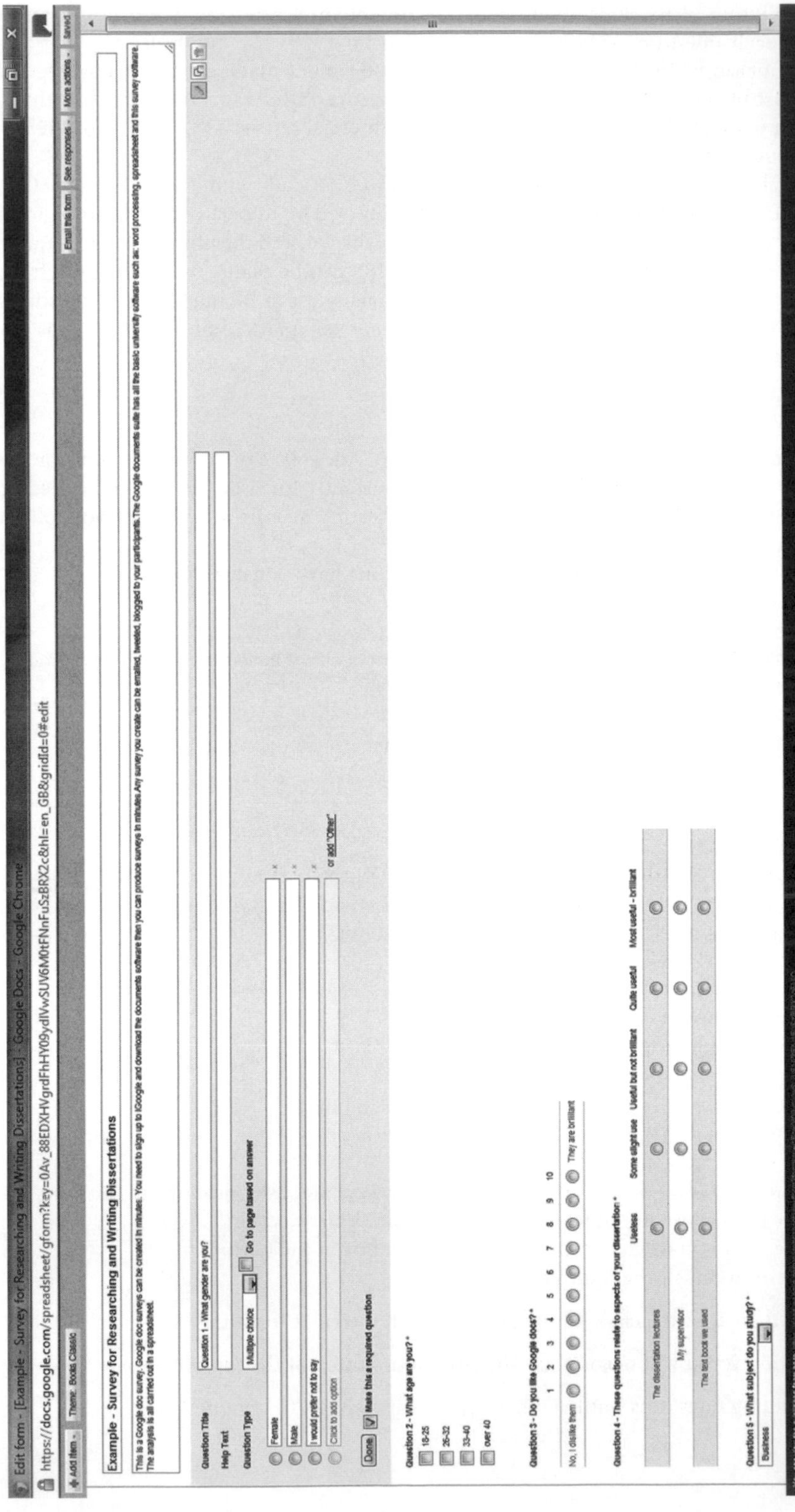

You should now have a survey that looks something like the example in Figure 13.

You can now send the questionnaire to your friends or classmates to complete and create some data for analysis.

- In the topline right-hand menu find the box **Email this form**: click on it.
- Add email addresses or choose them from **Contacts**.
- Then **Send**.

After a short while you will find that your survey is accumulating data.

The survey your friends or classmates receive looks like the image in Figure 14. You can change the look of it using the **Theme** button.

Figure 14 Google doc survey form (2)

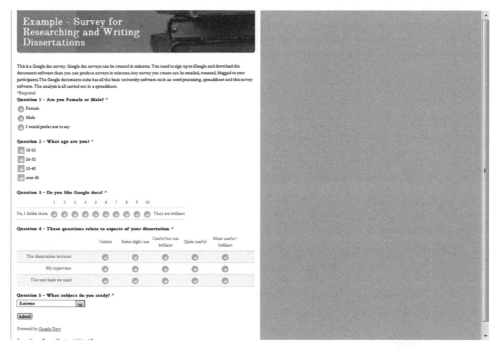

When you have input some data from participants, the survey will look like Figure 15.

Figure 15 Google doc survey form (3)

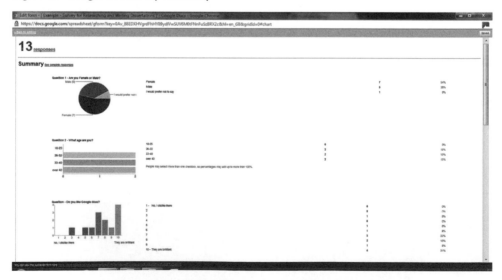

Figure 15 presents a spreadsheet view of your data. You can obtain a more visually useful summary of the data if you:

- click on **Forms** and then on **Summary of responses**.

My example data looks like Figure 16.

Figure 16 Google doc survey summary

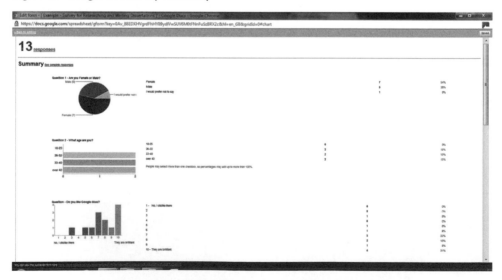

If you want to post your survey on a social network site or other website, the URL address is to be found by editing the form, and the address is at the bottom of the window.

7.5 INTERVIEWS

The demarcation between questionnaires and interviews is not very distinct. When questionnaires are administered in person by the researcher, the skills of interviewing are very much to the fore. This section firstly considers the skills required to carry out successful interviews, and then considers the types of interview that can be used.

Interviews are normally classified as a qualitative method for gathering data, but as is evident from the statement in the introduction to the section they can be quantitative. This classification may become clearer if we consider the nature of qualitative research. The difference between these two approaches is not always clear or distinct, but qualitative research quite often focuses on and displays the following characteristics:

- It is exploratory in nature.
- It uses natural, existing, settings and contexts.
- It is interested in meanings, perceptions, understandings.
- The research focus is often on processes, not outputs.
- It uses induction for the analysis of data.
- It produces specific rather than generalised data.
- Research findings are specific to the context.

The qualitative approach is often used when the area being researched is not well defined or is not well understood by current theory or research. This can occur because the research is in new settings or contexts or because there has been little research focus on an area. But sometimes well researched areas can be looked at afresh, revealing new insights and solutions, when a more exploratory approach is undertaken.

Qualitative research seeks data and understandings from natural organisational settings. The methods chosen need to disrupt these natural settings as little as possible. If your study proposes (for example) to look at illicit sexual affairs in the workplace, it will require a method that does not disrupt this activity. Interviews would not be very suitable – but you might consider observation, analysis of document records, personal diaries or social networking spaces.

Qualitative research is interested in exploring meanings, perceptions and understandings – interviews can be a very effective instrument for gathering this type of data. If the object of the study is group understanding, a group interview is the appropriate instrument. Qualitative research often focuses on processes, not outputs. Observation is an effective tool for understanding process, and interviews can be used so that respondents can explain their understandings of processes.

Qualitative research using an inductive approach researches the general and then focuses down to the specific. The outcomes of qualitative research are therefore often not generalisable to larger populations. The findings are specific to particular contexts. This can mean that qualitative research findings can be disseminated to be used in different contexts, but the contexts must be similar.

THE SKILLS REQUIRED FOR INTERVIEWING

In questionnaire research the survey is the instrument, but in interviewing the researcher is the instrument. It is essential therefore to plan, develop and pilot the interview with great care. The skills required for successful interviewing are different from the skills required for preparing a questionnaire. The essential skill is the ability to build a successful relationship quickly that will allow for valid good-quality data to be collected.

Interviews are predominantly about listening, and you must develop the skill of active listening. You do not say very much but the person speaking is very aware that you are listening intently to every word he or she is saying. This is achieved with body language – see below – and with small interventions in the discussion to show that you are both listening and understanding what is being said. These interventions will also be needed to steer the discussions along the lines of your prepared interview schedule, if there is one.

Body language is very important in interviews: posture, eye contact, and hand movements. In preparing to carry out interviews, do some 'dry runs' with friends or colleagues. If you can, video these, and then ask your colleague to assist you in analysing your body language. All the body language issues are about balance – too much eye contact and you will seem too intent, nervous or aggressive; too little eye contact and you will seem disinterested. Body language, like most aspects of interviewing, is about a relationship. Some interviewees will favour a lot of eye contact and some will favour just a little. Take your cues from the interviewee and modify your behaviour from your reading of the cues. Reflecting the behaviour of the interviewee is a very successful strategy for putting them at ease and gaining the best data possible. If the interviewee is not at ease, the data you get will be short and stilted and probably not a true reflection of their views.

The use of clear and understandable language is an important skill – using precise and direct questions will ensure a successful interview. If you intend asking specific questions, try them out in a pilot before the first interview is conducted. It is amazing how often the question you thought was straightforward – indeed, simple – turns out to be confusing or unclear the first time you use it. Avoid using jargon and abbreviations: they will make your interviewee ill at ease if he or she does not know them. Compound questions, where there is more than one question, should be avoided. There will be an opportunity after the first response to a question to develop it, or ask supplementary questions, but ensure that the first question in an area is simple and clear. If you are using an interview schedule, you can format the questions in such a way that the first question is simple and clear, and supplementary questions are more involved and complex. In qualitative interviews do not be afraid to modify the questions you ask to reflect the answers that the interviewee has given. This is quite normal practice and often reveals the most interesting data.

Empathy might be defined as identification and understanding of an interviewee's situation, feelings and motives. Empathy and trust are an important building-block of relationships and the relationship in an interview must be developed quickly. It is important that interviewees feel that you have a deep-seated understanding of their feelings; if they do not feel this, their responses are likely to be less 'rich' or 'deep'. It is also important so that you can get beyond the surface content of what they are saying, and better understand the underlying values, thoughts and feelings.

Social settings management is the skill of achieving your aims in different social settings. These skills will come to the fore in interviews involving more than one person. The skills are very similar to the skills needed to manage a meeting. Phrasing brief introductions that set the scene and the purpose of the interview are essential. You can develop this skill using groups of friends or by leading in tutorial group discussions. In interviews with more than one person it is important to control the environment so that everyone in the group feels able to participate. This is a more difficult skill to develop, but being aware of the need and developing personal strategies to include everyone in group interviews should work well. Summarising the interview at various points is also an important skill, as is the skill of dealing with feedback from the group about the accuracy of the summary. In lively group interviews your summary is likely to be challenged and debated by the group. It is as well to practise this aspect with friends before you conduct a live group interview.

Logistical skills are needed to set up, arrive, conduct the interview, and leave in the agreed time frame. There are whole sets of skills involved in arranging and conducting interviews that relate to being organised, precise and logical, and communicating clearly.

Observation skills are required to focus on and record the unsaid aspects of any interview. Taking notes in interviews will record these observations, such as facial expressions, shrugs, sighs, eye movements and pauses. Recording skills can be developed so that you can engage in conversation with the interviewee and record observations, insights, comments at the same time. Normally, handwritten notes are made of the interview as it progresses. This is important because such notes record a set of information that is different from the audio recordings that are customarily made. Once the interview is complete, these observations, insights and inferences should be fully recorded as quickly as possible. Your memory of these details will be volatile, and after even a few hours they will not be remembered.

Being insightful is the skill of seeing new things in the mundane parts of the interview. It requires alertness to the unusual statement, or the hesitation in a speech pattern that can reveal an underlying feeling, view or emotion that is not at the surface level. Following up on these small insightful points can uncover valuable data that would go unnoticed if the interviewer were not alert to such things.

As the interview progresses it is important to use probing questions to understand more fully significant areas of the interview. The significant areas are those that relate to your research questions. Once an answer has been given, it is normal to explore the answer more fully using questions like:

- Why did you do that?
- Can you elaborate?
- What evidence led you to …?
- What did you think?
- When did this happen?
- How did you feel?

You can probably see from above, the key words for probing questions are *why, can, what, when*, and *how*.

TYPES OF INTERVIEW

Interviews can be classified along many dimensions, but for clarity just two major dimensions are considered here. The first dimension measures the structure of interviews. This can vary from the highly structured to the totally unstructured. Highly structured interviews often appear more like the administration of a questionnaire in that all interactions revolve around predetermined questions; both open and closed questions can be used. The classification moves towards the less structured as more periods of interaction occur that are not centred on the predetermined questions. Finally, at the unstructured end of this continuum no formal questions are used – the interview consists of a free-flowing discussion around the topic area introduced by the researcher.

Structured interviews are used in situations where the research problem is well defined and the theoretical 'drivers' are well understood. In these circumstances, the interview is testing the various aspects of the theory or research problem. It would be normal to use the same type of data requirement sheet that was suggested for questionnaires. This would allow for all the aspects of the theory or research problem to be explored systematically and would assist in the analysis of the data collected.

Unstructured interviews are used in circumstances where the research is broad, wide-ranging or not well defined. They allow respondents to express their view without the constraint of a predetermined list of questions. The interviewer's main task is to explain the nature of the research and then to listen and observe. The respondent should be free to take the discussion to any area that he/she wishes to go, and sometimes respondents may seem to be explaining matters far removed from the researcher's view of the research. If using the unstructured approach, this wide-ranging explanation must be welcomed because it may well throw up new insights. Although interviewers may have a mental list of areas that the interview may cover, this should not be imposed on the interviewee, even if, when the discussion slows, it is permissible to introduce some of those pre-prepared questions into the discussion. Preparation for an unstructured interview should include listing the possible areas for discussion so that there is a tentative interview schedule, and developing a considered opening statement that explains the research.

The interview guide opening statement should say the minimum possible that allows an interviewee to understand the nature of your inquiry. The more that is said about the research in the opening statement, the more the respondent will tend to answer the implicit questions contained in the statement.

EXAMPLE: INTERVIEW OPENING STATEMENT

Frankie was investigating self-esteem in organisations using unstructured interviews to broadly explore what it meant to people. There was a real worry that anything said at the beginning of the interview would restrict the possible range of discussions that might result from the interview. In the first interview Frankie explained at some length what self-esteem was, and how it could be manifest in organisations. The interviewee then made some brief statements about the areas that Frankie had suggested, and the interview came to an end quite quickly. Frankie thought to herself, 'Eighteen minutes – and I spoke for about nine of those minutes.' Later, Frankie discussed this with a number of people and finally concluded that her introduction had been too wide-ranging.

In the second interview the introduction was quite short, but the interviewee asked what self-esteem was, and a discussion took place. The thought that went through Frankie's mind after this interview was, 'Twenty-four minutes – four minutes of my introduction, and 12 minutes to try to explain what self-esteem was. So only eight minutes of real interview.'

After some further reflection Frankie settled for the following opening statement – 'I would like your views on self-esteem.' If an interviewee asked what self-esteem was, the response was always: 'That depends on your view.' Once Frankie approached the interviews from this stance, the interviews often lasted for over an hour.

The size of the interview grouping is another important dimension to be considered. Interviewing individuals provides very specific and detailed information but is very time-consuming and the respondent is providing a non-relationship and personal perspective. Individual interviews are used when the required data is of the specific, detailed and individual perspective.

Group interviews

Group interviews should be used for specific research purposes. Some of the specific reasons for using group interviews are:

- to investigate the dynamics of a group
- to explore the reality of group membership
- to debate group issues as a collective
- to discover the methods and dynamics of group cohesion
- to explore shared meanings
- to investigate the roles played by group members
- to discover the processes of constructing realities in groups.

What can be seen from this list of reasons is that group interviews are not designed to be a cheap and quick way of gathering data. If individual views are sought, individual interviews would be used. If group views are sought, group interviews would be used. Group interviews present quite a few logistical and analytical problems for a researcher. Because the researcher is mainly focused on controlling and facilitating the group, it will not be possible to record any written information in the course of the group interview. It is quite normal to have one or several note-takers sitting in the room but outside of the group to record body language, group dynamic issues, important narrative, interaction and support structures. For a group of 12 participants, there might be a lead researcher and two to four assistant researchers. After the group interview is complete, the notes from the researchers would be amalgamated into a real-time record of observations. The lead researcher must develop skills in controlling and facilitating a group interview. It would be helpful if he or she had completed some group interviews as one of the assistant researchers.

The conduct of the group interview normally follows a semi-structured or structured format, with questions 'triggering' the group responses. There must be freedom for the group to respond in the ways that best express the group's views. Participants are selected because of their involvement in a particular group or groups.

The group interview should be recorded using multiple recording equipment. Group interviews are normally videotaped via three machines. More machines are needed if the group is larger than 12 participants. It is necessary to video group interviews so that you can be sure who is speaking, and what the other group members are doing. The video evidence, with the notes from the assistant researchers, is then analysed using one of the qualitative methods discussed in the later data analysis chapter.

Focus groups

Focus groups are often used to test participants' reactions to products. However, this type of interview is also useful in gathering data about topics, feelings and meanings. Whereas a group interview focuses on the aspect of a topic related to groups, the focus group is concerned with the research question as content rather than as process. Participants are selected because of their common interest in a topic, idea, approach or course of action. Focus groups are typically of 8 to 12 people. Any larger and it becomes difficult to control the group, to keep them focused on the topic and to record the information they provide.

The recording arrangements are similar to group interviews in that multiple recording is required.

Longitudinal interviews

Longitudinal interviews are normally one-to-one interviews, but more than one is conducted over a period of time. They are particularly suited to the study of change over time. The conduct of the interview is essentially the same as any one-to-one qualitative interview. The main methodology decision is to decide on the length of the study and the interval between interviews. Some classic social studies have continued for in excess of 10 years, with interviews every year. In dissertation research these time-scales would be inappropriate, but the technique can be used to gather data over a period of months, especially if the research questions are focusing on the changing nature of an organisational phenomenon.

7.6 COMMONLY-USED METHODS

OBSERVATION

It is important to distinguish between what human participants say happened and what actually happened. Human memory is selective in perception and in recall, and therefore what an interviewee might say about a situation and what actually happened (from an observer's standpoint) may be quite different. This difference between what is said and what happens is not normally a deliberate ploy to mislead researchers – it occurs because of the normal human processes of perception and memory recall. The role of observation studies can be as a primary research data-collecting technique or it can be as part of a multi-method technique. When used as a part of a multi-method approach, the observations are used to corroborate the data already collected from interviews.

Observation studies are often conducted over long periods of time, and can be either 'objective observer' type or 'participant observer' type. When the observer is objective, he or she is not part of the activity being observed – the study is then a direct observation study, in that participants are aware that they are being observed. Behaviour at the commencement of an observation can often be non-typical due to the observation effect, but most people forget they are being observed after some time and behaviour can then be regarded as normal. The other type of research observation is unobtrusive observation, where participants are unaware that they are being observed. This type of observation has important ethical dimensions that must be considered prior to the commencement of any study. Unobtrusive observations always require approval by an ethics committee.

One final type of observation is the participant observation where the researcher takes part in the activity being observed. This provides a privileged and intimate vantage point from which to observe behaviour. It does, however, present issues around recording data from the observation. This is normally done by keeping a research journal filled in after the daily activity is complete. Participant observations are sometimes direct observations, but are more often unobtrusive observations and so will require ethical approval.

There are two possible time-frames for observations: either continuous observing where all activity in a day or event is seen and recorded, or time allocation monitoring is carried out. The key question in time allocation monitoring is what interval of time to use. This may range from an opportunity time frame where the researcher observes an organisational or social scene until a saturated record has been made through to predetermined sampling of maybe ten minutes in every hour.

What is observed in these studies?

Descriptive observational data requires you to observe something and note down what has been seen. Inferential observational data requires the researcher to make inferences about what is observed and the underlying emotion. Thus, if we see someone shouting, we may record the shouting and note down the inference that the person was angry. Care must be taken with inferences, because (in this example) the person may have been shouting simply to get someone's attention. When actions are observed, it may be necessary to note down several possible inferences and the probability of each. Evaluative observational data requires the researcher to make a descriptive note, an inference and a judgement of the observed behaviour. The field notes made must describe the context, the nature of the setting and any other significant feature, because all these things are capable of changing the behaviour observed. Data analysis from these field notes is considered in the following chapter.

ETHNOGRAPHIC STUDIES

The key element of ethnographic studies is that they research the whole system, arguing that it is not possible to research parts of a system to understand the whole. Classic ethnography studied social cultures, took many years, and provided very detailed accounts of all elements of a society or social grouping. Modern organisational research has adopted this approach for the study of organisational cultures. The time scale is shorter, but the underlying premise that the whole system must be studied remains. Ethnography uses a mixture of mostly qualitative techniques such as:

- direct, first-hand observation of daily behaviour
- participant observation
- informal and formal conversations
- studies of small-talk and gossip
- interviews
- studies of relationships in organisations
- detailed work with key players in organisations
- in-depth interviewing

- discovery of local beliefs, values and perceptions
- critical incident analysis
- problem-oriented research
- longitudinal research of aspects of the organisation.

Because of the long-term nature of ethnography, it is not used extensively in dissertation research. But adopting the holistic nature of ethnography can offer a valuable method when researching groups, and organisations. It would be possible to devise a method that involved three months' ethnographic study of some part of an organisation. Tony Watson (2000) developed a book from his ethnographic study of managers striving to cope in changing organisational circumstances.

REPERTORY GRID TECHNIQUE

Repertory gird technique is based on the theory of personal constructs which suggests that each person interprets the world in terms of their own personal set of constructs – ideas about how the world works. Constructs are ways of seeing and interpreting the world that are personal, although personal construct systems may well align with others' personal constructs. The repertory grid is a way of exploring and understanding personal constructs used in relation to an event or circumstance. The technique normally involves two phases: the elicitation of constructs in use, and the rating of the constructs. Software for analysis is available to assist in the data analysis phase. See the section in Chapter 9 for more details of the technique and the analysis method.

DIARIES

Diaries can be used to collect detailed and rich self-reflection data from participants in a research study. They typically contain detail about events, motives, feelings, thoughts, and the behaviour of the diarist and others. They can often be an alternative to traditional interviews and have some advantages over that method. Diaries are now mostly kept as computer documents, so the time taken by the researcher to collect data is very low. The entries are likely to be both more revealing and more accurate than the data that might be collected in an interview. Diary-keeping can be paired with interviewing to create a reliable and valid multi-method approach. Diaries can be open-format or category-structured. Open-format allows for the most expressive accounts to be given, but the analysis is labour-intensive. Pre-categorised diaries provide a more restricted account but reduce the time required to analyse the data. Pre-categorised diaries need extensive piloting to ensure that they are grounded in theory and are effective in use.

A modern variation on diaries for data collection is the audio diary or the video diary, made popular by reality television programmes. These methods offer a fast and effective way to record huge amounts of personal data very quickly and cheaply. Of course, the equipment problems have to be overcome, such as cost, loss of equipment and technical difficulties. But the major problem arises at the analysis stage. Participants can be provided with guidelines for the study indicating what areas of their lives should be recorded, but in all probability you will be provided with a very large amount of unstructured data. The time required to analyse this unstructured data will be very large. One developing technique for audio data is to use voice recognition software. Once you have trained the system to your voice, you read the audio data out and the software will translate it into text. The accuracy will not be perfect – you will have to do some editing – but it will save a lot of time.

RELIVING

Witkin and Poupart (1985) in 'Running a commentary on imaginatively re-lived events: a method for obtaining qualitatively rich data' provided the raw ingredients for an approach to the gathering of qualitatively rich data (page 79).

The method replaces the normal interview with one in which the researcher encourages and assists the subject to develop a 'commentary' in the present tense on imaginatively relived events that are deemed to be of significance in the life world or work of the subject. Literally, the subject is asked to imagine that the events are happening now, and to run a commentary on them so as to make them 'visible' to the researcher.

They go on to explain that good storytellers follow the approach when communicating. The role of the researcher is to create an environment in which the participant can relive an event that is qualitatively rich, and relevant to the research area. It is a technique that is most suited to exploratory studies. The reliving is recorded and later transcribed, providing qualitative data that is analysed by developing categories of statements, feelings, values or behaviours.

ACTION RESEARCH AND PARTICIPATORY RESEARCH

The characteristics of participatory research are:

- People are the subjects of research: the dichotomy between the subject and the researcher is broken.
- Participants themselves collect the data, and then process and analyse the information using methods easily understood by them.
- The knowledge generated is used to promote actions for change or to improve existing local actions.
- The knowledge belongs to the participants and they are the primary beneficiaries of the knowledge creation.
- Research and action are inseparable.
- Research is a cycle of action – reflection where knowledge-creation supports action.
- There is a built-in mechanism to ensure authenticity and genuineness of the information that is generated.

These characteristics are very different from those of a 'normal' research study. Researchers normally act as assistant researchers on a study before they can successfully complete their own study. The role of the researcher in action research or participant action research is to facilitate a rigorous investigative process. This often involves devising simple research approaches that engage and energise the participant group.

ROLE PLAY

Research that investigates human behaviour can place 'actors' in settings and observe their behaviour. Research has been conducted on interviewing job applicants, performance appraisals and leadership influence. The basic business and psychological processes are also studied using role-playing methods. These include decision-making, business processes such as inbox activities, and judging other people's behaviour. Sophisticated virtual worlds such as Second Life offer interesting role-playing arenas for dissertation research, with a ready supply of subjects.

ORAL HISTORY TECHNIQUES

The Oral History Society offers excellent advice on carrying out oral history studies. Oral history involves people in telling their own life stories. The role of the researcher is to focus the study or develop the theme and then to seek out those with histories to give. Emmett (2007) reports on the oral histories of the University of Chicago Economics Department between the 1930s and the 1980s. He records the oral histories of professors, lecturers and students, building up a multifaceted view of the organisation during this period. If you are carrying out an oral history study, be sure to check on the technical detail of any recordings you make. The theme in Emmett's work was a single place over time: Chicago University's economics department,

1930–1980. Shorter themes or event themes are more suitable for dissertation research. So, for instance, a study might be on oral histories of a merger or acquisition, or oral histories of crisis points such as the Northern Rock credit crisis.

NARRATIVE RESEARCH

Narrative research focuses on the construction and dissemination of stories. The focus of attention for business research is on individual or organisational stories. Stories exist in all areas of human interaction and can be researched by investigating:

- written and recorded stories of organisational settings
- individual life stories
- group-created stories
- fairy stories and stories from history.

Once a story has been uncovered, elicited or otherwise recorded, there are several forms of analysis that can be conducted.

Narrative analysis

Narrative analysis is analysis of a chronologically-told story, with a focus on how elements are sequenced. The analysis also asks why some elements are evaluated differently from others, and how the past shapes perceptions of the present. Narrative analysis is an in-depth qualitative technique.

Content analysis

Content analysis is a systematic method for analysing text or stories and developing categories based on explicit rules for coding. Content analysis is a method for revealing the messages and ideas carried in written forms. For instance, a study could be made of the content of organisational mission statements. To fulfil the requirements of reliability and validity the precision of the codes used for analysis is the key feature. This technique is used for analysis of qualitative data and is thoroughly covered in the next two chapters.

7.7 NOTES AND DEFINITIONS IN THE RESEARCH PROCESS

TRIANGULATION

Triangulation is a well-used and confused term. It seems as if no dissertation is complete without inclusion of the word 'triangulation'. There are at least four ways to use the term. *Methodological triangulation* is covered below. *Data triangulation* involves collecting different types of data related to the research. It is quite common to collect data at different times. This will add some sense of reliability to the data collection – assuming the two sets of data concur. If the two sets of data turn out to be dissimilar, an investigation of the causes will be required. Strictly the term 'triangulation' requires three (or more) perspectives. We can also achieve a measure of data triangulation by using three sets of 'matched' participants. We could then argue that because the data from three different but closely matched sets of participants are similar, the research is generating some measure of reliability.

Researcher triangulation uses three or more researchers to conduct and view the research. The most frequently-used example of this is where three researchers independently of each other observe a research event. Post-event analysis will focus on the similarities and differences between the accounts of the three researchers. Researcher bias is always present, and this approach helps to surface specific bias and also by analysis to mitigate its effects.

Theory triangulation involves investigations that adopt three different 'driving theories' (defined elsewhere as synthesised theory). This approach allows for multiple explanations and recommendations to be given. Typically, one synthesised theory will emerge as having greater explanatory power than the others.

Triangulation is not a panacea for poorly structured and reasoned research. It is criticised as presenting a naive idea that there is only one 'correct' way to understand a phenomenon. The general trend of *constructionism* is that each person and group constructs the world in a way that is particular to them. So from a constructivist approach there is not, and can never be, one agreed 'true' explanation. In practice, for dissertation research, any form of triangulation often creates confusion and a lack of clarity rather than the intended outcome of validity and reliability.

MULTIPLE METHODS

It should be noted that using just one method – a mono method – is a perfectly sound research approach. When used in dissertation research, it has the merit of being simple to understand and explain and being speedy to complete. Quantitative mono methods such as questionnaires rely on sampling and statistical techniques (covered in this and other chapters) to establish the validity of the outcomes. Qualitative research cannot rely on these two aspects, because they are often small opportunity samples of interview or observational data.

Methodological triangulation

As remarked above, triangulation is a means of improving the validity of qualitative research, and to a lesser extent of quantitative research. Triangulation involves a research method that collects data using three (or more) distinct methods. A multi-method approach uses more than one method to gather data – most often a two-method approach – and should ensure improved confidence in the outcomes.

Mixed methods

If the research design combined quantitative and qualitative research, we would call it a mixed-method approach. There are several approaches that use mixed methods depending on the research philosophy. Mixed methods are often used sequentially, one after the other in a two-phase design.

- *Qualitative method informs the quantitative method*, often following inductive reasoning. When an area is not well researched and/or is lacking in well-developed theory, it may be difficult to construct a questionnaire or form a hypothesis. A qualitative method, such as interviews or focus groups, would then be used to explore the issues. The analysis of the data would then provide issues and ideas for the quantitative study to explore.
- *Quantitative method followed by the qualitative method*: in this approach the qualitative method is used to explore interesting or complex issues raised by the questionnaire study. This approach would be broadly following the deductive method. If the quantitative data is finding confused or irregular-looking outcomes, a qualitative study – often interviews – can be used to follow up and explore these unusual outcomes. In general, when we see confusing or unusual findings it is a signal to investigate more fully.

Multi-method approaches

Multi-method approaches use more than one method to research the same thing. For example, if research were conducted on retail stock losses, it would be possible to design a study with the following elements:

- statistical analysis of the stock records
- interviews with staff
- analysis of security video
- interviews with convicted shoplifters.

Confidence in any findings would be improved if the findings of one element of the design agreed with the findings of one or more of the other elements.

When planning the methodological approach, beware of the time constraint in dissertation research. It is all very well having a complex and elegant multi-phase multi-method design, but complexity slows down the research process. Your aim in dissertation research is to create a method that is simple, is do-able and will produce outputs that are viewed with confidence.

PRIMARY AND SECONDARY DATA AND SOURCES

There is considerable confusion around what is meant by 'primary' and 'secondary' data and literature. This section is intended to present a clear and simple statement about how to use these terms.

Primary data refers to data that has been collected for the study in which it is used. Your findings will thus be primary data. Funded research produces primary data where it collects quantitative or qualitative data.

Secondary data refers to data that is being included in research or academic writing that has not been collected as part of that study. Thus, if you have carried out a re-analysis of the data produced from a CIPD research study, you would be using secondary data.

In many dissertations there is primary data (that collected by the research) and secondary data (that which was not collected by the research). In writing about data, be sure to make clear if you are using primary data that you have collected or secondary data that came from a published source or another research study.

Do not use the terms 'primary' and 'secondary' for any purpose other than defining data. You will often come across the terms used for source material (as in 'primary literature' and 'secondary literature'). You are advised not to follow this convention. If you need to express the status of literature, it would be better to describe it as 'literature containing primary data' or 'literature containing secondary data'.

7.8 ETHICS

It is important to consult your university regulations relating to the ethical standards of conducting research. These will be unique to the institution, but the sections set out below cover most of the major areas that must be considered. Ensure that your research proposal has a section addressing ethics. If you are in any doubt, consult with your dissertation supervisor. Depending on the nature and context of your research you may have to seek and gain ethics approval from your university or workplace ethics committee. There are specific requirements for each institution, but the section below sets out a general introduction.

ETHICAL CONSIDERATIONS FOR RESEARCH INVOLVING HUMAN PARTICIPANTS

The main aim of ethical standards and the issues highlighted here are that your research should DO NO HARM. It is preferable for your research to do some good. The methodology section must set out the detail and argument of an ethical case for your research. It must weigh up the potential good against the possible harm. There are special rules for carrying out research with children or those who are unable to give informed consent – if your research involves either of these groups, you must discuss it fully with your supervisor. Although students over 18 years of age are considered to be able to give informed consent, it is worth considering carefully the impact of any study on this group of relatively life-inexperienced people. Informed consent will be required for all research. This may be as simple as asking if respondents are comfortable with completing a questionnaire, or as complicated as a full, research ethics committee approved consent form.

In this respect the Economic and Social Research Council has set out six key principles:

1 Research should be designed, reviewed and undertaken to ensure integrity, quality and transparency.

2 Research staff and participants must normally be informed fully about the purpose, methods and intended possible uses of the research, what their participation in the research entails and what risks, if any, are involved.

3 The confidentiality of information supplied by research participants and the anonymity of respondents must be respected.

4 Research participants must take part voluntarily, free from any coercion.

5 Harm to research participants must be avoided in all instances.

6 The independence of research must be clear, and any conflicts of interest or partiality must be explicit.

JUDGEMENTS ABOUT HARMING PARTICIPANTS

Making a judgement about the possible harm that could occur from a study is not an easy process. Careful consideration must be given to any effects on the well-being of participants. It is vital that no physical harm come to participants. If a study involves physical activities, these will have to be piloted with skilled participants and a suitable risk assessment carried out. In the majority of business research studies, it is the psychological well-being of participants that must be protected. Because each participant may perceive a question in possibly specific damaging ways, it is not easy to predict possible damage to well-being. One approach is to seek ethical judgements about the effect of any instrument on the participants of the pilot study. Judgements must be made about each question. Asking about preferred chocolate bars does not seem very intrusive, but to an anorexic such a question may be damaging.

The research method chosen must be justified by the potential risk to participants. If less risky methods can be used, there must be a compelling case for using a more risky method. This is one of the reasons that research methods must be fully discussed and evaluated in a methodology section.

When working with a diverse group of participants, great care should be taken to handle the differences in gender, age, religions and cultures with great sensitivity. This is especially important in the wording of questions in questionnaires, because these cannot easily be adjusted to the participants' circumstance, unlike interviews where adjustment and sensitivity to the participants' diversity is relatively easy.

OBTAINING INFORMED CONSENT

Potential participants have the right to a clear understanding of the research. Research information sheets are often used that set out:

- the title of the study
- the purpose of the study
- why the participant was selected for the study
- a description of procedures, the purpose, the length of time required, and how participants will be involved
- a statement of any likely inconveniences expected
- the possible risks to the participants, and details of any support mechanisms
- the possible benefits to the participants and society
- details of any payments, prize draws, feedback from the study
- how confidentiality, anonymity and privacy will be maintained

- the right of participants to refuse to participate or to withdraw at any time for any reason
- contact details of the university ethics group, and the researcher
- details of the care, use and storage of the data collected from the study
- the signature of the researcher and the participant.

Example layout of a Research Information Sheet
- Title of study
- *Information Sheet for Participants*
- The information sheet should be written for a lay person to understand and should cover the following topics:
- The purpose of the research
- What is involved in participating
- Benefits and risks – including a statement that the participant may not benefit directly from the research
- Terms for withdrawal:
  - participants have a right to withdraw at any time without prejudice and without providing a reason
  - thought should be given to what will happen to existing, already provided data in the event of withdrawal
- Use of the data:
  - during research
  - dissemination
  - storage, archiving, sharing and reuse of data
- Strategies for assuring ethical use of the data:
  - procedures for maintaining confidentiality
  - anonymising data where necessary, especially in relation to data archiving
- Details of the research:
  - the funding source
  - the sponsoring institution
  - the name of the project
  - contact details for researchers
- An invitation to ask for more information, with researchers' names and contact details.

EXAMPLE OF A SIMPLE CONSENT FORM

Stress Research at ARTO Incorporated

Thank you for considering taking part in this research. If you have any questions, please ask a member of the research team before you decide whether to take part. You will be given a copy of this Consent Form to keep and refer to at any time. Please tick, as appropriate:

 I confirm that I have read and understood the Information Sheet for Participants dated January 2012 (version 122/12) for the above study. I have had the opportunity to consider the information, ask questions and have had these answered satisfactorily.

 I understand that my participation is voluntary and that I am free to withdraw at any time without giving any reason, without my care or legal rights being affected.

 I understand that if I withdraw from the study, the data collected from me up to that point will be destroyed.

> ☑ I agree to take part in the study.
>
> Participant's name: .... Signed: ....
>
> Researcher's name: .... Signed: ....
>
> Dated: ....

The following is a more involved consent form. Note that although it covers more points and represents an approved form of consent, it may be more off-putting for participants. I would suggest in practice that you introduce elements of both into your own consent forms.

MODEL CONSENT FORM

Name of study

Please tick the appropriate boxes

I have read and understood the project information sheet   ☐

I have been given the opportunity to ask questions about the project   ☐

I agree to take part in the project. Taking part in the project will include [*indicate form of participation, eg being interviewed and recorded (audio or video)*]   ☐

I understand that my taking part is voluntary; I can withdraw from the study at any time and I will not be asked questions about why I no longer want to take part   ☐

Select only ONE of the next two options:

I would like my name stated against any information I have said or written as part of this study that will be used in reports, publications and other research outputs, so that anything I have contributed to this project can be recognised   ☐

OR

I do not want my name used in this project   ☐

I understand my personal details such as phone number or address will not be revealed to people outside this project   ☐

I understand that my words may be quoted in publications, reports, web pages, and other research outputs but my name will not be used unless I requested it above   ☐

I agree for the data I provided to be archived at the UK Data Archive   ☐
[*include this where required by the funding body; more detail may be provided here so that decisions can be made separately about audio, video, transcripts, etc*]

I understand that other researchers will have access to these data only if they agree to preserve the confidentiality of the data   ☐

I understand that other researchers may use my words in publications, reports, web pages and other research outputs   ☐

I agree to assign the copyright I hold in any materials related to this project to [*name of researcher*]   ☐

On this basis I am happy to participate in the [*name of project*] study

Name of Participant .... Signature .... Date ....

Name of Researcher .... Signature .... Date ....

If you have any queries or concerns, please contact: [*insert names, phone, email address, etc*]

One copy to be kept by the participant; one to be kept by the researcher

The informed consent can be recorded in a number of other ways dependent on the type of research instrument. When using questionnaires, a simple statement at the end requiring a tick in a consent box or a signature will be sufficient. In interviews a small tear-off tab may be provided at the end of the research information sheet – the participant would sign this and return it to the researcher. Participants must be well-informed and free to give their consent without any coercive behaviour by the researcher.

It is sometimes necessary to seek approval for your study from an organisation before carrying out the research. This would normally be covered at the same time as access to the participants in an organisation is granted. A signed agreement as to the nature of the access and the grant of approval to carry out the research is important, and may prove essential in the continuation of your access if organisational circumstances change.

Some research requires the formal approval by a university ethics committee. Most universities use a two-stage process for ethics approval. Stage 1 is designed to check if a formal approval is required. Stage 2 details the research and the risks to enable a formal committee to give approval.

Stage 1 requires the following typical questions to be answered and then countersigned by your supervisor.

EXAMPLE OF A STAGE 1 ETHICS APPROVAL FORM

Ethical review form for research involving human participants

No data with human participants should be collected until ethical approval has been formally given.

Name of student:

Project title:

Overall aim of the research project: [*3–4 sentences*]

Proposed research methods:

Intended participants:

Signature of student: ....

Signature of supervisor: ....

Please complete all sections by ringing the appropriate answer.

1. RISKS

	YES	NO
Do any aspects of the study pose a possible risk to participants' physical well-being (eg use of substances such as alcohol or extreme situations such as sleep deprivation)?		

Are there any aspects of the study that participants might find embarrassing or emotionally upsetting?	YES	NO
Are there likely to be culturally-sensitive issues (eg age, gender, ethnicity, etc)?	YES	NO
Does the study require access to confidential sources of information (eg medical, criminal, educational records, etc)?	YES	NO
Might conducting the study expose the researcher to any risks (eg collecting data in potentially dangerous environments)?	YES	NO
Does the intended research involve vulnerable groups (eg prisoners, children, older or disabled people, victims of crime, etc)	YES	NO

2. DISCLOSURE

Does the study involve covert methods?	YES	NO
Please confirm that the study does not involve the use of deception, either in the form of withholding essential information about the study or intentionally misinforming participants about aspects of the study.	YES deception is involved	NO deception is not involved

3. DEBRIEFING

Do the planned procedures include an opportunity for participants to ask questions and/or obtain general feedback about the study after they have concluded their part in it?	YES	NO	N.A.

4. INFORMED PARTICIPATION/CONSENT

Will participants in the study be given accessible information outlining a) the general purpose of the study; b) what participants will be expected to do; and c) individuals' right to refuse or withdraw at any time?	YES	NO	N.A.
Will participants have an opportunity to ask questions prior to agreeing to participate?	YES	NO	N.A.
Have appropriate authorities given their permission for participants to be recruited from or data collected on their premises (eg shop managers, head teachers, classroom lecturers)?	YES	NO	N.A.

5. ANONYMITY AND CONFIDENTIALITY

Is participation in the study anonymous?	YES	NO	
If anonymity has been promised, do the general procedures ensure that individuals cannot be identified indirectly (eg via other information that is taken)?	YES	NO	N.A.
Have participants been promised confidentiality?	YES	NO	N.A.
If confidentiality has been promised, do the procedures ensure that the information collected is truly confidential (eg that it will not be quoted verbatim)?	YES	NO	N.A.
Will data be stored in a secure place which is inaccessible to people other than the researcher?	YES	NO	N.A.
If participants' identities are being recorded, will the data be coded (to disguise identity) before computer data entry?	YES	NO	N.A.

6. SUMMARY OF ETHICAL CONCERNS

If any of the boxes below requires a tick, you should complete the relevant sections in the Stage 2 ethics documentation. If none of the boxes requires a tick, it is reasonable to expect approval.

If you have answered 'YES' to any of the questions in Section 1 (risks), please tick the box.	
If you have answered 'YES' to any of the questions in Section 2 (disclosure/covert methods), please tick the box.	
If you have answered 'NO' to any of the questions in Section 3 (debriefing), please tick the box.	
If you have answered 'NO' to any of the questions in Section 4 (consent), please tick the box.	
If you have answered 'NO' to any of the questions in Section 5 (confidentiality), please tick the box.	

Student signature: ....   Date: ....

APPROVAL: ....   Date: ....

Project supervisor

If any aspect of the research requires further ethical investigation, further details are provided using a document rather like the example below.

EXAMPLE OF A STAGE 2 APPROVAL FORM

Name of student:

Project title:

Ethical Considerations
If you have ticked any of the boxes in Section 6 of Approval Stage,1 please give details below of how you will address each issue in your research.

Section 1 – Risks

Section 2 – Disclosure/covert methods

Section 3 – Debriefing

Section 4 – Consent

Section 5 – Confidentiality

Signature of student:

Signature of supervisor:

If in the supervisor's judgement the research will require full ethics committee approval, the form should be annotated with the words 'referred for full ethics approval' and a copy kept on file. The student should be asked to fill in the full ethics approval form.

When completed, this form **MUST** be countersigned by your supervisor. A signed copy should be kept on file by the University. You are also advised to keep a signed copy for your own records.

If full ethics approval is required, your university will have a specific forms and arrangements. The example below displays the types of area that will have to be explained for approval to be granted. Full ethical approval normally takes several weeks but can take months. In practical terms it may be a sensible strategy to adjust the research to avoid the requirement of a full ethics approval.

EXAMPLE OF AN ETHICS PRO-FORMA

GUIDELINES AND PRO-FORMA FOR PROPOSED RESEARCH PROJECTS

For submission to the Ethics Committee

The Pro-Forma is to assist members of the Research Ethics Committee. It is therefore essential that the following questions are individually answered by researchers before the research projects are considered by the Committee. To aid clarity, it is suggested that the questions are retained in bold with the answers added in italics. Please remember that the Ethics Committee is made up of diverse individuals and therefore give your answers in clear language.

Particular emphasis is placed on the Participant Information Sheet and the Consent Form, which must accompany all submissions.

Ethics Committee approval is for a limited period, which will be stated on the approval. At the end of this period the researcher should request an extension, if necessary. If the basis of the research has not altered and it is progressing satisfactorily, there should be no difficulty about extending Ethics Committee approval.

In order to comply with the National Research Ethics Service application form and guidelines, we have adopted certain procedures. The Ethics Committee will continue to request a progress report at six-monthly intervals from the month in which approval was given. The report will be sent out to you when it becomes due. The same form will be required on completion of your project. Please request a copy from the Committee Secretary.

You are advised to refer to the National Research Ethics Service (NRES) guidelines and appendices before you complete your application. A reference copy of this is available online at http://www.nres.npsa.nhs.uk/.

On all Participant Information Sheets and Consent Forms a **principal contact and telephone number must be identified.**

Participants in the study are to be sent **two copies of documentation** which they are required to sign with instructions for them to **keep a copy for themselves and a second copy to be returned to the sender.**

Principal investigator/research details

Title		Forename		Surname	
Post held:					
Department:		Email: Tel. no./Ext Fax no.			
Organisation:					
Full postal address (including postcode):					

Co-applicants

NAME	POST HELD	ORGANISATION

Full title of project:

Justification of the research

Explain the rationale for carrying out this project. Please include any literature review to support the research.

Total cost (if applicable)

£

Proposed duration: [*months*]

'Plain language' summary

Please summarise your proposal in non-scientific language, using words and terms that can be easily understood by non-research communities. Do not use acronyms or abbreviations. Your summary must include a clear statement of the purpose of your research, how it will build on existing evidence where available, and its intended benefits to patients and the public. It must also describe how the research will be conducted and how patients and the public will be involved, both as research participants and partners.

Please indicate the methodological design(s) and other features of your study

☐ Literature review	☐ Clinical Trial
☐ Clinical Trial	☐ Randomised
☐ Scoping/mapping study	☐ Controlled
☐ Policy analysis/service evaluation	☐ Single blind
☐ Case-control study	☐ Double blind
☐ Survey	☐ Incidence/prevalence study
☐ Cohort study	☐ Systematic review/meta analysis
☐ Economic evaluation	☐ Qualitative (please elaborate using the 'Other' box below)

Other (*please use this box if your proposal is qualitative research **or** if your quantitative method is not listed above*)

Sampling procedure

Please include sample size and sample calculation (if applicable). Sufficient detail should be given to enable any calculation to be repeated.

Study procedures

Please describe study methods, including all measurements and outcomes, processes and the follow-up.

Planned analysis

How will you analyse your data?

Have you taken statistical advice?

Yes ☐ From whom?	No ☐ Please justify	N/A ☐

Have you taken analytical advice?

Yes ☐ From whom?	No ☐ Please justify	N/A ☐

References

Cite up to 10 academic references that reflect your literature review.

Dissemination

Please state your plans for disseminating your research findings.

Project plan and milestones

List of key tasks	*Timing (in months)*

eg 1) Organise focus groups
    2) Data collection
    3) Data entry
	Months 1–2
	Months 2–5
	Months 3–6

Who will conduct the study?

Who will be responsible?

Who will actually do the research?

What other members of helpers will be included?

Who will be undertaking the study, and what will their role be?

Are they competent to undertake this work?

Has the person named received adequate training?

For those yet to be assigned to the study, will they be receiving training prior to investigation?

What practical procedures will the participants undergo?

Details and frequency of interventions – to what extent are they part of normal activities?

What are the degrees of inconvenience/pain/discomfort for the participants?

What are the possible adverse effects/complications, and what are the chances of their occurring?

How will participants be selected and approached?

State if minors, elderly, pregnant or lactating women, or mentally incapacitated people will be included.

State if participant exclusion in the light of possible adverse effects from practical activies.

Please include a list of:
Subject inclusion criteria

Subject exclusion criteria

Have those responsible for the participants (eg employer, lecturer) given their approval?

Yes ☐	No ☐	N/A ☐

How will the research be funded?

*We need to know the costs of carrying out **each stage** of the research*

Consent

Please use the following as a checklist before providing a full statement
Who will ask for consent?
Consent must be obtained in writing.
A consent form should normally be given to the participant at least 24 hours before it is expected to be returned.
A consent form must be signed by all participants.
The consent form must state that the information sheet has been read and understood.
It is the responsibility of the researcher to ensure that the participant fully comprehends and interprets the content of the information sheet used for the project as it is intended.
Participants with reading difficulties may have problems in understanding the information sheet. In these circumstances the content must be fully explained to the participant.
If/when the research is to be carried out on under-18s or people of clouded judgement, we would like to know what methods will be used to obtain consent.

Readability evaluations for the consent form and participant information sheet

To assist in the participant's understanding, the information sheet should be clear and comprehensive. We suggest using Gunning's FOGG Test, aiming for a maximum score of 10. Typeface should be a minimum of 12pt Arial, and illustrations and diagrams used wherever possible.

Arrangements for indemnity insurance

Please enclose any documents relating to indemnity insurance (if required) with your submission.

Data Protection Act

Does your study involve the use of computerised participants' records?
☐ Yes
☐ No
If Yes, *have you complied with the requirements of the Data Protection Act?*

Authorisation

For undergraduates, master's and research students:
Please ask your supervisor to sign that they have read the application form and that they accept responsibility for the applicant who is undertaking the work.

Signed ....
                        Supervisor

I, as the Supervisor, recognise the benefit of attending the Ethics Committee meeting with the student.

Signed ....
                        Supervisor

Date..

Outcome:
The research proposal is approved
The research proposal cannot be approved at this time and is referred back to the supervisor.

Approval period from: ....

Approval ceases: ....

Signed (Chair of the Ethics Committee): .... Date ....

Checklist for Applicant

☐ *the Ethics Application Pro-forma*
☐ *the Participant Information Sheet*
☐ *the Consent Form*

RELATIONSHIPS CHARACTERISED BY HONESTY

In all research relationships, honesty should be the defining characteristic. Honesty is grounded on providing accurate and full information for participants, organisations and supervisors. There may be certain specific circumstances in which a measure of deception is needed to collect the data required to fulfil the research questions. In such circumstances this should always be discussed and agreed by the university ethics committee, and explained fully to participants on completion of the study.

When you have given participants assurances about confidentiality and privacy, these must be maintained. Personal data should never be released to third parties without the written consent of the participants. There is also a necessity to analyse data in honest ways so that the integrity of the study is not damaged. Findings should only be reported when they can be evidenced with data and supported by known theory and secondary data. Data must be protected in safe and secure environments so that unauthorised access is not possible.

Using the following practices can protect participant confidentiality:

- securing individual confidentiality statements from all people involved in the conduct of the study
- coding data with numbers instead of names to protect the identity of participants
- using codes for the identification of participants when transcribing data, and destroying interview records on completion of transcription
- storing data with any identifying information in a secure password-protected file to which only one or two people have access

- using pseudonyms for participants, agencies and geographical settings in the publishing of the findings
- carefully disposing of information that can reveal the identity of participants or places, for example by security shredding.

In the spirit of honesty, participants should be given access to the summary findings of the research study. There should also be provision for participants to comment on the accuracy of the data and the relationship to the findings.

THE DATA PROTECTION ACT

The collection and storage of research data is subject to the regulation by the Data Protection Act 1998. If you are unsure of your responsibilities under this Act, refer to the link in the weblink section or contact your tutor or your faculty librarian. Universities normally have a set of guidelines relating to the implementation of the Data Protection Act in the particular institution – consult these before completing the methodology section of your dissertation.

Researchers must be aware of the risks to anonymity, privacy and confidentiality posed by all kinds of personal information storage and processing, including computer and paper files, email records, audio and videotapes, or any other information which directly identifies an participant. Provisions have to be made to prevent accidental breaches of the Act. These could include the use of locked files, password-protected files, or storage of multimedia files in such a way that assess is restricted to researchers involved in the project. Procedures must be in place that will quickly and effectively deal with any breach of data protection.

PETRA

CASE STUDY

Petra is a postgraduate student carrying out her research in training and development. She also works part-time at Concorde Industries, a large IT and engineering provider. One of the directors, Mrs Jade Gemini, asks if she would like to carry out some research for the company. Each year the company spends in the region of £1.5 million on training and development activities. Some of this is in-house training and most of it is supplied by about eight external agencies. The board of directors has become concerned at the sums being spent and has asked Jade to justify these amounts and the benefits of training and development to the company. As one part of the review strategy, Petra is asked to research the views of departments using the training and development service – this has not been done before. The outcomes of the research are likely to lead to great changes, so Jade stresses that the outcomes of the research must be sound. She further emphasises that she does not want to find herself exposed at board level by weak or poor research findings. 'This has to be dead right,' she says.

The departments who use the training and development service vary in size from five people to the large engineering groups of over 100 people. There are 22 departments in total. There have been no complaints about the training and development service, but Jade feels 'We need to know what they think.' Jade is pretty sure Petra can do this with a survey. Jade's view is that she should avoid getting 'bogged down in too much theory'.

To think about ...

1 Comment on how useful a survey will be in discovering the views of the departments. If you were to use a survey, would one survey be suitable for all departments?

2 What other stakeholders ought to be included in the research?

3 Prepare a one-page 'action report' for Jade

setting out your proposed strategy for the research – a methods statement. Pay particular attention to Jade's stated need for the research to be 'sound'.

4 Comment on whether your strategy can be developed and implemented without getting 'bogged down in too much theory'.

KEY LEARNING POINTS

SUMMARY

The methodology chapter of your dissertation will be part of the 'backbone' of the finished work. It must address the following areas:

- Consider what philosophical approach your research will take, and address the issues around the epistemology of knowledge:

  - What will be regarded as new knowledge?

  - What philosophical stance will the research take?

  - Will the research be positivist or subjectivist?

  - Will the research be quantitative or qualitative?

  - Will the research test hypotheses or be exploratory?

  - Will you be part of the research or stand as an outside observer?

- If your study is not structured as a census, you will have to decide how you will choose participants:

  - Census or sample?

  - What is the population?

  - Have you built a sampling frame?

  - Random or non-random sample?

  - How effective is the chosen sampling process?

  - Will it be possible to generalise from your sample to a larger population?

- Choosing and justifying your method is an essential part of the dissertation. Commonly-used methods include:

  - questionnaires

  - interviews

  - observation

  - ethnography

  - experiment.

- Specific methods are:

  - repertory grid

  - diaries

  - reliving

  - action research

  - role play

  - narrative studies.

- The methodology section of the dissertation is a traditional place for a consideration of the ethics of the study:

  - judgements about any possible harm or risk

  - obtaining informed consent

  - developing honest and open relationships

  - the Data Protection Act 1998.

EXPLORE FURTHER

Emmett, R. (2007) 'Oral history and the historical reconstruction of Chicago Economics'. Interview transcript in *History of Political Economy*, Vol. 39, Supp. 1: 172–92

Eriksson, P. and Kovalainen, A. (2008) *Qualitative Methods in Business Research* (*Introducing Qualitative Methods* series). London: Sage

Fransella, F., Bell, R. and Bannister, D. (2003) *A Manual for Repertory Grid Technique*. Chichester: John Wiley & Sons

Israel, M. and Hay, I. (2006) *Research Ethics for Social Scientists*. London: Sage

Watson, T. (2000) *In Search of Management*. London: Thompson Learning

Witkin, R. and Poupart, R. (1985) 'Running a commentary on imaginatively re-lived events a method for obtaining qualitatively rich data', in Strati, A. (ed.) *The Symbolics of Skill*. Trento (Trent): University of Trento

Weblinks

The Oral History Society, home page: http://www.oralhistory.org.uk/

The Data Protection Act (1998): http://www.legislation.gov.uk/ukpga/1998/ 29/contents

ESRC Framework of ethics: http://www.esrc.ac.uk/_images/Framework_ for_Research_Ethics_tcm8-4586.pdf

Google docs YouTube tutorials: http://www.youtube.com/watch?v=OBh8bMC7XEU

Google docs overview tour: http://www.google.com/google-d-s/tour1.html

Policy and Code of Conduct on the Governance of Good Research Conduct: http://www.rcuk.ac.uk/Publications/ researchers/Pages/grc.aspx

Socio-Legal Studies Association: http://www.slsa.ac.uk/

Data, and How to Analyse It

8.1 INTRODUCTION

By the time you read this chapter it is to be hoped that you will have successfully carried out some research and are now faced with the problem of what to do with the data. If you have got this far in the book and the research, it may be reassuring to know that you are on the home straight. However, dealing with large amounts of data in a structured and efficient manner can be difficult, and this chapter aims to assist you in validating, inputting, organising and analysing your data. It looks firstly at how to enter data so that it is in a useful electronic form. Describing and displaying quantitative data is the first type of analysis for many dissertations – for some it will be the only analysis. Looking for and at relationships in data is covered in the following chapter. Qualitative data requires a different approach from data analysis, and this is covered in the latter part of this chapter and in Chapter 9. Good research always involves using theory in the analysis of data, and the links between data and theory are examined.

This chapter is designed to guide a 'new' researcher through the process of validating the data, inputting the data and beginning the process of analysis. For qualitative data it will guide you through the basic processes of analysis. Chapter 9 investigates ways to represent data, output data and carry out more elaborate analysis. All the sections are suitable for general business research. You may find it useful to read this chapter before you finalise the methodology section because a logical and coherent approach to asking questions should help make the data analysis easier.

8.2 PREPARING DATA

CODING CLOSED QUESTIONS

In Chapter 7, which dealt with methods, very little was said about coding data for input to a computer system. Each response to a question needs an individual code that allows for data analysis. For example, a common question is 'What gender are you?' This could be coded as Male or Female in a spreadsheet. However, subsequent analysis is easier and more accurate if a code is used – say, 1 male, 2 female. There must also be a code for a non-response or a missing response, and with gender it is sometimes useful to know the reason for a non-response. So the full coding of the question would be:

- 1 = male
- 2 = female
- 3 = would prefer not to respond
- 4 = is unwilling to be characterised in this manner
- 5 = this information is confidential
- 9 = missing

Note that 9, 99, 999 or 9999 is ordinarily used as the code for missing data.

If you are intending to use a secondary data source and carry out comparative analysis with that source, then coding your own research using the same coding system will make the comparison considerably easier. If you are collecting data on the socio-economic class of your respondents, you could use the standard national statistics classification. Any subsequent analysis with your own sets will be easier. If your dissertation is in a well-researched area, you will normally be able to find a well-thought out existing mode of data classification.

The analytical socio-economic classes are:

- 1 Higher managerial and professional occupations
  1.1 Large employers and higher managerial occupations
  1.2 Higher professional occupations
- 2 Lower managerial and professional occupations
- 3 Intermediate occupations
- 4 Small employers and own-account workers
- 5 Lower supervisory and technical occupations
- 6 Semi-routine occupations
- 7 Routine occupations
- 8 Never worked, and long-term unemployed.

You may immediately see the problem with using data coding from secondary research. Some classes that you might want to carry out analysis on are missing. If you wished, or your hypothesis suggested, that students might do something differently from the main population of the UK, you would not have a category 'student'. In summary, it is useful to use categories from secondary research if you will be carrying out comparative analysis, but using these categories restricts your own primary analysis of the data.

In survey or questionnaire research there are often many closed questions and scaled items. For these items it is easy to develop a pre-coded questionnaire. The answers are marked with the code, often in subscript after the answer:

- Male $_1$
- Female $_2$
- Non-response $_3$
- Missing data $_9$

For a scaled question such as 'How enjoyable did you find your university studies? Answer on the scale 1–6', answer codes might be:

- Very enjoyable $_1$
- Quite enjoyable $_2$
- Mostly enjoyable $_3$
- Not very enjoyable $_4$
- Not enjoyable $_5$
- Dreadful $_6$

Once you have coded one question, the scale should remain the same for similar questions. This will also allow for 'matrix' questions where the answer scale remains the same and the questions are listed in a column to the left. If the scale descriptions need to be changed, the hierarchy of codes should still flow in the same direction – that is, the most positive answer codes as 1, and the least positive codes as 5 or 6. This will make the data entry into electronic form easier, by not needing to use the 'transform' command, in SPSS, to recode the variable. There is, however, a phenomenon of 'trivial' answering by which respondents sense the flow of the answers to questions and very quickly and without much thought 'tick' their way through a questionnaire. Reversing the positive or negative flow of the answers can slow the respondent and encourage more reflective answering. But, importantly, the coding remains the same – it is only the layout of the questions that may be changed. Statements can also be expressed as positive or negative, and the balance of these should be about 50% positive and 50% negative. The flow of the positive and negative questions should be varied to keep the interest and attention of the respondent (see Chapter 7, section 7.4). Likert scales are used to test the agreement or disagreement of a respondent to a proposition. A Likert scale question is coded in the same way as other scaled questions:

- Agree $_1$
- Tend to agree $_2$
- Tend to disagree $_3$
- Disagree $_4$

If you are using survey or questionnaire software, such as Snap or Survey monkey, the data coding is done automatically. When you enter the data into a spreadsheet the cells will contain only the code number. A narrative reminder of the coding of the question is often present in the column heading. When using SPSS you set up the variables and their characteristics as you enter the data.

CODING OPEN QUESTIONS

Even in a questionnaire-based study it is common to find open questions – those that do not have predetermined answers. The most commonly-occurring open question is represented by the word 'Other', which allows for a response that has not been predetermined. For example:

Q What motivated you to join your current employer?
Mark the most important motivator (one answer only)

- Salary $_1$
- More responsibility $_2$
- Employer's reputation $_3$
- Desire for a change $_4$
- Improved fringe benefits $_5$
- More interesting job role $_6$
- More flexible working arrangements $_7$
- Other – please state $_8$
  . . . .
  . . . .

Note that the 'Other' response is still coded 8 in this example, but will also have a text entry column in the data table for the other motivation(s).

What sort of things might be entered in 'Other'? Such things as:

- My partner moved jobs to a different part of the country.
- The transport links to my old job were just so poor.
- I wanted a shorter journey to work.
- Two of my friends worked at the same company.

- My mum is the managing director.
- I worked here before and I really liked it.
- This job is completely different from my last job. I was a teacher and now I am an administrator.

The possible answers to this question are endless. The structured answers in the first part of the question may well be 'driven' by a known motivation theory. The respondents' responses are driven by their own experience. Often in dissertation research the 'Other' question is asked, but the data it reveals goes unanalysed, or is analysed by listing all the responses. This may be because analysing large amounts of open data can be problematic – yet with a little thought and a sound technique it need not be particularly troublesome.

The most common way to deal with open data is to create code categories for the responses, so that the data above is entered into electronic form as:

- Geographical change of area $_{11}$
- Transport problems $_{12}$
- Shorter journeys to work $_{13}$
- Social connection to existing workers $_{14}$
- Kinship relationship to existing worker $_{15}$
- Previously employed at the organisation and enjoyed the experience $_{16}$
- Change of career $_{17}$

One main question often asked of supervisors is 'Do I set up a category for every response?' This is an important question and requires a measure of balance in answering. If you simply code every response with a new category, you will have done little more than list all the responses, which was the original unanalysed position. However, if you encounter a similar response more than once – let's say,

- The buses are terrible to my current place of work
- The traffic to that part of town is unimaginably bad
- The train line to work is dangerous and I don't feel safe
- The bus stop is about a mile away from work, and I am fed up with getting drenched walking the last mile

– these responses would all be coded as 'Transport problems' and the number of responses recorded. This analysis provides a more general set of problems and the frequency of the problem. The final data would be 'Transport problems – 4 responses'. Interestingly, there will be no loss of data in this aggregation, because if 'transport' appears to be an important issue in explaining employer selection, it will be easy to return and consider the detail of each respondent's transport problems. Using this type of approach for coding open questions allows a higher level of analysis to take place. The output into your chapter, probably entitled 'Analysis of findings', will be the developed category names and the frequency of occurrence. But what should be done with the single reasons for joining a new employer? When thinking about the nature of research it is easy to adopt the approach that suggests that data is more important if it occurs more frequently. The majority view is the dominant view and we should act and make recommendations from those consensus views.

OPEN QUESTION FREQUENCY TABLE
Analysis of 'Other' responses to the question
What motivated you to join your current employer?
Mark the most important motivator! (one answer only)

Category	Frequency
Geographical change of area	12
Transport problems	6
Shorter journeys to work	2
Social connection to existing workers	9
Kinship relationship to existing worker	3
Previously employed at the organisation and enjoyed the experience	7
Change of career	11

If we were to adopt a different stance, it could be that we would value most highly the unusual and individual responses, rather than the general responses. So don't discard the individual and unique responses – list them in full in your findings, and consider on an individual basis the value and merit of each statement.

8.3 CONTENT ANALYSIS

A more formal and systematic method for analysing open questions or qualitative data is content analysis. Content analysis is a research tool used to determine the presence of certain words or concepts. The technique quantifies and analyses the presence, meanings and relationships of words and concepts, then makes inferences about the messages within the source. There are many aspects of organisations and people that can be analysed using content analysis, such as memos, emails, agendas, reports, newsletters, books and conversations. Content analysis is a versatile technique and can be used in many circumstances where media, texts or the spoken words require analysis. The approach in the section below is restricted to its use in analysing open questions.

The first step in content analysis is to select the 'units' to be analysed. It is important to realise that any given set of answers to open questions can be analysed several times using different units – the analysis will reveal different aspects depending on the unit chosen for analysis. What sorts of units are there?

- Syntactical units focus on words and word use, and the symbols of words.
- Referential units focus on people, events, objects.
- Propositional units focus on relationships such as manager–subordinate, seller–buyer, harasser–harassed.
- Thematic units are higher-order units like those we looked at above, and are abstractions from the open questions. Themes that might emerge are the past and the present, work and home, self and organisation.

The units you select to use for analysis should be closely related to your research questions. If a research question is investigating work–life balance, for example, a propositional or thematic unit of 'work–home' would be appropriate. To conduct a content analysis the open question answer is coded, or broken down into several categories, if the answer is long or contains more than one idea. The codes can be at several levels, such as word, word-sense, phrase, sentence, or theme. The coded sections are then analysed using either conceptual analysis or relational analysis.

Conceptual analysis can be carried out by following these steps:

1 Decide on the level of analysis – word, phrase, theme.

2 Decide whether to have an exhaustive set of codes, or codes related only to the research question.

3 Decide whether to code for presence of a concept or the number of times the concept is used.

4 Decide on a set of coding rules so that you can work out when something is one category or another.

5 Develop a simple set of rules to code the source.

6 Decide what to do, if anything, with words that are not coded.

7 Code the source document.

8 Analyse your results.

Relational analysis can be based on two fundamental ideas – the emotional inferences of statements or phrases, and the occurrence of two concepts in close proximity to each other. The emotional evaluation is called 'affect extraction'. Evaluating the occurrence of two concepts in close proximity is called 'proximity analysis'. In affect extraction we are exploring the emotional or psychological state of the speaker or writer, and some of the standard psychological scales can be useful. We could, for instance, code a sentence as positive–negative, and this would reveal the emotion of the respondent. It would then be possible to relate this emotion to another emotion, to note whether (for example) respondents who had given positive statements had also given a statement that was coded as empathetic.

Relational analysis is carried out using these steps:

1 Determine the type of analysis – affect or proximity.

2 Reduce the source to categories and code for words or patterns.

3 Explore the emotion or relationships between concepts.

4 Code the relationships.

5 Analyse the emotion or relationship.

6 Explore or map the emotions or map out the relationships.

The outcome of proximity analysis is a co-occurring words or phrases map. The outcome of affective analysis is a relationship map – this is not unlike a mind map.

The following probably takes the analysis to too complex a level for use with open questions, but the technique is useful for analysing larger passages of source material. The extension technique to the two ideas above – that of conceptual and relational analysis – is to combine the techniques. We would then create a mental model of the concepts and the relationships between concepts. Internal mental models are created as people draw inferences and gather information about the world. Mental models offer a more specific approach to mapping because they go beyond extraction and comparison.

The main steps in creating mental models are:

1 Identify concepts in use.

2 Define possible relationships.

3 Code the text on the basis of **1** and **2** above.

4 Code the statements.

5 Graphically display and analyse the resulting maps.

To create the diagram of the mental model, you convert the source into a map of concepts and relations. The map is then analysed on the level of constructs, where a construct consists of two concepts and their possible relationship. There is software available to create mental model maps or, as they are often known, 'mind maps': the qualitative software analysis tool NVivo can create these types of maps.

Using content analysis is a useful way to extend the systematic analysis of the answers to open questions. If you are analysing larger quantities of qualitative data, there is software available to assist the analysis. NVivo is probably the most widely-used qualitative data analysis software. But for dissertation research where time is always limited, it is important to realise that NVivo takes some time to learn, and full functionality with the software may take a few months.

8.4 VALIDATING DATA

In dissertation research the amount of data you gather will not be very large and it is therefore feasible to validate the data 'visually' before you start entering it. Typically, you will have questionnaire data from between 30 and 80 questionnaires with around 20–30 questions on each questionnaire. There are two stages to the validation process.

'In the field' is a research term used to describe the actual collection of data. It is very seldom actually in a field. In dissertation research you are very likely to be the person collecting the data. Field editing, or checking the validity of the data at the point of entry, is vital. Following a questionnaire and asking people the questions on the form looks like a simple and straightforward task. However, it is always slightly pressured and the answers given often need minor interpretation or clarification. This is one reason why questionnaires should be piloted. Any confusing issues or pressure points for the interviewer – you – can be recognised and removed.

STUDENT COMMENT

When I created my questionnaire, I didn't give a thought to how I might use it in the field. I had asked a lot of quite complicated questions that had lots of possible answers. When I piloted the questionnaire, no one could quite understand the questions and I felt under real pressure because I could not make them understand the questions. Also, I got a lot of long answers and some answers were very different. And it was taking about 25–30 seconds on average to ask each question. The people responding just glazed over and I felt under more pressure to hold their attention. The answers they gave tended not to fit into my categories very well, either, so I had to work hard and ask for clarity to get an answer I could use. I was really glad it was just the pilot. I changed the questions and answer categories a lot before I used the questionnaire on the main sample.

The key issues in field editing are to get accurate answers, record an answer to every question, and ensure that any writing is legible. If you are asking the respondent the questions, plan for about two to three minutes between the respondents so that you can check and correct the entries on the completed form. You will be surprised how often after only a few seconds you cannot quite read or remember the answer just given.

When the respondent is self-completing the questionnaire, you must check the form before the person walks away. It should only take a minute to look over the form but if anything is not clear or is missing, you will have the chance to ask if your respondent missed the question or chose not to respond. You may also need to ask the question: 'What does that say?'

Check through this list after every respondent's questionnaire completion:

- All questions have been answered or a non-response given.

- Answers are in the correct format.
- Inappropriate answers have been identified and corrected.
- Answers in the wrong place on the form have been replaced correctly.
- Open questions' answers are legible.
- Biographical data is present and 'visually' looks correct.
- Any note the interviewer has made is legible.

Brief as these checks are, they may save an otherwise sound questionnaire from being discarded from the data due to errors. It is not too much of a problem if one or two questions have been omitted, but if the whole biographical data section has been missed, the questionnaire is unusable. Even a simple error in the biographical data will lead to inaccurate results. If by error a male respondent is entered as female, for example, it will have a significant effect on the average respondent pattern of female respondents. Cross-tabulations of answers invariably correspond to biographical elements such as age, gender, and years worked at an organisation.

Office editing involves a more thorough check of the questionnaire for the same items in the checklist above. This editing process can make small corrections to 'obvious' errors such as marking the answers in the wrong format, or putting the answer in the wrong place, or using the wrong data format. But this editing process should never be adding missing answers that you think the respondent would have made – in academic dissertations this would be regarded as a form of falsification for which there are harsh penalties.

Errors can occur when data is entered and once entered are quite difficult to find and remove. Standard transposition errors can occur frequently and create havoc in your data. A transposition error occurs where the entry of two digits is reversed. Because questionnaires use codes for data, there are plenty of opportunities to create havoc. The code 12 is certainly a possible code for a question with a large number of possible answers. The code 21 is not likely to represent useful data. When entering data on a numeric keypad it is very easy to enter 21 for the code 12. Most of the analysis software mentioned below can set up 'input masks' that significantly reduce the possibility of entering data wrongly. An input mask restricts the data that can be entered to a predetermined range. So if a question has 14 answers and uses 15 for missing data, the input mask can restrict the entry of data in that cell to the range 1–15. You will note the problem of using 9, 99, 999 for missing data when using an input mask. The transposition error 21 for 12 would be stopped with the input mask set to accept only numbers 1–15, but if the codes range was 1–14 for the answers and 99 for missing data, the error would be allowed. It is for this reason that we sometimes do not use 9, 99, 999 for missing data. Input masks can also ensure that data is entered in the correct and consistent format, dates being particularly troublesome in this respect. In SPSS, the variables table can be used in a similar and more flexible way, to control data entry.

WEIGHTING CASES

When you have sampling strata, such as in a stratified random sample (see Chapter 7, section 7.3), you may decide to 'weight' the cases. This is a technique designed to create equal-response effects in strata that do not have the same number of respondents.

For example: Kat had decided to sample male and female responses as a stratified sample, as she had argued that gender was an important and significant variable in understanding her research question. The methodology indicated that the strata would have 30 male and 30 female respondents. After collecting the data she was troubled by having 30 female respondents, but only 15 male respondents. After attempting to collect more data from male respondents, without success, she gave up. Her tutor suggested solving the problem by 'weighting' the data she had. This would need a reflective discussion about the effects on the data, but was a practical solution to the problem.

In Kat's example, the responses from male respondents would each count for two cases in her analysis.

The weighting is calculated like this. The percentage of respondents in each stratum is:

Female 30/30 = 100%   Male 15/30 = 50%

The higher stratum is divided by the lower stratum, thus

$$\frac{100\% \text{ (female)}}{50\% \text{ (male)}} = 2$$

So the weighting for male respondents is 2, and for female respondents 1.

8.5 CHOOSING THE TOOL FOR ANALYSIS

Questionnaire data analysis is normally undertaken using one of the following software products:

- Excel spreadsheet
- Access database
- Survey software, such as Google docs forms, Snap or Survey monkey
- SPSS software.

The tool that you choose for analysis will depend on your experience of using it, and on your data analysis needs. Whatever software you use, there will be some functionality to exchange data between different software. Dissertation research is most frequently carried out using the free specialist software.

SURVEY SOFTWARE

There is a wide range of survey software on the market for designing questionnaires and for data analysis of the answers. In the previous chapter we carried out a short exercise creating

Figure 17 Screenshot of Snap software in questionnaire design mode

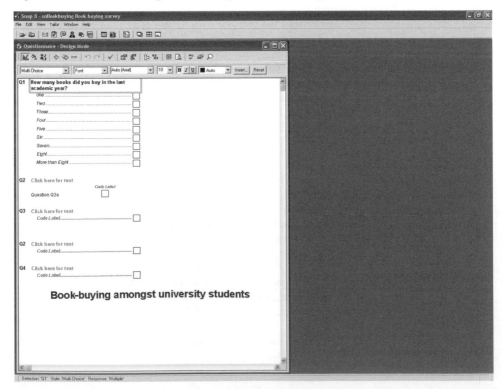

a Google doc survey. Your university will probably have a licence to use one of the main survey packages, and you should seek help from your computer support personnel if you are not sure about any aspects of this software. Many university courses have a set of structured tutorials to introduce an appropriate survey package. This may be through e-learning or face-to-face teaching. One such survey package is Snap surveys. This is a software package that generates attractive questionnaires and allows for the recording of data and for data analysis. It also has enhanced functionality for web-based surveys and mobile interviewing. There is an evaluation copy and quick tutorial available at the web address given at the end of the chapter.

In Snap the data entry process actually starts at one stage earlier – when you design the questionnaire. As you build the questionnaire, Snap also builds the data entry structure. When you have results from your survey, it is very easy to use one of the Snap data entry modes. The software automatically produces a data code sheet as you design the questionnaire (see Figure 17).

In questionnaire data entry mode (see Figure 18) you will be able to talk to respondents and enter the data as they respond. This is a quick and efficient way to enter data and removes some of the possible coding and other errors that can occur with a paper-based survey. It is also cheap to administer and the lack of paper copies is environmentally friendly.

Figure 18 Screenshot of Snap software in questionnaire data entry mode

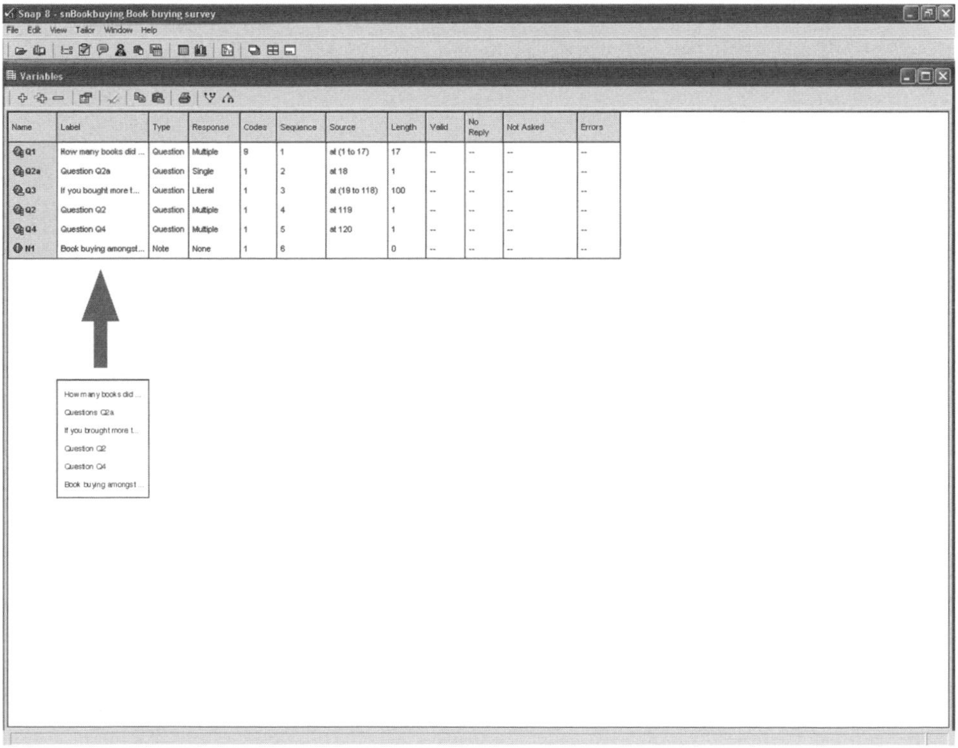

These survey software packages have a reasonable range of analysis tools that can generate cross-tab tables and statistical output. They also produce a range of graphic outputs.

The advantages and disadvantages of using survey software for data entry

Advantages	Disadvantages
• This software is more than just a data entry tool. • It is relatively easy to learn in about 2–4 hours. • It is easy to generate questionnaires, data output and charts. • It is easy to post them to websites and social media sites	• It has limited statistical power. • It does not offer a complete range of statistical tests. • It is harder to export the data to other software. • Student licences and university licences limit the number of cases (this is not often a major problem in dissertation research).

There is a large range of survey software available, and the main suppliers are:

- Survey monkey
- Snap
- Google docs forms
- Survey Gizmo
- Freeonlinesurveys
- Forecast
- Statpac
- LimeSurvey
- VT Survey
- QuestionPro
- Smart Survey
- WinSurvey
- Cool Surveys
- Zap Survey
- Feedback Farm
- Mysurveylab
- Instantsurvey
- Ultimatesurvey
- Surveymethods
- Zoomerang

All these tools have an online site at which you can try out the software. Some, such as Snap surveys, are available on most university campuses. My advice is to try out the software during the year before your dissertation, so that you can hit the ground running when you do actually start your dissertation.

EXCEL SPREADSHEET

Excel is a well-known generic program – Google has an alternative – that you are likely to have had experience of using during your earlier studies and that should therefore involve very little learning time for you. Dissertation research is always time-restricted, so using a familiar piece of software makes a lot of sense. A standard 'worksheet' is used to enter the data, with respondents in rows, and answers or 'variables' in columns.

Excel is also rather useful if you have a record of the population of your study and you wish to select a random sample. The spreadsheet has the population names or ID numbers in the first column, one row per member of the population. Let's say you have obtained 100 names from an organisation and these represent every member of staff in the organisation. Time constraints mean that you will only be able to use a questionnaire and interview 33 of this population. You intend to use simple random sampling. Enter this data using three columns:

Column A: Participant ID number
Column B: Family name
Column C: First name

In a fourth column you can now carry out a random selection of 33 of this population.

Column D: Enter the following formula exactly as it appears here

=RAND()<=33%

Then highlight the cell D2, **Copy** it, and **Paste** it to the cells D3 to D101.

Your population data of ID, Family Name, First Name will now have an additional column reading TRUE or FALSE. TRUE represents those people chosen to be respondents. Because of the manner in which Excel generates random numbers with this formula, this may not amount to a sample of exactly 33.

Figure 19 Screenshot of Excel spreadsheet

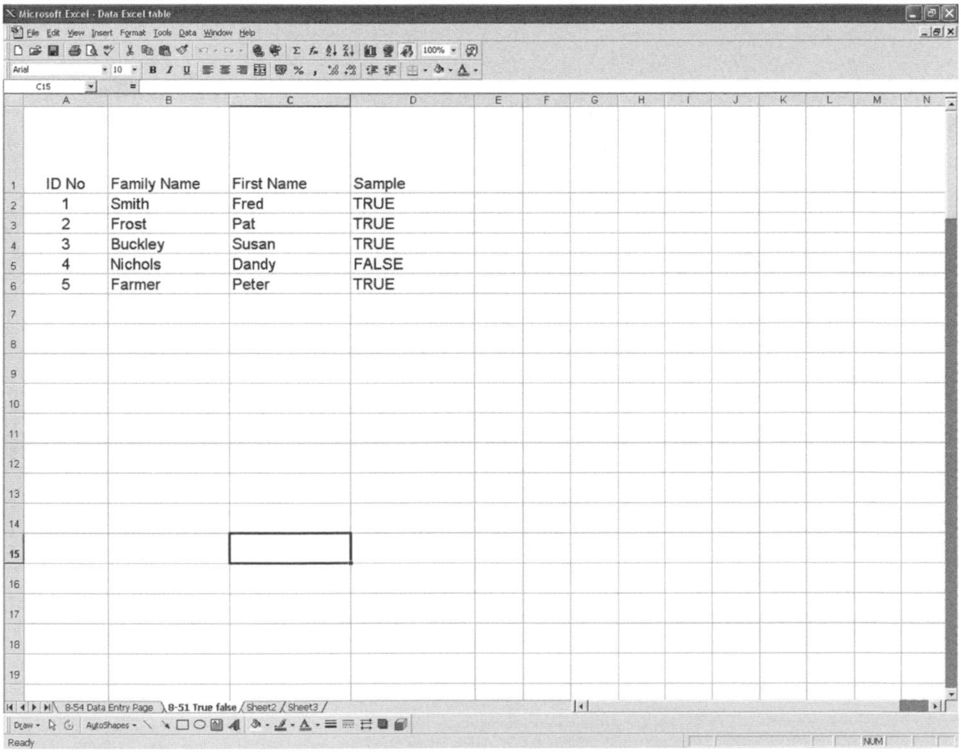

ID No	Family Name	First Name	Sample
1	Smith	Fred	TRUE
2	Frost	Pat	TRUE
3	Buckley	Susan	TRUE
4	Nichols	Dandy	FALSE
5	Farmer	Peter	TRUE

Excel is a versatile and well-known tool for entering and analysing your data and probably requires little or no learning on your part. The downside is that you must understand basic statistics to generate any meaningful data output because you will have to set up the functions that create your analysis. Excel generates 'pivot tables' very easily, and these are often the most-used element in displaying data. Displaying the data you have entered is also easy and versatile.

If you are choosing to carry on and enter your data in an Excel spreadsheet, each subsequent column will be labelled with one variable from your questionnaire. It is not possible within the scope of this book to set out the detail of the complete data entry process using Excel. There is a very effective Help system within Excel, and there are many related web articles to assist if this is your chosen tool of analysis.

Once you have specified the variables in the first row of your spreadsheet, Excel will be able to provide a data entry form for entering the results. This is a very quick and accurate way to enter data. The way to do it is:

- Highlight the first row cells containing the variables,
- then click on **Data**
- then on **Form**.

You will now have a form on the screen for entering data, accurately and quickly. Using the numeric keypad will further improve the speed and accuracy of the data entry. Move between cells with **Tab**, and at the end of each record use **Return**.

Figure 20 Excel spreadsheet with data entry form

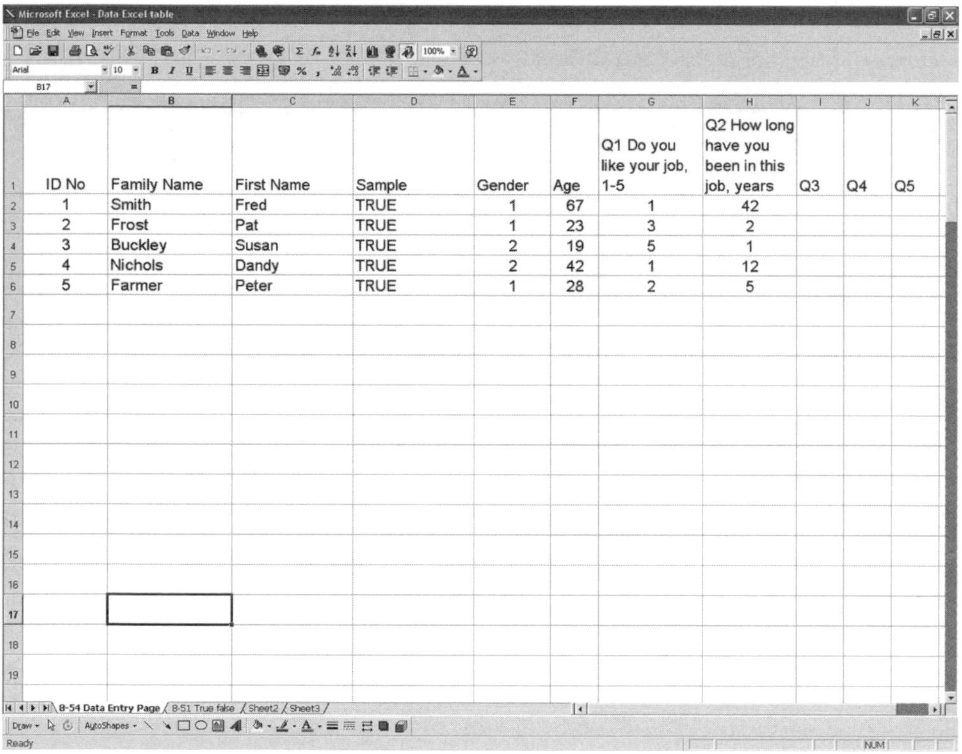

ID No	Family Name	First Name	Sample	Gender	Age	Q1 Do you like your job, 1-5	Q2 How long have you been in this job, years	Q3	Q4	Q5
1	Smith	Fred	TRUE	1	67	1	42			
2	Frost	Pat	TRUE	1	23	3	2			
3	Buckley	Susan	TRUE	2	19	5	1			
4	Nichols	Dandy	TRUE	2	42	1	12			
5	Farmer	Peter	TRUE	1	28	2	5			

The advantages and disadvantages of using Excel

Advantages	Disadvantages
• You will probably have prior knowledge of this software. • You can see your data at all times in the worksheet you are using. • The software is powerful enough for dissertation research, and flexible. • Computations can be carried out quickly on medium-sized data sets. • It uses some quick and easy data entry, validation and analysis procedures. • Pivot tables can be produced quickly and easily with 'drag and drop' procedures.	• It is somewhat cumbersome when the data set is large. • Complex data can be difficult to manage. • You need a reasonable understanding of the data tests you want to carry out. • It is easy to distort and corrupt data, and it is therefore important to back up data and outputs regularly.

ACCESS DATABASE

Depending on your work experience and course of study, you may have experience of using databases. Access – part of the Microsoft Office suite of programs – will be loaded on all your university's computers and you will probably also have a copy on your personal computer. It is a widely available program and provides more structure and security for your data. The data is stored in 'tables' and these tables are linked together in 'relationships'. The software can carry out complex queries into the results of your research, but entering the data and generating the outputs is more complex and to some extent less flexible than with Excel. Yet your data once entered can be exported easily to Excel, where it is easier to create and manipulate graphs and tables.

The advantages and disadvantages of using databases for research results

Advantages	Disadvantages
• A more formal structuring of your data is forced on you (this is a good thing). • The data is secure in the tables and not easily lost or corrupted. • Powerful queries can be used for analysis. • It provides a relatively permanent archive of your data. • It copes well with large and complex data sets.	• You will need some experience of using the software. • It takes a reasonable amount of time to learn. • The data output is less flexible, but exporting to Excel can ameliorate this. • It offers no practical help in producing the questionnaire.

SPSS SOFTWARE

SPSS stands for Statistical Package for Social Sciences, and offers a comprehensive suite of tests and data analysis for questionnaires. You will need some training and a little time to become used to the data entry and analysis modes. But it does offer a complete set of statistical tests for quantified data. If you are importing a data set from secondary research, there will be a translator to SPSS. Your university may arrange training in SPSS, and if you have a quantitative study, it would be a wise move to undertake the training. SPSS is not difficult to learn, but it does take 6–8 hours of study to become a proficient user – and there is still a huge amount to learn about SPSS even after this amount of time has been spent on understanding the package.

The primary data entry mode is in the SPSS Data Editor screen (see Figure 17). This looks like a spreadsheet with two worksheets. You will note that they are called Data View and Variable View. When you first start to enter data, you should list the variables in the Variable View sheet. The variables are the characteristics of your respondents – like age, gender, etc – and the answers to the questions you have asked. When the variables have been created that represent your questions, you can move to the Data sheet and enter your data. This approach is straightforward and feels as if you are working on a spreadsheet, which appeals to most users. Missing data is handled in a flexible and precise manner, this being specified in the Variable sheet and allowing for up to three discrete entries.

Once the data has been entered for all your cases, you can then proceed to the analysis section. SPSS has an excellent range of statistical tests covering descriptive and inferential statistics. The selection and use of these tests is covered in the following chapter. Descriptive statistics will depend on the type of data you are trying to describe.

Different descriptive statistics are appropriate for different types of data, depending on the level of measurement:

Categorical data has a limited number of distinct values or categories (for example, gender or marital status). Categorical variables can be text (called string data) data or numerical data that uses numeric codes to represent categories (for example, 1 = male and 2 = female). There are two basic types of categorical data:

- Nominal data has no inherent order to the categories. For example, the job category of human resource management is not higher or lower than a job category of marketing or research.
- Ordinal data is where there is a meaningful order of categories but there is not a measurable distance between categories. For example, there is an order to the values high, medium, and low, but the 'distance' between the values cannot be calculated.

Figure 21 Screenshot of SPSS variable sheet view

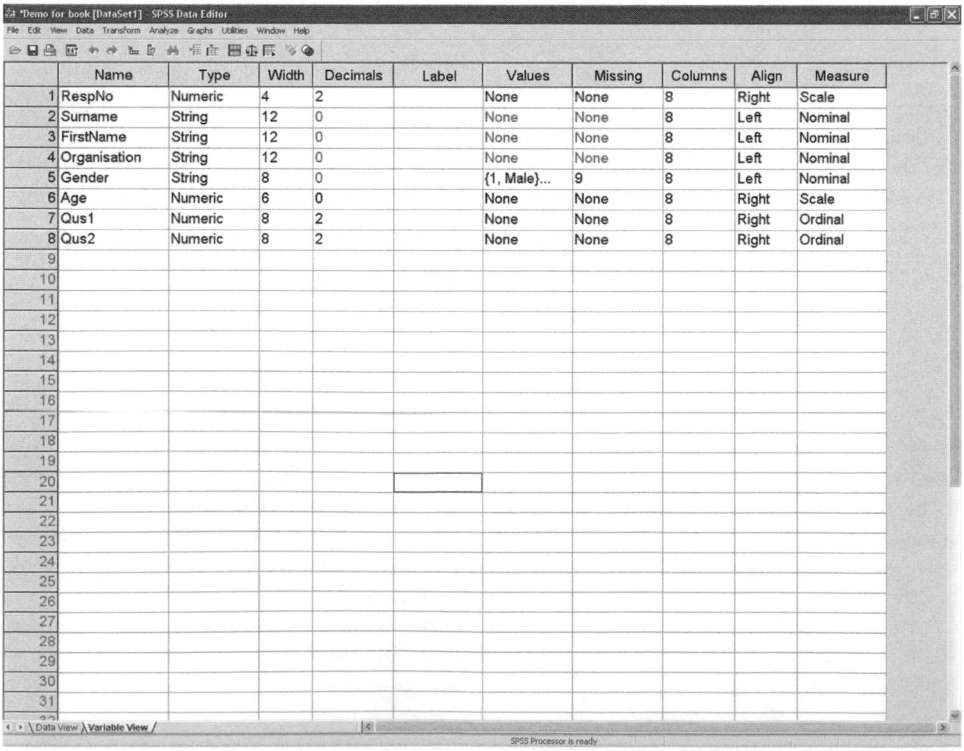

	Name	Type	Width	Decimals	Label	Values	Missing	Columns	Align	Measure
1	RespNo	Numeric	4	2		None	None	8	Right	Scale
2	Surname	String	12	0		None	None	8	Left	Nominal
3	FirstName	String	12	0		None	None	8	Left	Nominal
4	Organisation	String	12	0		None	None	8	Left	Nominal
5	Gender	String	8	0		{1, Male}...	9	8	Left	Nominal
6	Age	Numeric	6	0		None	None	8	Right	Scale
7	Qus1	Numeric	8	2		None	None	8	Right	Ordinal
8	Qus2	Numeric	8	2		None	None	8	Right	Ordinal

For categorical data, the most common descriptive statistic is the number or percentage of cases in each category. The mode is the category with the greatest number of cases. For ordinal data, the median (the value at which half of the cases fall above and below) may also be a useful summary measure if there is a large number of categories.

Scale data is measured on an interval or ratio scale, where the data values indicate both the order of values and the distance between values. For example, a salary of £34,600 is higher than a salary of £24,600, and the distance between the two values is £10,000.

The SPSS' Frequencies procedure produces frequency tables that display both the number and percentage of cases for each observed value of a variable. You carry out this procedure in SPSS by clicking successively on:

- **Analyse**, in the top menu
- then **Descriptive Statistics**
- then **Frequencies**.

Figure 22 Screenshot of SPSS frequency table

→ Frequencies

[DataSet0]

Statistics

Q1

N	Valid	500
	Missing	1

Q1

		Frequency	Percent	Valid Percent	Cumulative Percent
Valid	1.00	105	21.0	21.0	21.0
	2.00	154	30.7	30.8	51.8
	3.00	106	21.2	21.2	73.0
	4.00	117	23.4	23.4	96.4
	9.00	18	3.6	3.6	100.0
	Total	500	99.8	100.0	
Missing	System	1	.2		
Total		501	100.0		

SPSS and other packages provide a range of descriptive summary statistics, measures of central tendency and measures of dispersion.

The most common measures of central tendency are:

- mean – the calculated average
- median – the value at which half the values fall below and half fall above.
- Measures of dispersion or spread of the data from the mean are:
- standard deviation
- minimum
- maximum
- range.

8.6 QUALITATIVE DATA

So far this chapter has focused on validating and entering predominantly quantitative data. If you have carried out a largely qualitative study, you will have non-numerical sources, such as:

- in-depth/unstructured interviews
- semi-structured interviews
- structured interview questionnaires containing substantial open comments
- focus group records
- unstructured or semi-structured diaries
- observation field notes/technical fieldwork notes
- case study notes
- minutes of meetings
- personal documents (eg letters, personal diaries, correspondence)
- press clippings
- photographs or any other type of media material
- critical incident logs
- emails
- memos and notes
- videos
- audio recordings.

All the sources will have slight variations in how they are represented, but if we ignore the multimedia sources, the rest could be characterised in two camps:

- sources already in a text format (emails, meeting minutes, some diary entries and notes)
- sources in a non-text format (interview tapes, handwritten diaries, notes and incident logs).

THE TRANSCRIPTION OF NON-TEXT SOURCES

There is no easy way to address these next few points. If you are carrying out a qualitative study, it is highly likely you will have to tackle the problem of transcribing non-text sources into text. This most commonly occurs with interviews where the 'normal' procedure is to record the interview and analyse the data after the interview has concluded. Most analysis requires the data to be in text form, and preferably as computer files. If you are intending to use software to assist with the analysis, it is vital that the interviews or other sources are in text files – a Word document being the most popular form.

You might think that by this stage of the twenty-first century, transcription would be an automated process – but it is not. The closest to an automated process is to use speech recognition software (SRS) to read documents into a Word document, or to repeat the narrative of transcripts into the SRS. Neither of these approaches is very accurate and considerable editing has to take place after the process to correct the tense and grammar errors that are introduced. Typically, each hour of interview takes between three and four hours to transcribe.

The normal transcription process may be said to have some eleven steps.

1 Start the tape. Use a foot-pedal machine to stop and start the tape if one is available (they are called transcribers). A normal tape or digital recorder will work but it will take longer. Use the pause button to stop and start the recorder. Digital files can be played back on the computer while you use the Word software; a foot-pedal control can be purchased.

2 Start typing as soon as the tape starts. You won't be able to type as fast as respondents speak, so you'll have to stop the recorder each time you fall behind. You will quickly develop a technique for doing this effectively. One technique is to listen first to a sentence, then 'Pause' the recorder and type it. Accuracy is very important, so be sure to transcribe all the words during the pauses. The more accurate you are in the first pass, the less editing you will have to do.

3   If a passage is difficult to decipher, listen to it several times. If you are still having trouble, make a note of the counter number on the recorder and go back to it later. Sometimes the context of an interview will help you interpret that section later.

4   Transcribe the interview exactly as it was recorded. Pauses may be indicated by . . . . between words – the longer the . . . ., the longer the pause. If you cannot decipher a word or passage, use ****** to indicate this. It is also normal to add gestures and other expressions in [square brackets], such as [laughs]. You may need your field note record to transcribe all of these.

5   Abbreviate speakers' names to the first or first two initials, with a colon following. (eg V: What other jobs have you done? C: I've done three jobs.)

6   Use a new paragraph to separate the speaker's ideas and always when a new speaker commences.

7   When you have finished typing the initial draft, listen to the recording again. At the same time, read along with what you have typed. The versions should match exactly. Make corrections to the transcript as you listen and read along. It is sometimes useful to get another person to do this task. (It saves you time and it may correct any 'hearing glitches' you have made.)

8   It may be necessary to return to the problem areas that were not deciphered during the second playing of the recording. If the dialogue is impossible to decipher, and the answer is an important fact or comment, do your best to verify the information with the original speaker.

9   If you are unable to verify the words, put your best guess in brackets in the final copy, to show that it is your text, not the original source's verbatim words.

10   Don't forget to save the Word document regularly and to back up the document to a flash drive or other medium when you have finished. Each interview should be on a separate Word file.

11   The interview is now ready for manual analysis or import into qualitative analysis software.

ALTERNATIVES TO FULL TRANSCRIPTION

There are some ways to analyse qualitative data that do not involve transcription of the non-text sources.

Part-audio transcription

In this technique you will have to fully transcribe the first few – maybe between two and seven – interviews and then carry out the free coding of the respondents' ideas (see later for the detail of coding narrative). After coding the first few interviews you will have a set of codes probably formed as a table of the code (concept or idea) and a specification (details of the features and characteristics of the code). Once the main codes have been created and specified, further cases are analysed by listening to the recordings of interviews and only transcribing the sections that relate to the existing codes, or to new codes that emerge from the recording. This technique saves a lot of time in transcribing large chunks of interviews that will later not be coded. But at the stage of audio coding there is a tendency to be reluctant to create any new codes – this is because the motivation of the moment is to get on with coding the recordings. It is a major flaw in this system. One technique to combat this flaw is to give the coding sheet, the transcribed sections and the original recording to another person and ask them to listen and check the coding. They would have the specific instruction to report back if they think there was other material that should have been coded, and to identify the code they would have used. Getting an independent review of your data coding is good practice anyway, but essential if you have followed the part-audio transcription technique.

Outsource the transcription

Transcribing interview data is predominantly a routine, time-consuming and unskilled task. It is possible to outsource this part of the dissertation. Two possibilities arise. One is to use a professional outsourcing transcription service. This is fast and efficient but also expensive. It normally requires the data to be in a digital recording format, but analogue tapes can be handled. An alternative is to enlist willing and able members of your family and friends. While you are striving to improve your qualifications, many of your family will be sympathetic to assisting you in any way that they can. A skilled and experienced typist will work at up to three times the speed of an average computer-user when transcribing data from recordings.

Qualitative analysis software

The most frequently-used software for qualitative data analysis is NVivo. This is a software package for the coding, analysis and representation of qualitative data. Importantly, the latest versions allow the coding of data directly from audio, or indeed video, recordings. It is still possible to use transcripts as well, but in time-restricted dissertations this is a valuable tool for timely and successful completion. Coding on audio files is relatively straightforward, but the source document does have to be a digital audio file.

Figure 23 Screenshot of NVivo audio mode

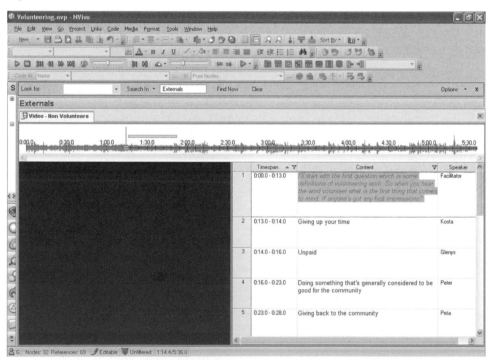

In audio mode you listen to the transcript. Then when you find a section that is represented by a code, you **Start Selection**, and finally when finished you **Finish Selection**. From the **Code** menu you select how you want to code the selection.

Although there are ways to avoid transcribing large amounts of data, as noted here, carrying out the analysis manually on a transcript is the best way for a new researcher to become proficient at analysing qualitative data. Dissertation research rarely produces more than about 50 hours of interview data, and in most cases a good deal less. You can get assistance in transcribing the data – and this should be the preferred approach for most dissertations.

THE GREAT BOOK-BUYING SURVEY

CASE STUDY

This case study is based on using Snap survey software. It can also be accomplished using Excel or SPSS or any other survey software. It is a large case study and will take several days of work – but when you have completed it, you will have experience of a number of important aspects of collecting, recording and representing data.

Tom works during the vacations at a large well-known publisher based in London. He was asked by the Vice-President to carry out a pilot survey of higher education students and their book-buying habits. When he carried out a literature search he was surprised to find that there was practically no data on the book-buying habits of HE students. He had been given a tight time scale to complete the pilot study. The VP indicated that a pilot study of 50 students would be sufficient. Tom was worried about the implications of the restricted amount of literature and lack of previous studies, and discussed this with his friend Wendy. He was very worried about the small sample size, and discussed this with Wendy as well. But eventually he put these issues aside to carry out the survey.

To think about ...

Stage 1 – Questionnaire design
Prepare a survey using Snap or other similar software. You must discover a number of biographical factors:

- age
- gender
- course of study
- subject area
- level of study
- how much money a person earns from part-time jobs
- how much money a person has in total each month or week

- year of study
- any other biographical details that you think might explain a person's spending on books.

In terms of people's book-buying habits, the following may be worthy of investigation:

- recommendations by tutors
- subject practice – eg do law students buy more books than business students?
- the cost of the books
- the number of modules that have to be studied each semester
- how much is spent on books in total
- how many books are purchased
- the average cost of each book (calculated from the two items above)
- the preferred method of purchasing
- any other details you think important.

Stage 2 – Gathering data

Administer your questionnaire to the required 50 participants.

Field-validate your data.

Note down the types of errors that were occurring.

Stage 3 – Data entry

Validate the data in the office.

Enter the data into Snap.

Stage 4 – Data output

Devise ways of displaying the average amount of money spent by students on books, the frequency distribution of the spending habit, measures of dispersion for average spend.

Produce graphs and tables to illustrate the average spend on books of HE students by the following variables:

- age

- gender
- level of course
- subject area
- income level.

Stage 5 – Reflections

1 Reflect on how accurate these findings are likely to be.

2 What aspects of book-buying would you want to investigate further?

3 What amendments would you make to the pilot survey before it was rolled out to thousands of respondents?

4 How would you find out about the person-centred aspects of book-buying?

5 How different do you think are your findings from those of the qualitative case study below? Compare and reflect on your findings and those from someone who has completed the qualitative case study.

6 Is there any merit in combining the quantitative technique with the qualitative technique below?

(You may find it helpful to look at some of the sections in Chapter 9 that deal with these types of analysis in more detail.)

WHY I BUY BOOKS

CASE STUDY

This case study does not require any software to complete. It is suitable for those who are intending to carry out a qualitative study. On the other hand, if you have a personal copy or access to an institutional copy of NVivo, it can be used to assist the management and analysis of this case study. Wendy works part-time for a well-known London publisher. The Director of Research has asked her to investigate why HE students buy books. The Director is not very interested in 'some sterile numbers' – she wants to know why students buy books. She thinks that five interviews will give an adequate picture of this homogeneous group. After all, she says 'Students are all the same.' Wendy had a brief chat with her friend Tom about what she thought was a major problem – the complete lack of literature about why people, and especially students, buy books. She also expressed real concern that her Director of Research thought that students were all the same. But eventually she put these worries behind her and got on with her research.

Stage 1 – Interview design

Design a short set of interview questions to get to the heart of why students buy books. There is very little literature to guide

you so you may have to think the issue through and speak to a few students before you decide on the questions. When you have the questions, decide how much time students might give to being interviewed on this topic. Remember: interview bribes help locate and keep interviewees – a cup of coffee will often give you interview access for 30 minutes. Once you have decided how long the interviews will be, trim the questions to fit the time available. Remember to collect some biographical data. Because time will be short and the sample will be small, an opportunity sample will do for this case study.

Stage 2 – Collecting data

Decide how you will record the interview. The traditional approach is to write down the responses – but now it is fairly normal to record the interviews. Some mobile phones are capable of doing this. If you need a recorder, your university department may be able to loan you one. Conduct the interviews with the five participants, making brief field notes as you proceed.

Stage 3 – Data entry

If you have recorded the respondents' answers to your questions, type them up and store them in separate Word files. If you have recorded the interviews, you must now decide how to proceed – see section 8.5.

Stage 4 – Data analysis

Use simple content analysis to analyse the data. Look through the transcripts or notes or listen to the recordings looking for concepts and relationships.

Stage 5 – Representing data

Create a 'mind map' of the concepts you have found and the relationship of those concepts. This can be done in Word using Autoshapes and adding text in a Textbox to each shape. There are also software packages for creating mind maps, and some of these are free or have free evaluation periods. See the link in the web resources section to SmartDraw. If you are using NVivo, you can produce a mind map from that software.

Stage 6 – Reflections

1 Reflect on the process of gathering qualitative data and consider possible ways to improve the process you have followed.

2 How representative of the general body of students are the views you discovered?

3 How can you represent the findings of the project to the Director of Research?

4 How different do you think are your findings from those of the quantitative case study above? Compare and reflect on your findings and those from someone who has completed the quantitative case study.

5 Is there any merit in combining the qualitative technique with the quantitative technique?

(You may find it helpful to look at some of the sections in Chapter 9 that deal with these types of analysis in more detail.)

SUMMARY

- Data must be carefully checked and validated before entry.

- Content analysis can be used to analyse open questions.

- You will have to choose a software tool to analyse your data:
  - Excel spreadsheet
  - Access database
  - Survey software, such as snap
  - SPSS software.

- Consider whether you should transcribe all your qualitative data.

- The transcription of large amounts of qualitative data is a time-consuming process. Consider ways to reduce the time it takes by:
  - using audo analysis direct in NVivo
  - getting specialist help in carrying out the process
  - coding data from digital recordings.

KEY LEARNING POINTS

EXPLORE FURTHER

Dancey, C. and Riedy, J. (2011) *Statistics without Maths for Psychology*. London: Prentice Hall

Field, A. (2009) *Discovering Statistics Using SPSS* (*Introducing Statistical Methods* series). London: Sage

Bryman, A. (2008) *Social Research Methods*. Oxford: Oxford University Press

Weblinks

National statistics socio-economic classification: www.esds.ac.uk/government/ dv/nssec/ nssecdetails.doc

Mr Excel dot.com on research data in Excel: http://www.mrexcel.com/tip125.shtml

University of Reading good practice guide for using Excel: http://www.reading.ac.uk/ssc/n/ SADC%20DVD/Resources/Excel%20guide/

SSC%20Introduction%20to%20data%20 handling%20in%20Excel%20SADC%20version. pdf

Snap survey software: http://www.snapsurveys. com/

LSE Online SPSS tutorials: http://www2.lse.ac. uk/methodologyInstitute/tutorials/SPSS/home. aspx

NVivo 8 website: http://www.qsrinternational. com/products_nvivo.aspx

SmartDraw business graphics software: http:// www.smartdraw.com/specials/smartdraw.asp?id =35545&gclid=CNjCv4mk1KsCFcIKfAod6mU9PA

Google docs online tutorials: http://edutech. msu.edu/online/googledocs/googledocs.html

CHAPTER 9

Data Analysis and Representation

What will I learn in this chapter?

- The nature of analysis: how to break down and explain
- How to describe quantitative data
- How to explore trends, distributions and proportions in data
- How to explore relationships in data
- How to represent data in tables, graphs and other forms
- The nature of qualitative data
- Techniques for analysing qualitative data
- The links between data analysis and theory

9.1 INTRODUCTION

In this chapter we look in more detail at ways to describe, represent and analyse data. First, the main descriptive statistics that are typically used in dissertation research are considered. Then some elements of analysis are examined. Dealing with quantitative data occupies the first part of the chapter, and dealing with qualitative data is covered in the final part of the chapter. This chapter is best used when you have your data in a suitable electronic form and you are focusing on what sort of analysis to carry out. Quantitative data is often represented in graphs and tables, and these are covered within the analysis section.

Qualitative data has outputs that are distinct from quantitative data. Concepts and relationships are often graphically represented in mind maps, tables, and other diagrams. Some of these standard outputs are covered in the latter half of the chapter.

If you have a good working knowledge of statistics, the first section can be skipped because it corresponds to an introduction to statistical measures. If you are carrying out a predominantly quantitative study, the first half of the chapter is of more interest. If you are carrying out a qualitative study, on the other hand, the second half of the chapter is of more interest.

Excel and SPSS have a huge range of tests, statistics and correlations that can be used on your dissertation data. The aim of this chapter is to explain some of the important elements of data analysis and to provide an overview of the possibilities for analysis.

9.2 ANALYSIS AND EXPLAINING: AN OVERVIEW

If you have come this far in the book and the research process, you will have expended considerable effort to frame your research, conduct it and enter the data. The section in your dissertation that analyses the data and represents the analysis is vital to its success. The effort you have expended so far can be lost or dissipated with a weak or illogical data analysis section. We covered the nature of analysis in an earlier chapter. There, it was described as:

- the study of the constituent parts and the interrelationship of the parts
- the breaking down and separation of the whole into constituent parts
- simplifying the whole into parts to display the logical structure
- an explanation of a process and the parts of that process.

Let's look at these again now that we have some data to analyse. The first three bullets all have an element of separation or breaking down into parts. This is a primary task of data analysis. There will be considerable quantities of data from your research, and in its raw format it will mean very little to anyone, including you. If you don't believe me, open up your spreadsheet or other software and take a look at the Data view of your research. You will see rows and columns of data – but what do they mean or represent? Data analysis does two important things: it separates out the data, as when we look at the responses from female and male groups, but it also groups things together, as when we add together the responses to a question – for example, to create age categories. Technically this is 'synthesis', but you don't often hear people say they are going to analyse and synthesise their data.

In the first bullet point there is a reference to discovering, uncovering, the interrelationship of the parts. Quantitative and qualitative data analysis searches out the important relationships in the data. In quantitative approaches we have some standard tests that ask the question 'Is this thing related to that thing?' We can also judge the strength of a relationship and, with advanced techniques, the nature of the relationship. In qualitative analysis we are looking for important concepts and the interrelationship of the concepts.

 STUDENT COMMENT

I was just trying to finish off my dissertation. I was doing the data analysis stuff. My sister came home from university for the weekend and asked what I was doing. I said, 'Trying to finish off this dissertation I started a year ago.' She asked if she could have a look. When I showed her, she said, 'That is so boring! It is all numbers and charts.' 'Yes,' I said. 'That is statistics.' She was doing critical studies, and she said, 'But what is the story?' That took me back a bit, and I thought about it for a while and then realised there was no story. The statistics were there, and the graphs – but there was no story. It was then that it really dawned on me that my job was to tell the story. When I submitted the work, I got a distinction. My sister may not have realised it but she was probably responsible for that great grade.

In the fourth bullet point the notion of explanation occurs. Your data analysis section is an explanation of your data and what that data represents. When you explain, you tell a story. If readers or listeners believe the story, your explanation has been successful. In the data analysis section of your dissertation you must tell a story. Statistics can look very good on paper but they do not tell a story. Your task in the data analysis section is to tell the story of the statistics or the qualitative data. This is where it is important to understand the reader of your dissertation – in this case, the marker. The marker will be expecting a certain type of story, such as:

1 This is a problem.

2 The problem has these parts.

3 People say these things about the problem.

4 If people did this or that, the problem would lessen or even be solved.

Now take a second look at that story. Does it look like your dissertation?

Your data story should:

- be simple, brief and relevant
- have a beginning, middle and end
- have a 'punchline', a discovery
- have data and evidence to support the story (but only to support the story)
- be specific and appropriate to the research study
- offer improvement and solutions
- illustrate how it all might be relevant to a wider audience.

Below, these points are elaborated on to see how they can help in analysing and explaining your data.

Be simple, brief and relevant

Now this immediately presents a problem. How can all your research and effort be simple and brief? The answer is that it must be expressed in this way if it is to be understandable and clear to the reader. The simple and brief characteristic is achieved by separating up the important outcomes of the analysis. One main idea creates one main story, then the next idea and story, and so on. Normal structuring of the writing then conveys to the reader a set of simple and brief data stories. The relevance aspect is a judgement call that relies on two other ideas. The data story should be significant in that it should tell a story about something important in the dissertation. How do you know it is important? This would be judged against the stated research aims and objectives. Remember them? In terms of analysis and explaining, they are the important things you are trying to investigate. Print the aims and objectives and constantly check that your data stories are relevant to them.

Have a beginning, a middle, an end – and a punchline, and evidence

Normal story structure follows this format and your data stories must follow this format if you want to successfully explain your research. What does this look like for a data story?

- Beginning – Analysis showed that (for example) there was a significant difference between the book-buying habits of law students in comparison with business students.
- Middle – Explore this in more detail using data evidence such as tables and graphs. Ask questions about why this might be occurring. Relate the issue to any known theory from the literature review. Create a punchline in the middle section – a 'wow event', if you like.
- End – Find a conclusion to your story, also a summary – and if the data story presents a problem, say what the solution might be. Relate the conclusion to the punchline.
- Data evidence to support the story – The important thing here is to be sure that the data evidence supports the story. The data can never be the story.

Be specific and appropriate to the research study

At the beginning of your research you should set out some aims, objectives, research questions or hypotheses – all your stories should relate to these. It is best if this relationship is made explicit. One of the marking criteria for your dissertation will be how well you have met the aims, objectives, research questions or hypotheses. Making the link explicit in the stories will address that issue in an integrated and effective manner.

Offer improvements and solutions

Some stories have a moral conclusion, and your data stories must have a similar thing. In the data stories you will conclude with improvements, solutions or recommendations. This will allow you a 'handle' in the data section that you can return to in the conclusion of your work.

Illustrate the significance to a wider audience

Your data stories are specific to your research, but depending on the philosophical stance your research takes, may have useful implications for groups beyond your data. Even specific qualitative data may have general points that are worthy of mention.

This section has tried to encourage an approach to data analysis that tells stories of the data rather than just producing data tables or graphs. The data can never speak for itself. Your job is the job of the storyteller.

9.3 DESCRIBING QUANTITATIVE DATA

All research that generates quantitative data should start the analysis with a set of descriptive statistics. These are normally simple to produce (mostly automatically from the software) and serve two purposes. Firstly, descriptive statistics will summarise your data in a manner that anyone can understand. Secondly, it will allow you to compare your data with other data. Although an overview of the measures and some brief information about the formula to calculate the statistics appear below, you do not have to worry unduly about the calculations – they should be performed automatically by any of the software listed in Chapter 8. The explanations are given here for the very important reason that you should understand what each statistic or test is designed to achieve.

In dissertation research a range of different data is collected. It is important to have a general idea of what tests apply to which types of data. If you have (for example) coded your gender data as 1 male, 2 female and 9 missing, it is quite possible to generate an average statistic of, therefore, 3.234. Generating ridiculous and inappropriate values with Excel and SPSS is very easy. If you have an understanding of the various tests and statistics, you are less likely to do this. If you find yourself explaining that the average gender of your sample is 3.234, then you have a problem. That example is a very obviously inappropriate statistic. Without a basic knowledge of the tests and statistics and their appropriate use, you can generate ridiculous and inappropriate statistics and try to explain them in your dissertation.

THE AVERAGE

This is more correctly called the mean. It is the first statistic that you generate and it is the most commonly-used statistic to find the centre of your data. It should only be used on interval or ratio data (see section 7.4). The mean is calculated by adding all the values in your data and dividing by the total number of values.

So, for example, if we have the values for age of 23, 18, 36, 45, 68, 21, and 32, we add them together and divide by the number of values (7). This gives us 34.71.

This is a simple statistic, easy to calculate, but also very useful for describing your data, and is essential for calculating other statistics.

Excel uses the following function to calculate the mean:

AVERAGE(a1:a5)

– where the data is held in cells a1 to a5.

THE MEDIAN

The median literally means a line dividing something down the middle. In statistics that is the middle value of a set of values. If we reorder the numbers we used above into a rank order lowest to highest, we will easily see the middle value.

18, 21, 23, 32, 36, 45, 68

The median of this set of values is 32. Note that this is different from the average of 34.71.

The median is easy to find in a set of data with an odd number of values.

Where the range of values is even, the median will fall between two values. If one value is added to the range of values above, you will see the problem.

18, 21, 23, 32, 36, 45, 51, 68

What is the median value?

It falls half-way between 32 and 36 – so the median of this range of values is 34.

With the extra value in the range the mean/average is now 36.75.

The median is just as acceptable as the mean for describing the centre of your data. You would use the median if you wanted to know the typical age of a group in a data set. You would use the mean if you wanted to know the average.

If we add one more value to this set of data, we can see one further advantage of using the median. We will add 101 to the age values. Now we have:

18, 21, 23, 32, 36, 45, 51, 68, 101

The mean is 43.89. The median is 36.

The effect of what we might call an 'outlying' or 'extreme' value is to move the mean up by 7.14. The median has moved up by 2. The mean value of a set of data is very sensitive to outlying data.

THE MODE

The mode is the most frequently occurring value in a data set. The mode is mostly used with ordinal data so that if one of your questions was 'My favourite colour is ... ?', a descriptive statistic of the centre of the data might be the mode, the most often-given answer, which might in this case have been 'purple'. With categories and opinion scales, the mode is the only expression of the centre of the data that means anything. Yet if you were not careful about this point and you coded the favourite colour with a number, you could end up explaining that the average colour is 6.42. Use the mode for opinions, category data and ordinal data.

This section has introduced statistics that explain what the middle of your data looks like. To offer a complete picture of your data you must also offer statistics about the spread of the data.

THE RANGE

The range is only used with interval or ratio data and expresses the lowest and the highest value of a data set. Using our example above, the original range of values was:

18, 21, 23, 32, 36, 45, 68

The range is indicated by 18–68. The range is often forgotten as a way of expressing the spread of the data, but it does convey useful information.

The inter-quartile range

Don't be put off by this rather grand and confusing name – it merely implies separating the data into quarters. The statistic is normally calculated for ranked data (values in a list in ranked order – eg 1, 12, 15, 18, 25, 36, 42, 65). The main number that is returned is the inter-quartile range – that is, the range that consists of the middle two quarters – in other words, the middle half of your data, ignoring the highest and lowest quarters.

Figure 24 The inter-quartile range

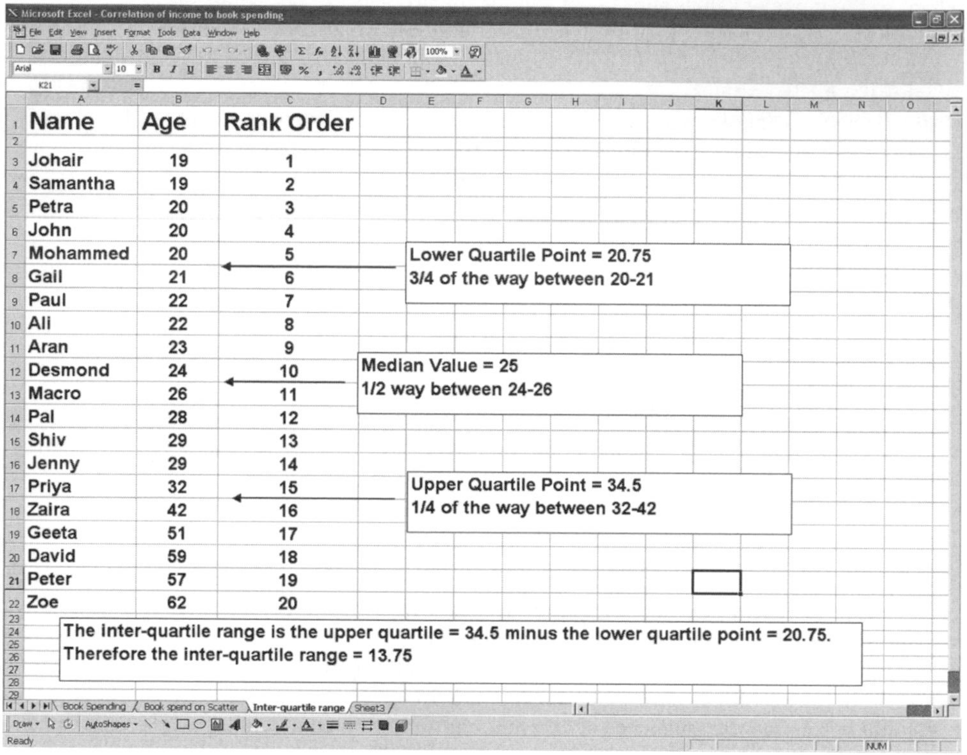

Name	Age	Rank Order
Johair	19	1
Samantha	19	2
Petra	20	3
John	20	4
Mohammed	20	5
Gail	21	6
Paul	22	7
Ali	22	8
Aran	23	9
Desmond	24	10
Macro	26	11
Pal	28	12
Shiv	29	13
Jenny	29	14
Priya	32	15
Zaira	42	16
Geeta	51	17
David	59	18
Peter	57	19
Zoe	62	20

We have already been alerted to the problem of 'outlying' or 'extreme values'. Using the inter-quartile range overcomes the effect of these extreme values by excluding them.

In Excel this can be calculated using the quartile function:

QUARTILE(a3:a12,1)

The first numbers inside the brackets are the values in the range of cells a3 to a12.

The number at the end should correspond to whichever quartile you want.

Remember to put the data in rank order (smallest to largest) – this is easy in Excel using the sort command.

1 First quartile (25th percentile)

2 Median value (50th percentile)

3 Third quartile (75th percentile).

To calculate the inter-quartile range, you would subtract the (in Excel's terms) third quartile from the first quartile, or the upper quartile from the lower quartile.

THE STANDARD DEVIATION

The standard deviation expresses your data spread in a slightly different and more useful manner. Each value in your data is compared to the mean value for all the data.

So for the range of values:

18, 21, 23, 32, 36, 45, 68

the mean is 34.71.

The standard deviation calculates how far each value is away from the mean.

For example,

18 is –16.71 away from the mean

68 is +33.29 away from the mean

and so on

To avoid negative numbers being generated, the difference is squared – multiplied by itself – so that we now have:

18 is –16.71 away from the mean; –16.71 × –16.71 = 279.22

68 is +33.29 away from the mean; +33.29 × +33.29 = 1,108.22

and so on

Then the amount of each squared deviation from the mean is added together, and then averaged. Finally, the square root of the number is calculated – and this is the *standard deviation*.

You will note in the Table of values below that there are two ways to calculate the standard deviation. In column E you will notice that we calculate the standard deviation of the population. This is not the usual calculation – most dissertation research uses a sample. In column F we calculate the standard deviation of a sample of the population: this is much more frequently used in dissertation research. The difference in these functions is to estimate better the standard deviation from a sample, and involves carrying out the standard calculation, but using n–1 as the denominator.

Figure 25 Table of values, and the calculation of standard deviation

	A	B	C	D	E	F	G	H	I	J
1	Table of values and the Standard Deviation calculation									
2		Value	Mean	Difference between mean and value	Square of the difference	Square of the difference				
3	Value 1	18	34.71	-16.71	279.37	279.37				
4	Value 2	21	34.71	-13.71	188.08	188.08				
5	Value 3	23	34.71	-11.71	137.22	137.22				
6	Value 4	32	34.71	-2.71	7.37	7.37				
7	Value 5	36	34.71	1.29	1.65	1.65				
8	Value 6	45	34.71	10.29	105.80	105.80				
9	Value 7	68	34.71	33.29	1107.94	1107.94				
10										
11	Average	34.71								
12								Average based on Sum/n-1		
13	Sum of the differences				1827.43	1827.43				
14										
15	Average of the differences				261.06	304.57				
16										
17	Squareroot of the differences				16.16	17.45				
18										
19										
20	Excel calculation of Standard Deviation of the Sample					17.45				
21	Excel calculation of the Standard Deviation of the poulation				16.16					
22										
23										
24										
25										
26										
27										
28										
29										
30										
31										
32										
33										
34										
35										
36										
37										

Excel has two functions to calculate standard deviations:

=STDEV(b3:b9), which is the calculation from the Table of values above in the F column, and calculates the standard deviation of the sample

=STDEVP(b3:b9), which is the calculation of the standard deviation of the population, and is shown in the Table of values in the E column

– where the data is held in the cells b3 to b9.

USING THE STANDARD DEVIATION: A WORKED EXAMPLE

CASE STUDY

Fifteen members of three MBA groups are having lunch together when the question of grades comes up in the discussion. Each group has looked at the overall results posted by their tutor on their e-learning site in a spreadsheet. Natural boasting starts, and one group says its grades are better than the others' grades. The challenge issued, they decide to use the data they have to decide which group is 'best'. The 15 class members are part of larger groups of students, but feel it would not be right to include the grades of classmates not present nor involved in this debate.

Each of the groups took the same examination set by the same tutor. The grades for the five people in each of the three groups were:

	Group 1	Group 2	Group 3
	82	82	67
	78	82	66
	70	82	66
	58	42	66
	42	42	65
Mean:	66	66	66

The mean of each group is 66%. This causes some concern, because they are unable to answer the question of 'which group is best' using the mean.

They decide to make the judgement on the range that the different groups display.

	Group 1	Group 2	Group 3
Range:	82–42 (40)	82–42 (40)	67–65 (2)

This output also proves to be problematic in that whereas Group 3 claims that because its range is the smallest it must be the best, both Groups 1 and 2 state that they have the highest score, so that must be nonsense.

They look for another measure that may help them decide which is the 'best group'. They remember that their research methods tutor discussed using the standard deviation.

	Group 1	Group 2	Group 3
	82	82	67
	78	82	66
	70	82	66
	58	42	66
	42	42	65
Mean:	66	66	66
Standard deviation:	16.25	21.91	0.71

The debate then moves to whether the standard deviation should be of the population or whether the members count as a sample. The original reason for doing the calculation gets forgotten at this point when one of them says: 'Why do you calculate the standard deviation of a sample using the denominator of n–1?'

At this point their tutor comes in for her lunch – and they stop her and ask why the standard deviation of a sample is different from that of a population. She sighs. 'I'll get my lunch and then explain.' Seated with her lunch she explains the issue thus:

'The reason that the denominator in the calculation of the standard deviation of a sample is n21 deserves some thought.

'To look at it let's change the example. Suppose that I am interested in the number of hours per day that university students in the UK spend doing their dissertations. The "population" of interest is all master's students in the UK – a very large number of people. Let's call this number N. The real interest is the mean and standard deviation of this population, as once we know this we could compare "you lot" with the population.

'Rather than trying to deal with this large population, a researcher would usually select a "sample" of students – say n of them – and perform calculations on this smaller data set to estimate the mean and the standard deviation. Here n might be 25 or 30, or 100, or maybe even 1,000 – but certainly much smaller than N. To estimate the standard deviation of the sample it seems natural to use the mean of the sample. Likewise to estimate the standard deviation of the sample it seems reasonable to use n – the number in the sample – but this quantity tends to underestimate the standard deviation of the population that we are trying to work out. This problem is particularly acute for small values of n. From research it works out that using n–1 as the denominator provides a much better estimate of the standard deviation of the population.

'Can I eat my lunch now?'

Returning to their original question, the 15 decide that it is not possible to decide which group is 'best'. They do agree that:

- Group 1 and 2 have the highest examination scores: 82

- Group 3 comprises the most consistent performers: std dev 0.71

They also decide that they must in future frame their questions more precisely.

In the research setting, the standard deviation and the mean are useful in understanding if the data has a *normal distribution*. A 'normal' distribution is one in which the data displays a 'bell-shaped' frequency curve. The empirical rule states that 68% of the data will lie within one standard deviation either side of the mean, and 95.4% of the data will lie within two standard deviations either side of the mean, and that 99.7% of the data will lie within three standard deviations either side of the mean.

The table in Figure 27 shows the completion times of dissertations for a group of 20 students. Take a look at the data and consider what these values mean, and how we might predict things from the data. It is possible to say that the mean time to complete a dissertation for this sample is 26 weeks. You might want to work out the median figure for this data – what does this tell you about the data? Using the empirical rule it is possible to say that 68% of the students would complete their dissertations in 1 standard deviation either side of the mean. This would give us two-thirds of the students completing their dissertations in the range 20–32 weeks; 96% of the students would complete in the range 15–37 weeks. In practical terms, it might be an effective idea to provide extra support and advice for students who are taking longer than 37 weeks to complete their dissertations. You might also be able to predict that this extra support would be needed only by 2.3% of students.

Figure 26 The standard distribution curve

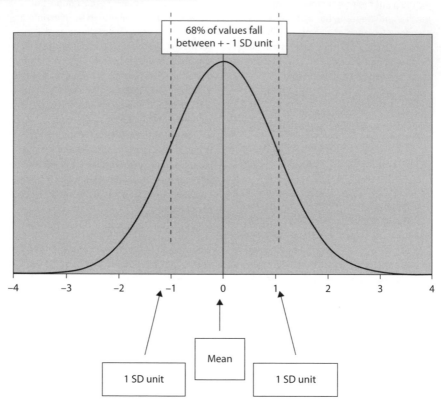

Figure 27 Screenshot table of completion times of dissertations in weeks

	A	B	C	D	E	F	G	H	I	J	K	L
1	Table of the time taken to complete a masters dissertation											
2	Student ID	Time to complete the dissertation										
3		Weeks										
4	20.6145	17										
5	20.5448	18										
6	20.5896	19										
7	20.6254	20										
8	20.5689	22										
9	20.6321	22										
10	20.5887	23										
11	20.6451	24										
12	20.5778	25										
13	20.5899	25										
14	20.5874	27										
15	20.5881	27										
16	20.6522	28										
17	20.7811	28										
18	20.7544	29										
19	20.5495	30										
20	20.5892	31										
21	20.6102	32										
22	20.5621	35										
23	20.5863	38										
24												
25	Std Dev Sample	5.61										
26												
27	Mean	26										
28												
29												

THE PREDICTED EXTRA SUPPORT NEEDED

Reflect on why the extra support would be required only by 2.3% of the students.

You might have expected the support to be provided for 4.6% of the students

– those lying outside the range of two standard deviations from the mean, as specified by the empirical rule …

9.4 TRENDS, DISTRIBUTIONS AND PROPORTIONS IN QUANTITATIVE DATA

Raw data is stored in software in rows and columns – normally, a row for each respondent and a column for each answer. In any data that occupies more than a few rows and columns, it will be impossible to see any trends in the data. To see better the trends in your data you will have to represent parts of the data in tables or graphs. This is useful in at least two circumstances. The first is for your own exploration of the data. Once the data is entered into software, do not be afraid to generate tables and graphs using a wide range of types – it will throw up 'interesting' connections of ideas. We might call this 'playing' with the data, and it is really important that time is spent just 'playing' with outputs for tables and graphs. Once you generate a table or graph, ask several questions of what you see:

- Does it look like a true reflection of the data?
- Is it clear and understandable?
- What is it telling me about the data?
- Can I adapt it to generate a clearer message?
- Is it going to be useful in my data analysis section?

Does it look like a true reflection of the data?

It is very easy with the powerful software used for analysis to generate either rubbish or representations that are wrong. For instance, look at Figure 24: when the frequency distribution is first produced, it will probably show the output of the category numbers, not the data in the next column. Ask the simple question: 'Is there enough cumulative data in the in the table?' You are looking for about 500 responses. If the table is showing maybe only 19 responses, something is wrong. Investigate before you use the data output. You can also add some simple checks to tables by summing and averaging data. This will often make clear when something is slightly wrong.

Is it clear and understandable?

Problems occur when you have a lot of categories with small numbers in them and when tables and charts are trying to display too much data. Give some thought to the type of display that is best for displaying the data or message in the data. Summary charts tend to be pie charts and bar charts; detailed charts tend to be line-and scatter-graphs. If you try to display 500 responses to a four-answer question, you will create a chart that does not tell you much. Try it! Consider whether you need a table or a chart, or both – all the software that have been mentioned can create these outputs.

What is it telling me about the data?

When you have a clear and accurate chart, ask yourself what it tells you about the question you asked. Figure 24 has a table and a pie chart of the data – it is indicating several very clear messages. First, very few respondents chose to not answer the question. Secondly, the largest group agreed with the statement in the question. Thirdly, over half the respondents agreed or strongly agreed with the statement. Fourthly, and more worryingly, just under half the respondents disagreed or strongly disagreed with the statement. At this stage you are looking for descriptive elements that could be included in the narrative of the data analysis section, and areas that require or would benefit from further analysis.

Can I adapt it to generate a clearer message?

This is an extension of the above point, but useful and relative outputs that can explain a 'story' are what are required. In most dissertations there are always more data and more potential stories about the data and the behaviour behind the data than can ever be told. You need strong, bold stories that answer your research question or that are directly connected to your testable hypotheses.

FREQUENCY TABLES

Frequency tables and frequency distributions summarise the number of respondents that gave a certain answer – in statistical language, the number of cases in each category. The output can be varied by the settings you make in the software, but the minimum output will be the categories of answer and the number of respondents that so answered. You would normally include an entry for missing data, because this is an important consideration in relation to the validity of the question and the answers. If you had asked a very personal question and the frequency table data had shown that 72 out of 100 respondents did not answer the question, it would be unwise to include this question in any analysis and any subsequent recommendations. Frequency tables are an important source of data for the subsequent analysis using inferential statistics.

When you have developed the frequency table, it is a relatively easy matter to generate a more visual chart of the frequency table (see Figures 23 and 24). Figure 23 is generated from SPSS and shows the answer to Question 1 of a survey that asked 500 respondents to rate their agreement with the following statement: 'My research methods course was useful in training me for dissertation research' on a four-point scale of 'Strongly agree' to 'Strongly disagree'. The SPSS table in Figure 23 shows in the first column the number of respondents answering 'Strongly agree' – this being 105. Column 2 shows this as a percentage of all respondents (500). Column 3 shows the percentage of answers ignoring the missing data (482). The fourth column shows the cumulative percentage. Figure 24 shows the same data but in Excel, with a simple frequency table and a pie chart of that table's output. Note that the table data would be more useful for further statistical work, and the pie chart would be more useful for visually representing the data.

CREATING CATEGORIES FROM DATA

Collecting data with continuous variables (those that can take any value) often causes difficulties in data analysis. There will be times when you need to convert a continuous variable into categories to display data more clearly and to carry out some forms of analysis. Imagine that the data we used above – 500 responses to Question 1 – also has data about each respondent's age. Whereas it is not possible to have 500 different responses, assuming age is expressed in years, it is possible that there will be 50 different answers. It might be useful to your research question to know if different age groups respond differently to the question relating to the usefulness of research methods.

It can be achieved using a lookup table in Excel, where you have the age data in column D, insert a new column as E, then use the **Lookup** command in the form Look in cell d6, Check this number against a set of categories, Return the number of the category, eg 1, 2, 3, 4, ... or 18–21, 22–27, 28–32, ...

In SPSS you would use the **Transform**, **Compute variable** command. You will then have turned your continuous data for age into a set of categories and can then calculate the frequency in each category. Importantly, you would also have the continuous data if you wanted to investigate the relationship between age and individual responses. Note the link to the questionnaire design. If age categories had been designed into the questionnaire, this data transformation would not be necessary.

Figure 28 SPSS frequency table for Q1

'My research methods course was useful in training me for dissertation research'

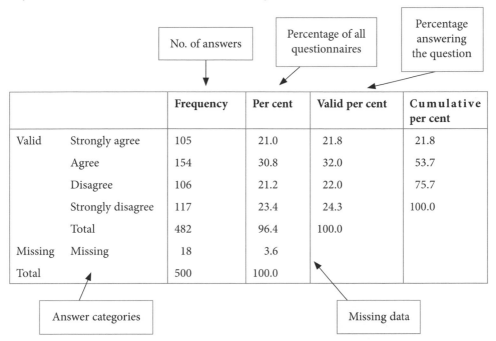

		Frequency	Per cent	Valid per cent	Cumulative per cent
Valid	Strongly agree	105	21.0	21.8	21.8
	Agree	154	30.8	32.0	53.7
	Disagree	106	21.2	22.0	75.7
	Strongly disagree	117	23.4	24.3	100.0
	Total	482	96.4	100.0	
Missing	Missing	18	3.6		
Total		500	100.0		

Figure 29 Excel screenshot for Q1 with frequency table and pie chart

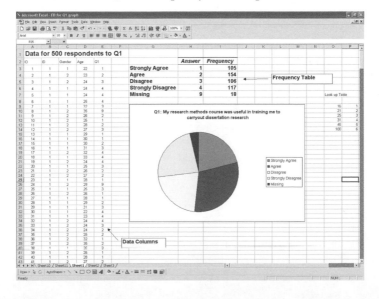

Continuous data can also be represented directly using a histogram; the chart in Figure 30 was produced in SPSS and represents the frequency distribution of the age of the same 500 responses considered above.

Figure 30 Histogram of the answers to Q1

▶ Graph

[DataSet0]

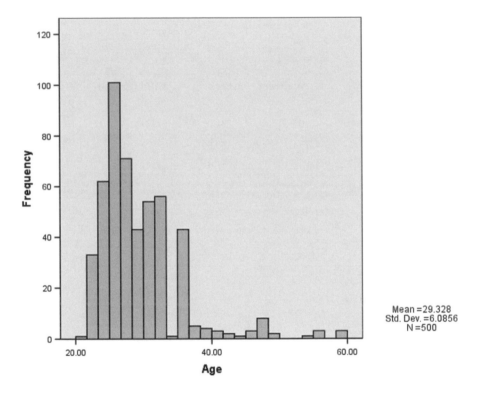

Once you have data in Excel or SPSS, a range of interesting charts can be produced. Figure 31 is a chart of the age frequency by response to Question 1.

Figure 31 Area chart of the age of respondents to Q1 in each category

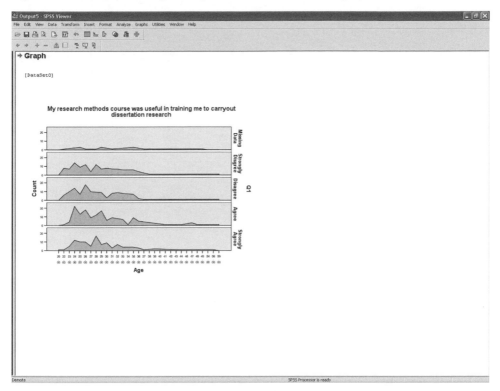

Pictograms replace bars and areas with small pictures, as in Figure 32.

Figure 32 Pictograms showing frequency of age of respondents to Q1

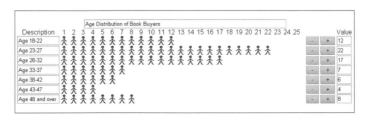

TRENDS

Some of your data may well have been collected over a period of time. Some examples might be test scores of students (carrying out the same test), absence rates, product failure rates, call-out times, delivery time. Trend data is normally presented in line-graphs using the variable measure along the vertical or y axis and the time along the horizontal or x axis. The format of these charts makes a large visual difference, as can be seen in the same data shown in two formats. Figure 33 is formatted to show a rather effective drop in working days lost to absence. Figure 34 shows a more natural representation of the data.

Figure 33 Line-graph of working days lost to absence 1985–2008

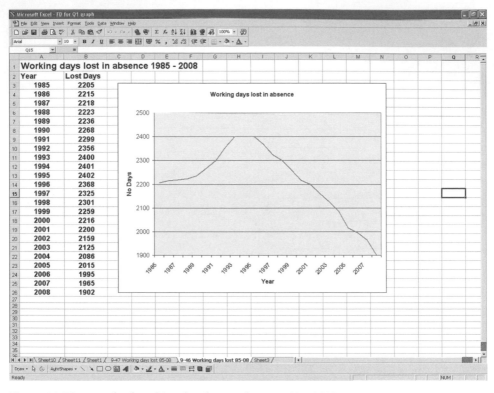

Figure 34 Line-graph of working days lost to absence 1985–2008

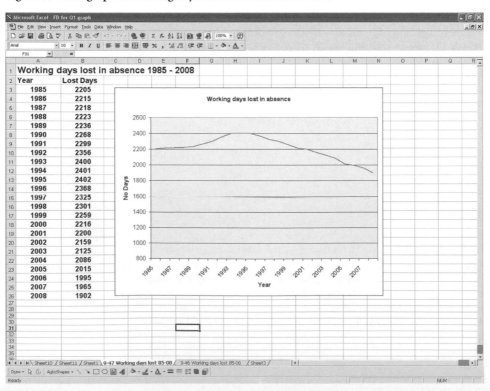

When creating charts of all kinds you must think about the scales used and the formatting of the object to display accurate, clear messages.

Scatter-graphs

Scatter-graphs present data by plotting one variable against another. Figure 35 shows two scenarios of income to book spending and the relationships between the variables. The normal approach is to plot the fixed variable (independent) against the horizontal or x axis and the variable that changes (dependent) against the vertical or y axis. The scatter-graph shows the relationship between the variables. In the left-hand scenario the relationship between income and book spend is almost a straight line. This indicates that there is a positive relationship between the variables – as income increases, so does book spending. In the right-hand scenario there appears to be no discernible relationship between the variables, although you might be able to see some of the scatter plots forming a rudimentary line above the income level of £12,000. In the next section we look at techniques to investigate these relationships statistically.

Figure 35 Scatter-graph of income to book spending

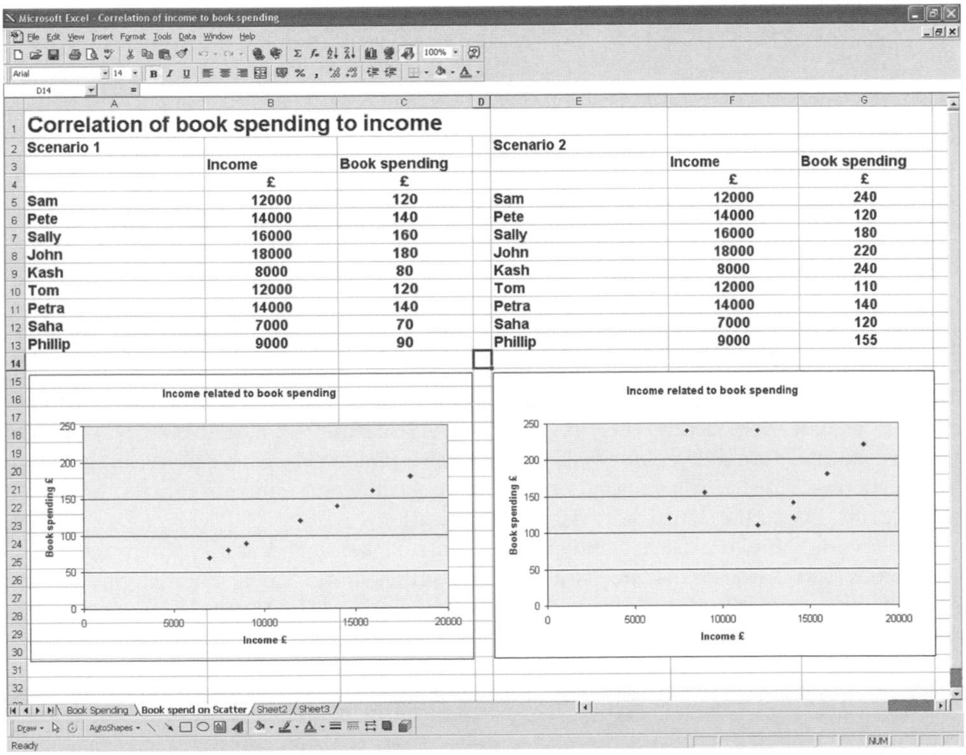

CROSS-TABULATIONS

Cross-tabulations are tables that present the data from two variables, one down the left (rows) and one across the top (columns). They can be useful for summarising and representing data from questions related to a biographical feature of the respondents, such as age, gender, experience, and income. It is important to create numerous cross-tabulations when you are exploring the data, so that the interesting and useful cross-tabulations of variables can be identified for explanation or further analysis. You can create multi-layer cross-tabulation tables, but it is advisable to master the simple tables before moving on to the more complex ones. In Excel these are called 'pivot tables'.

Figure 36 Cross-tabulation of age and gender of respondents to Q1

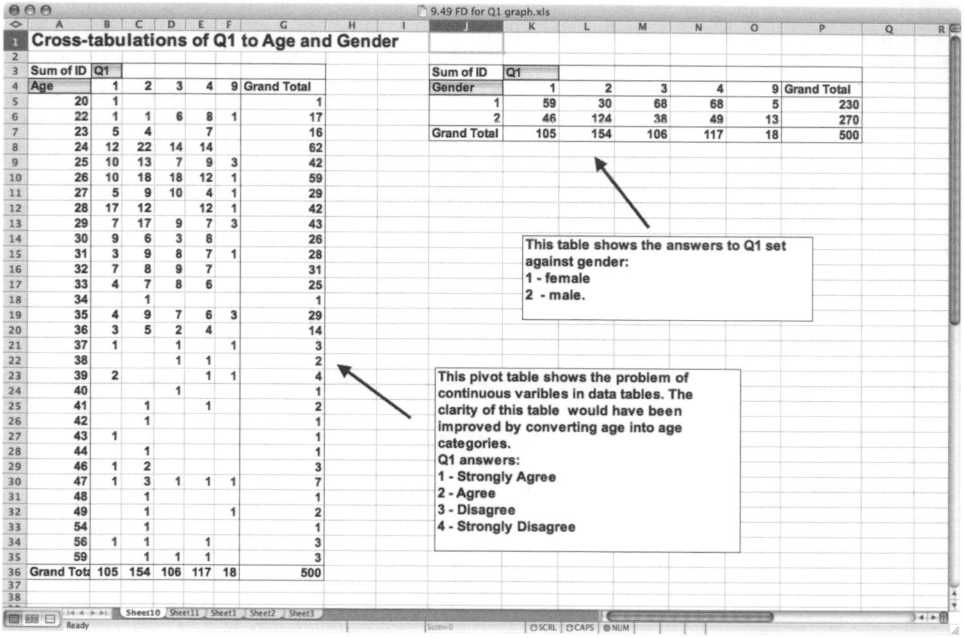

Cross-tabulations of Q1 to Age and Gender

Sum of ID	Q1					
Age	1	2	3	4	9	Grand Total
20	1					1
22	1	1	6	8	1	17
23	5	4		7		16
24	12	22	14	14		62
25	10	13	7	9	3	42
26	10	18	18	12	1	59
27	5	9	10	4	1	29
28	17	12		12	1	42
29	7	17	9	7	3	43
30	9	6	3	8		26
31	3	9	8	7	1	28
32	7	8	9	7		31
33	4	7	8	6		25
34		1				1
35	4	9	7	6	3	29
36	3	5	2	4		14
37	1		1		1	3
38			1	1		2
39	2			1	1	4
40			1			1
41		1		1		2
42		1				1
43	1					1
44		1				1
46	1	2				3
47	1	3	1	1	1	7
48		1				1
49		1			1	2
54		1				1
56	1	1		1		3
59		1	1	1		3
Grand Tota	105	154	106	117	18	500

Sum of ID	Q1					
Gender	1	2	3	4	9	Grand Total
1	59	30	68	68	5	230
2	46	124	38	49	13	270
Grand Total	105	154	106	117	18	500

The pivot table in Figure 36 shows two tables. One cross-tabulates gender to the answers given in Question 1. This table summarises 500 responses, so it condenses the data – but it is still unclear how gender relates to the answering of Question 1. A graph or chart may express this data more clearly. There is also another problem. Although it is evident that the response numbers are different for male and female respondents, we have no way of knowing if the pattern is statistically significant because there are different numbers of male and female respondents. Inferential statistics are dealt with in section 9.5.

The second table, on the left, indicates a problem, mentioned above, where tables use continuous data. There are an impossibly large number of age categories that confuse any possible 'messages' in the data. This problem would be improved by converting the continuous data into age categories.

9.5 INFERENTIAL STATISTICS

This section addresses the areas of analysis that considers differences between data and exploring relationships in data. It is important to remember that the claims you wish to make, evidenced by your data, will affect the sorts of inferences you need to make. If you have collected data on all the available cases of workers at the XYZ factory and you have no need to consider how this group might be represented in a wider population, you will have no need of inferential statistical tests. This situation would be described as a census (and was discussed in the methodology chapter under *Sampling*). However, if you have a sample of a population and want to make inferences from your sample to the wider population, you will have to use some of the ideas that follow. The first part of this section looks at some key concepts that you must understand.

PROBABILITY

Probability represents the likelihood that a particular finding or a relationship between variables will occur or has occurred. It is an easy way (once you are familiar with it) to express outcomes for inferential statistics. Your tutors will expect you to be familiar with expressing outcomes in this way. Probability statements are always expressed on the scale 0 to 1. A probability of 0 means an event or relationship is likely never to happen. A probability of 1 means it is always likely to happen. What do you think is the probability of going to the nearest tap and turning it on and finding that water runs from it? Yes, this probability is likely to be very near to 1 – let's say it is 0.9999. What do you think the probability of going to the tap, turning it on, and finding that red wine runs from it? Yes, the probability is likely to be very low – let's say 0.0001. If we think about these numbers a little further, we can equate them to everyday words and sayings. The probability we expressed above of finding water coming from a tap may also be expressed as 9,999 times out of 10,000 that water will run from the tap. In the red wine scenario 9,999 times out of 10,000 no red wine will come out of the tap.

In statistics, we express the probabilities as inequalities of something occurring by chance. So in the above scenarios we would say the probability of water coming from a tap when it is turned on is greater than 0.9999, written as $p > 0.9999$. The red wine scenario is that the probability of red wine coming from a tap is less than 0.0001, written as $p < 0.0001$. All the probabilities in dissertations are related to the probability of something occurring by chance.

The two statements above ($p >$ and $p <$) are the most frequently used probability situations, corresponding to being greater than something or being less than something. There are a few other 'operators' that you may want to use:

$p =$ the probability is equal to
$p \leq$ the probability is less than or equal to
$p \geq$ the probability is greater than or equal to.

CONFIDENCE

In research terms nothing is certain, and we need a way of expressing this uncertainty. Uncertainty is not normally what we express – we normally express the paired notion of confidence. There are two connected ideas when you are expressing confidence:

- the confidence level
- the confidence interval.

Confidence level

You may have collected data about the book-buying habits of students and found that 42% of students buy the recommended text for a taught module. Based on this data, you may report that 42% of students will buy the recommended text for a taught module. You might express the confidence level of this statement as that you are 95% (confidence level) certain that the prediction is accurate. This means that the 42% of students buying the recommended course text that you discovered in your sample would be represented in the whole population 95 times out of 100.

Confidence interval

The confidence interval is an estimate of how accurate the prediction of 42% is likely to be. So, from above, you might say that a nominal 42% of students will buy the course text and that this prediction is accurate to within plus or minus 2%. What this really means is that if multiple samples were taken (from the population), then results for students buying the course text would be found between 40% and 44%, 95 times out of 100.

So the full expression of confidence is 42%, plus or minus 2%, at 95% confidence level.

You might ask what the practical significance of confidence levels is. Confidence – or, as another way of putting it, margins of error – are related to sample size. Dissertations typically have low sample sizes, and so an understanding of confidence and an awareness of how it will affect your claims is important.

Sample size and margins of error

Survey sample size	Margin of error (%) at 95% confidence level
2,000	2
1,500	3
1,000	3
900	3
800	3
700	4
600	4
500	4
400	5
300	6
200	7
100	10
50	14
Note: These are approximations for a population larger than the sample	

What you can see from the table of Sample size and margins of error above is that if you have 50 respondents to your survey, any expressed confidence interval will be plus or minus 14%. At a sample of 100 the interval becomes plus or minus 10%. The 5% confidence interval does not come up until you have 400 in your sample. In summary, when making claims from samples of between 50 and 200, be very cautious because the confidence intervals are quite wide.

HYPOTHESES AND SIGNIFICANCE

Quantitative data often has research hypotheses that must be tested. For instance, to test if book buying by students is greater when they are employed than when they are surviving on grants alone. The results of research using samples always vary slightly from results using the whole population. Research outcomes will be making statements about the population based on the sample. Inferential statistics evaluate the probability that your sample data represents the entire population. We also use inferential statistics to evaluate and test research hypotheses.

Statistical significance

The data you collect for any hypotheses can occur simply by chance. Statistical significance will check whether this has happened or if it is more likely that the data represents a relationship between two variables. The assumption in these tests is that there is no difference between your sample and the population. This point stresses the importance of generating a representative sample (see the methodology chapter, Chapter 7).

This is a slightly unusual point and takes some getting used to, but significance tests work on the premise that there is no association between two variables. This means that the general assumption is that the data occurred by chance. If, however, it can be shown that the fact that data arose by pure chance is unlikely, that assumption may be rejected. This approach of assuming there is no relationship between variables is called the null hypothesis – taking it for granted that there is no association. The null hypothesis is referred to by the capital letter H and the subscript number $_0$, which together give us H_0.

To state that there is a significant relationship we would use an alternative hypothesis, initially abbreviated as H_1. The alternative hypothesis H_1 for our example might then be that employed students spend more money on book-buying than those without work. It is quite normal to have several hypotheses expressing possible relationships, and they are then referred to as H_1, H_2, H_3, and so on.

So from the example above, we may have a null hypothesis H_0 understood as 'There is no relationship between the book-buying habits of students and their being employed.' For the null hypothesis to be rejected corresponds to asserting that there is a significant relationship between the variables. Note that the correct way to express significance outcomes is to reject the null hypothesis or to not reject the null hypothesis. Do not simplify this to accepting the null hypothesis.

The calculation of the test results for significance between variables is mostly automatic within SPSS. If your research design is testing hypotheses, use this software. In Excel the test statistic can be calculated, but you will have to have a greater understanding of the test to generate the statistic.

THE CHI-SQUARE STATISTIC

The chi-squared statistic (the ch- of *chi* is pronounced as a k, and the word rhymes with 'I') is a test that is used on frequencies – in other words, the number of people or things that fall into a category. This proves useful for a lot of dissertation research where the sample is asked to respond to statements that fall into categories such as (for example), 'I spend less than 14 hours per week on dissertation research' or 'I spend more than 14 hours per week on dissertation research'. Our null hypothesis might be that there is no difference between the time that male and female students spend on dissertation research. If we asked 1,000 students carrying out dissertation research this question, we might get answers as shown in the table in Figure 37.

Figure 37 Excel screenshot table of 1,000 student responses for chi-square

	Less than 14 hrs/week	More than 14 hrs/week	Total	Less than 14 hrs/week	More than 14 hrs/week
	Observed	Observed		Expected	Observed
Female	267	343	610	295.85	314.15
Male	218	172	390	189.15	200.85
Total	485	515	1000		

Table of 1000 students and whether they spend more than or less than 14 hours per week on dissertation research

Chi-sq statistic	(observed value - expected value) x 2 / expected value		Carried out four times for the four cells	
		Chi-sq statistic		
Chi-sq b5:e5	(267-295.85) sq / 295.85	2.81		
Chi-sq c5:f5	(343-314.15) sq / 314.15	2.65		
Chi-sq b6:e6	(218-189.15) sq/ 189.15	4.40		
Chi-sq c6:f6	(172-200.85) sq / 200.85	4.14		
	Chi-squared total	14.01	Chitest	0.000182

Expected values = Row total*Column total / Table total

Cell E5 = 610*485 / 1000
Cell F5 = 610*515 / 1000
Cell E6 = 485*515 / 1000
Cell F6 = 390*515 / 1000

This Excel table shows a number of things:

Columns A, B, C, rows 4, 5 show the data from the survey.

D, 5, 6 are the row totals.

E, F, 5, 6 are the calculated expected values (see A 23, 24, 25, 26 for the calculation).

A, B, C, 13, 14, 15, 16 are the calculations of the chi-square statistic.

D, E, 18 is the chi-test statistic as calculated by Excel.

How should we interpret this result? If you calculated the chi-square statistic manually as in cells A, B, C, 13–16 and added these together, you would have a result of 14.01. This number is now looked up on a critical values table (see weblink) and for 1 degree of freedom would return a probability of less than 0.0005. The chi-test statistic does the same thing automatically in the Excel spreadsheet and returns 0.000182. This number represents the likelihood of these results occurring by chance, and because this is around 2 in 10,000 (very unlikely), the null hypothesis would be rejected. This means that the two variables of gender and time spent on dissertation research per week are significantly related.

The number of rows and columns in a chart make a difference to the critical value of the chi-square statistic in terms of 'degrees of freedom'. Degrees of freedom is calculated by multiplying the number of rows minus one, and the number of columns minus one. In our example, we had two rows and two columns, so the degrees of freedom (df) in this case corresponds to $(2 - 1) \times (2 - 1) = 1$. In Excel this is calculated automatically. For any set of frequency data, you must calculate the probability of the results' occurring by chance. This is done using the chi-square test and then looking up the probability that these results could have occurred by chance.

The null hypothesis would normally be rejected if the probability of the results occurring by chance is less than 0.05, or 1 in 20, or you can be 95% sure they did not occur by chance, expressed as $p < 0.05$.

The sample size makes a large difference in determining significant statistics for variables. In the example above of 1,000 respondents, it was relatively easy to find low probabilities below 0.05. When the sample size is reduced to 200 it becomes more difficult to find variables that are statistically useful. When the sample size is 100 or fewer it will be almost impossible to find any relationship that shows probabilities below 0.05. This is a dilemma for dissertation research, where there is normally too little time to produce data from large cohorts of respondents.

When using the chi-square test, you should be aware of the following conditions:

- The sample must be randomly drawn from the population.
- You must use the number of things or responses (frequency), not percentages.
- The categories must be mutually exclusive – each thing or response can fall into only one category.
- No expected values should be below 10 – and avoid observed frequencies of 5 or less.

Low expected and observed values can be controlled by combining rows or columns, effectively widening the criteria to include more things or responses. But check that the combined rows and columns create categories that are meaningful.

OTHER TESTS AND STATISTICS

There are a range of other tests and statistics for inferring differences between data variables.

Fisher's exact test tests the significance of variables in a 2×2 table that contains nominal data.

Spearman's rank correlation coefficient assesses the strength of the relationship between two sets of rankings.

Where you have tiered ranks you would use *Kendall's rank correlation coefficient*.

Correlation coefficients generate numbers between −1 and +1. 1 represents a perfect positive correlation: when one variable increases, so does the other variable. −1 means that the two variables are related perfectly but negatively: when one increases, the other decreases. 0 means that there is no correlation between the variables. It is important to realise that this does not mean that one variable causes the other to change (causation). It is very difficult to prove causation – expressing the relationship clearly is important.

Ranking correlations and statistics are useful with category data such as the answers to opinion surveys. There is a different set of tests when numerical data has been collected.

t-tests

There are three types of t-test. They all test for significance adopting different reference points.

The *one-sample t-test* looks at the average of set of data and assesses the significance of any difference from an estimate. A university poll asking students how long they spend each week on dissertation research might have expected an answer of 18 hours per week. The average of the sample it took was only 14 hours per week. The one-sample t-test would assess the significance of this difference.

The same university polled a sample of dissertation students and discovered that the mean time they spend on dissertation research each week was 12 hours. Being somewhat worried by this rather low figure, it arranged some research days and provided for the development of good research habits. Some weeks after these development days they polled the students again and found that the average had gone up to 14 hours per week. The *paired t-test* would assess if this change was significant.

The university was still worried and decided to poll a group of dissertation students at another university. The mean for this group was 18 hours per week. The *independent groups t-test* would assess whether this difference is significant.

Your data analysis software can make the calculations. The key data outputs will be:

(A) Hypothesized Mean Difference   0
(B) P(T<=t) two-tail   0.0386

(A) The test will 'ask' what the probability of obtaining our given results by chance is if there is no difference between the population means. 0 indicates there is no chance.

(B) The probability of these results occurring by chance, 0.039, is less than 0.05 (the 5% limit), so we would reject any null hypothesis.

Correlation between variables

One key relationship that researchers want to explore is the correlation between variables. This would allow analysis output that suggests one variable is related to another and displays the strength of that relationship. Remember, you can never say that one variable *causes* another to change.

Pearson's product moment correlation coefficient (Pearson's r) assesses the strength of relationship between two numerical variables. The calculation is carried out by the software you are using – your role will be to interpret the output. The analysis should be in two stages, one assessing the possibility that this output could have occurred by chance using a t-test of means. If the output could not have occurred by chance, the next step is to calculate the person's r coefficient. This will return a figure between −1 and +1.

Figure 38 Excel screenshot spreadsheet of the correlation of income with book buying

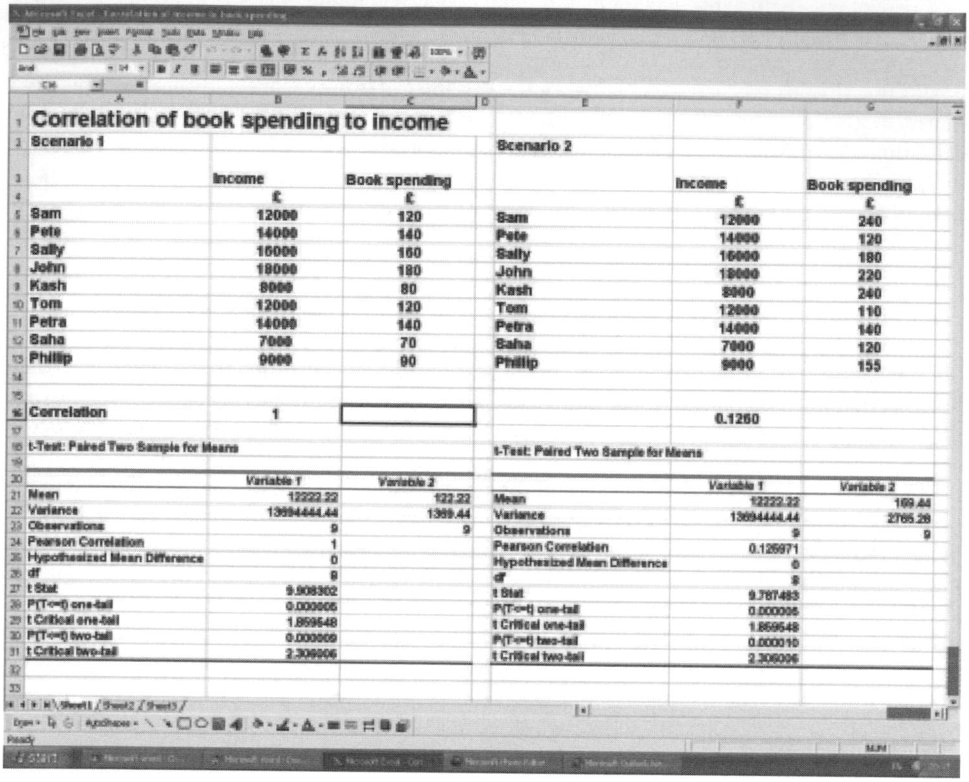

Correlation of book spending to income						
Scenario 1				Scenario 2		
	Income	Book spending			Income	Book spending
	£	£			£	£
Sam	12000	120		Sam	12000	240
Pete	14000	140		Pete	14000	120
Sally	16000	160		Sally	16000	180
John	18000	180		John	18000	220
Kash	8000	80		Kash	8000	240
Tom	12000	120		Tom	12000	110
Petra	14000	140		Petra	14000	140
Saha	7000	70		Saha	7000	120
Phillip	9000	90		Phillip	9000	155
Correlation	1				0.1260	
t-Test: Paired Two Sample for Means				t-Test: Paired Two Sample for Means		
	Variable 1	Variable 2			Variable 1	Variable 2
Mean	12222.22	122.22		Mean	12222.22	169.44
Variance	13694444.44	1369.44		Variance	13694444.44	2765.28
Observations	9	9		Observations	9	9
Pearson Correlation	1			Pearson Correlation	0.125971	
Hypothesized Mean Difference	0			Hypothesized Mean Difference	0	
df	8			df	8	
t Stat	9.908302			t Stat	9.787483	
P(T<=t) one-tail	0.000005			P(T<=t) one-tail	0.000005	
t Critical one-tail	1.859548			t Critical one-tail	1.859548	
P(T<=t) two-tail	0.000009			P(T<=t) two-tail	0.000010	
t Critical two-tail	2.306006			t Critical two-tail	2.306006	

In Figure 38 there are two variables, 'income' and 'book spending'. There are two scenarios. On the left-hand side the correlation is showing as 1.00, and on the right-hand side the correlation is showing as 0.1260. The left-hand scenario displays the relationship that is a perfect correlate – changes in income make proportionate changes in book spending. In the right-hand scenario the changes in income only weakly relate to changes in book spending. The lower half of the sheet calculates correlation again, and the t-test statistics. These show the two-tailed probability for this data being created by chance as $p < 0.000009$, so it was not likely to have occurred by chance. The null hypothesis is therefore rejected. Correlation outputs provide interesting and useful data to help explain the data and the behaviours, actions and views behind the data. But this test does not prove that one variable *causes* the other to change.

The coefficient of determination

The coefficient of determination (r^2) assesses the relationship between numerical variables in a randomly selected sample or a complete population. The coefficient of determination is the square of Pearson's r, and of course when anything is squared, the result can only be a positive number. Thus, the coefficient of determination returns a result in the range 0 to +1. It is also known as regression or the regression coefficient. It measures the proportion of one variable (dependent) that can be explained statistically by another variable (independent). When using Pearson's r it assesses whether two variables are related, but does not assess the cause-and-effect relationship. The coefficient of determination will do that, but you must express the variables precisely.

Figure 39 Independent and dependent variables

A coefficient of determination of +1 means that the variation in the dependent variable is fully explained by the independent variable. A coefficient of determination of 0 means that none of the variation in the dependent variable can be explained by the independent variable. This is sometimes expressed as a percentage:

0%	no variation in the dependent variable is explained by the independent variable (0)
25%	one quarter of the variation in the dependent variable is explained by the independent variable (0.25)
50%	half of the variation in the dependent variable is explained by the independent variable (0.50)
75%	three quarters of the variation in the dependent variable is explained by the independent variable (0.75)
100%	all of the variation in the dependent variable is explained by the independent variable (1).

Using the coefficient of determination would allow for statements such as:

- There was a statistically significant strong relationship between student income and the amount spent on books (r^2 0.75, $p < 0.05$), or 75% of the variation is explained by student income.
- There was a statistically significant but weaker relationship between student age and the amount spent on books (r^2 0.41, $p < 0.05$), or 41% of the variation is explained by age.
- There was no statistically significant relationship between gender and the amount spent on books (r^2 0.18, $p < 0.05$), or only 18% of the variation is explained by gender.

In Excel you would access this analysis by using the **Tools, Data analysis, Regression**.

9.6 QUALITATIVE DATA: AN OVERVIEW

The characteristics of qualitative data affect how you go about analysing it, how you describe it, and how you use it for answering your research questions. In this first section the characteristics of qualitative data are explored and the implications for analysis are considered. Your research study may well combine quantitative and qualitative data, so you may have to consider how the earlier part of this chapter can be integrated with the later part. It is also worth noting here that qualitative data can be presented as quantitative data and, depending on your method and epistemological stance, this may be an effective way to represent qualitative data. However, for many studies it is the 'rich' and in-depth accounts of events and ideas that are important. It cannot be stressed enough that the stance you take towards analysing and presenting qualitative data is wholly dependent on your research questions.

THE STRUCTURE OF DATA

Quantitative data is structured by the questionnaire used to collect it. Qualitative data is often collected by less-structured methods and therefore corresponds to data that is less structured. If you are interested in participants' notions of self-worth, the interview will probably be completely unstructured, more an informal conversation, and the outcome may well be 90 minutes of unstructured transcript. Clearly, this is at one extreme end of any qualitative data-gathering continuum. In semi-structured interviews there will be questions that create some structure, and in highly structured interviews the data will resemble the output from open questions in questionnaires. Where unstructured data is the output from the interview process, the role of the researcher is to create an analysis framework that enables the transcript to be analysed. This is more time-consuming than working with structured or semi-structured data. It leads back to the decisions that were made in the methodology section, where decisions around the structured nature of interviews affect the time taken and the complexity of the data analysis process. The techniques of analysis examined later in the chapter outline several methods for structuring and analysing unstructured transcripts.

VALIDITY

The validity of qualitative data becomes a much more subjective notion and is closely coupled to the sampling system that was used. The idea of construct validity is to evaluate how well the research process has generated data that is closely coupled to the research questions. Qualitative samples are often small, typically below 30, and the sampling system is often not random sampling. This puts much more emphasis on having a full and in-depth exploration of the participants. An in-depth explanation of how the sample was chosen and the characteristics of the participants should always be the first section in the analysis of qualitative data. Your aim is to convince the reader that the sample you chose has the right characteristics to address the research questions. It is always a partial explanation that can never be fully convincing, but the validity of the research is based on how convincing and reflective the author has been. Another technique for improving validity is to 'triangulate' the data, confirming the analysis from other sources. In a triangulation study this would have three viewpoints of the same issues, events, or behaviours.

Qualitative research can gain some validity by reporting back to the participants of a study the findings and asking if they recognise or associate with the findings. If it is practical, most dissertation studies should carry out this type of validity development – we might call it 'participant face validity'. A further way of increasing the validity of the findings is to seek out and reflect on evidence that has the potential to undermine what you want to make of the data. This approach places special emphasis on searching for evidence that contradicts your main findings, considering how and why such evidence might arise, and contemplating any implications it might have for your conclusions. Being reflective and open is important in convincing an audience that the findings of your research are sound and based on evidence.

SIZE

Qualitative data that is presented in transcript form is considerably larger and more difficult to handle than quantitative data. When quantitative data has been input on software it is easy to handle and manage. If qualitative data is being manually analysed, there is a large amount of transcript sheets to control and manage. One standard approach is to have each transcript as a separate Word file and then keep an index of the files. This can be complicated when the participants' confidentiality is protected by an anonymity arrangement. Here, each transcript has to be numbered, and the participants' details must be contained in a separate and 'distanced' file, sometimes held by a research officer. Manual analysis of interview data requires a close reading of the transcript, maybe several times, and then a number of analysis sessions in which the whole transcript is laid out for coding. This can be time-consuming and must be planned in the overall time available. Using a coding system will mark out some parts of the data as being included and other sections as not coded and therefore not part of the analysed data. Questions then arise over what should be done with the sections that are not coded – it is very unlikely that every word of a transcript will be coded. Excluded material must be retained, because a change in the coding structure may mean that the uncoded sections have to be revisited. Using software such as NVivo considerably reduces the burden of dealing with large data files and transcripts.

INDUCTIVE AND DEDUCTIVE

Qualitative data tends to have been collected from studies that are inductive rather than have the deductive nature of quantitative data collection. It requires a different mindset. In deductive studies there is a pre-formed theory or approach that the research aims to test and evaluate. In inductive research these ideas, notions, theories and approaches are not developed or not developed so fully at the beginning of the analysis process. The practical outcomes of this issue are that the researcher must keep an open and enquiring stance as the data is analysed. The process of analysis is also more dynamic in that the process often goes forward several steps and then has to retrace one or two of those steps and branch down a different line of analysis. In quantitative research the analysis process is much more linear. The need to be reflective and thoughtful is an important aspect of qualitative data analysis. The process is dynamic and creative – if you merely report what was said or done, the output is very 'flat'. Your role is to be interpretative and enquiring, bringing together ideas and explanations.

FOLLOW-UP RESEARCH

Most qualitative research requires areas and aspects of the original research to be developed. This predominantly comes from the inductive nature of most qualitative research. It is not normally possible to generalise from a small study to a wider population. But it is often possible to suggest areas for further development and new areas for related research. In the recommendation and conclusion sections, avoid suggesting (for example) that from your study of six people that the whole world should do this or that – but you can suggest that it would be valuable to investigate further this or that aspect of your dissertation research. Another form of follow-up research is to replicate the study and compare the findings of the first cohort of the study with the findings of the second cohort of the study. One further form of follow-up research is to investigate potentially undermining evidence in greater detail.

RESEARCH POINT OF VIEW

The data in a qualitative study has the point of view of the participants as the main view or focus. This requires the researcher to understand this and be sympathetic to the data. It is very easy to select and code qualitative data in such a way as to turn the participant's viewpoint into the view of either the researcher or the theory. Researchers come to research with a view on the phenomena under study. If this view is not 'surfaced' and made explicit, it can affect the research and especially the analysis in ways that will bring the validity of the outcomes into question. Qualitative data is rich and important because it comes predominantly from the view of the participants – this richness has to be guarded and protected. Allowing the researcher's view to 'overwrite' the original messages in the data is a form of bias. One way to check if this has occurred is to get another researcher to recode the raw data. Then the two outcomes of analysis are compared and contrasted to reveal any bias issues. Unfortunately, there is rarely time to carry out this second analysis in dissertation research. That means the researcher must take extra care to 'surface' and explain his or her own position on the phenomena (reflexivity). The researcher has to make explicit the detailed steps of analysis and the decisions taken in creating codes and themes. In general, it is very easy to incorporate unintentional bias into the collection and analysis of qualitative data.

9.7 QUALITATIVE DATA ANALYSIS

The possible ways that qualitative data can be analysed are infinite. Many research studies develop new methods and techniques of analysis and ways to display data outcomes. I mention this here so as to remind researchers that although some of the main methods for the analysis of qualitative data are listed below, the following sections are far from exhaustive and predominantly at an introductory level. You will in most cases be able to find textbooks written solely about your chosen method, and you will find research papers that explore, critique and evaluate your chosen approach.

This section outlines and evaluates the following approaches to analysing qualitative data:

- content analysis
- template analysis
- case study analysis
- repertory grid analysis
- grounded theory.

CONTENT ANALYSIS

Content analysis was partly covered in the quantitative analysis section of the previous chapter as a means of analysing open questionnaire answers. Content analysis is a technique for the objective, systematic and quantitative analysis of any research item. A 'research item' commonly means interview transcripts or open question answers, but the technique can be used on any research output, such as:

- memos
- meetings minutes
- diary entries
- audio recording of conversations or sales delivery
- video and other digital content
- historical documents
- books
- newspapers.

Or more unusually:

- office banter
- sex talk
- overheard conversations
- mental conversations with self
- reliving commentaries
- eye-witness accounts
- dreams.

Whatever the research output, content analysis could be a suitable technique for analysis. The main advantages of the technique are that it:

- looks directly at research outputs in many different forms
- can produce both quantitative and qualitative outcomes
- can provide a consistent means of analysing longitudinal accounts
- can function on categories and relationships and thereby provide integrated analysis
- produces outputs suitable for further statistical analysis
- can be used to 'trap' information for knowledge management systems
- is regarded as a systematic and replicable technique
- can produce effective analysis of complex human interactions, using categories and relationships
- can be used for cross-case analysis using predetermined research categories.

It is not all good news because there are disadvantages to this technique in that it:

- can be extremely time-consuming
- is subject to error, particularly when relational analysis is used to attain a higher level of interpretation

- can lack a theoretical base, or end up drawing significant inferences about relationships that may not exist
- is inherently reductive (reduces the meaning), particularly when dealing with complex issues, and can end up simply counting the themes rather than exploring the meanings
- often disregards, or underplays, the context that produced the research output.

Content analysis in its full form is a two-stage process but can be used as a one-stage process if time is short or if the complexity of the two-stage process is not required.

See sections 8.3 and 8.5 for the detail of how to carry out content analysis.

In dissertation research, it is possible to complete the first stage of conceptual analysis and then use this output to generate discussions of the findings. The main outputs of this stage are full and critical descriptions of the categories such that each is related to the research questions and is mutually exclusive – so that data cannot be coded into two categories. There may well be numerical data of counts of themes and categories. These can be statistically analysed. Carried out by one researcher in isolation, the proposed advantage of being objective is often lost. If two or three researchers develop the categories and then engage in discussion and comparison, a far more objective stance can be achieved. Using themes and categories developed in earlier research studies is an effective way to adopt a more objective stance and also allows for comparative study of the data set produced in the dissertation research and the published material. Categories are often developed by looking at only a few of the research outputs (this saves time) – maybe five or six interviews. The categories are then applied to the remaining interviews. If any significant amount of inconsistency arises, the categories can be added to or amended to include the new material.

A CONTENT ANALYSIS RESEARCH STUDY: EXAMPLE 1

In the study by Hassink, De Vries and Bollen (2007) entitled 'A content analysis of whistle-blowing policies of leading European companies', the authors used the following simple classification of two groups of observations:

- separate, specific policy documents and statements on whistle-blowing (sub-sample 1)
- whistle-blowing clauses in corporate codes of conduct or codes of ethics (sub-sample 2).

To get a better idea of the information the companies disclosed on whistle-blowing, supplementary information found on their websites was also included in the observations. Of the 56-company sample, 26 had separate policy documents and 30 had a code of conduct or ethics describing the company's policy on the subject.

All policies and codes were investigated for their contents. The range of information from the policies and codes was classified in seven groups of items:

- information concerning the policy's general contents, scope and tone
- the nature of the violations mentioned by the policy to be reported
- the contact persons to whom employees could directly report violations
- reporting guidelines and formalities
- details concerning confidentiality and anonymity
- details concerning protection from retaliation
- details about the investigation of the complaint.

A CONTENT ANALYSIS RESEARCH STUDY: EXAMPLE 2

In an article entitled 'Women paediatricians: what made them choose their career?', Martina Moorkamp in 2005 described the use of qualitative research in this way:

'Qualitative research looks at the world through the eyes of another person: it explores meanings, draws on subjective knowledge and works with feelings and values. These are the strengths of qualitative research methods (Burns and Grove, 1987). Interviews are the most common method of data collection and elicit the opinions of individual subjects. Semi-structured or unstructured interviews are usually employed. This also gives the subject a degree of control over what they say and ensures a higher degree of internal validity, which means lowering the chance of the results being affected by confounding bias. In-depth interviews give the respondents the chance to develop their opinions in more detail, especially the understanding and reasoning that lie behind them. Interviews that allow the respondents' own perspective to emerge more clearly can be demanding on the interviewer. It is important that the interviewer responds to the individual way in which the respondents interpret and answer questions while ensuring that a standard set of topics are covered (Boulton and Fitzpatrick, 1994).'

Source: Moorkamp, M. (2005) 'Women paediatricians: what made them choose their career?', *Journal of Health Organization and Management*, Vol. 19, No. 6: 478–93

The author developed only three themes from the content analysis:

- Theme 1: Women choose paediatrics because of the 'nicer' working atmosphere compared with any other medical specialty, and because paediatric colleagues are more supportive and approachable.
- Theme 2: Women choose paediatrics because they like working with children. Paediatrics

is a family- and team-oriented specialty and a fascinating subject. It welcomes certain characteristics that women possess more than men.

- Theme 3: Women choose paediatrics because of positive role models and mentors. There was a mixture of opinion among the women about role models. A few mentioned that they did not have any, but if they had, those role models would mostly be men. The majority of women stated that they had only worked with male consultants because there were hardly any women in higher positions. Role models had been a major influence in deciding to become a paediatrician.

Commentary

The research involved 10 interviews, and the content analysis results revealed just three main themes. This illustrates that content analysis does not need complex multi-level themes and concepts to be effective. Content analysis is a technique that takes a large volume of statements and thoughts and reduces it to themes and concepts and, if used, relationships. Clarity is the main aim of the analysis. Do not be afraid to present simple clear results as illustrated in this paper. There will always be the question of how to evidence your analysis. In this case there were around 10 direct quotes adding up to about 1,500 words of quote evidence for each theme. Something missing from this paper that would have improved the impression that the analysis was sound was a rationale of how the themes were discovered in the data, also some rationale of the characteristics of the themes. Further support could have been provided by some quantifiable statistics – the author notes that this would have moved counter to the epistemological stance but, remember, qualitative research requires stronger and numerous evidence sources to support the stated outcomes.

CARRYING OUT CONTENT ANALYSIS

The following transcript represents part of an interview with a female entrepreneur. The strained English is because the original interview was in Russian and the transcript has been translated. (Acknowledgement for data collection and translation is duly made to Anna Shuvalova.) It is useful to realise, however, that interview transcripts often contain errors, gaps, and confused thinking.

Scan the text for possible themes or concepts. If you are carrying out this analysis in a group setting, try to arrange for at least three groups to work independently.

Q: Why did you decided to become an entrepreneur?

A: Because I had to maintain my child.

Q: And if you did not have to maintain your child, do you think you would do something else?

A: No, I would do the same thing, but either as an employed or in a more relaxed conditions.

Q: And why did you decided to start a business and not to work as an employed?

A: I started business in 1989. That time this segment of the market where I started my business was not developed and there was no employment work of a high level in this sphere. I was among the pioneers in this sphere. I worked as an employed, as an editor. And that time my colleague offered me to start a cooperative but was afraid. I did not want to take so much responsibility. Because business is an enormous responsibility.

And when I started business it was because it was interesting in advertising. If I did not have this interest, if I was not curious, I would not do it. And that time there was not a structure or a company where I could work with advertising as an employer. And that is why I had to create this structure myself.

I had an interest in advertising from childhood.

My biggest merit is the presence of brains. And the biggest demerit – perfectionism. Because when you are improving something you must know to stop. And because you must require from people the possible and not the desirable.

Q: Do your acting experience in your youth helps you now?

A: It helps in the sense that I was taught to take the point of view of another person and developed the ability of the empathy. And this ability helps me in management. There are different types of managers – democratic, autocratic. But there is not net types, it is always the mixture. But the understanding of psychology is very important for any type of leadership.

Q: What pushing levers and motivation methods do you use?

A: They are different notions. All motivation methods are already known and written in the theory.

Q: Do you use the theory to motivate?

A: No, I am doing it intuitively and naturally, but I know how to call these methods. If we talk about management style, it is the command style and the position of a leader who is motivating on the result and on the objective is closer for me. But you have to remember that there is four levels of motivation and if you lose just one you lose people. And it is important to set up the priorities. There is no universal motivation method. Because every person has an individual motivation. And in order to succeed in business it is very important to find people for whom the material motivation would not be on the first place. Or to organise management in such a way that material motivation will be on the third place, and on the first place it will be self-fulfilment, self-actualisation and self-expression, and on the second place professional prestige, respect of the collective, and achievement of a certain final goal.

Q: Are you speaking about the top management or about any level of staff?

A: Any level. Even cleaners. Because imagine – she will be more pleased to clean in a nice office than in a dirty toilet.

In my last business there was 5,000 people.

There is a theory of motivation.

But also there is an entrepreneurial talent, and it is impossible to teach it. And it does not have anything to do with gender. People are born entrepreneurs, not become entrepreneurs. But some of them develop this genetic disposition and others do not. And it is a set of faculties.

Q: And what is the role of circumstances and of destiny? Do you believe in destiny?

A: I don't believe in destiny as something that is previewed in your life. I have another comprehension.

If you don't have this disposition to entrepreneurship, you should not try it. It is as if you don't have a pitch, you should not try singing.

Q: And what are the personal qualities which are necessary for an entrepreneur?

A: Entrepreneurship is a talent. There are different types of entrepreneurs. There are aggressors, who has analytical skills, and charismatic personalities. There are analysts, who can orient in the business space and construct the tactics. All are very different.

Q: And what type is you?

A: I am a charismatic leader.

Q: You mentioned that it is not right to have profit as an objective. And what objectives is it right to set?

A: Tactic precise objectives in that sphere where you work. No matter what is the sphere. If you are a baker, it can be the aim to make the best bread in a district. As for my business – advertising – it was always important that my company should be the best on the market, that the design that we make will work effectively. For somebody else this objective will be just to do something – not necessarily the best, it can be just something interesting, but something must go out, it has to be some result. So the objective must be not to earn money but to do something. The objective cannot be only material. Just because an intention to earn money is not exceptional – everybody wants it – if you will set up this goal you will be running with this crowd in the game without rules.

In business you are working with other people, and they would not share your objective to earn money, so you have to have other objectives. The objective to earn money is short and that is why it is not right. If you want to have money – steal.

TEMPLATE ANALYSIS

Template analysis is based on using themes to code interviews or other textual data. In this respect it is not dissimilar to content analysis. The themes can arise from previous research or 'emerge' from the transcript data. In dissertation research it speeds the analysis and grounds it in more established theory if existing codes are used. These may be identified, and perhaps modified, from published research that has been explored and critiqued in the literature review. The themes are coded for ease of analysis – you can use the existing coding or devise your own coding system. In dissertation research, it is sometimes useful to simplify the themes and coding systems because it may speed up the analysis process. The themes and codes are normally, but not always, arranged in hierarchical form. Each theme should have an accompanying theme definition, characteristics list and scope definition.

Template analysis is completed by taking the following steps:

1 Use existing theory and literature to define the themes and the codes.

2 Format the transcripts in such a way as to allow easy coding – a very large right-hand margin.

3 Code the transcript using the existing themes and codes.

4 Where part of the transcript does not fall under one of the existing codes, highlight or mark it as 'code pending'.

5 Complete the coding of the transcript in this manner.

6 Return to the 'code pending' sections and do one of the following:
   – Modify the definition of a code to include the uncoded section
   – Create a new theme and code.

In any transcript there will also be sections that are not significant and therefore do not require coding. Code even these sections (as 'uncoded') because later revisions may require a reanalysis of these sections.

Deciding when to start the analysis is crucial. The traditional approach is to collect all the data and then to carry out the analysis on all the cases. But because you will have a restricted time-scale you may want to start the analysis as soon as the first interview is completed. This may mean that you have to revisit some of the early cases to ensure that you are coding with the latest revised template.

The template must be revised in the following circumstances and for the following purposes:

- changing the definition or characteristics of a code – what it is
- changing the scope of a code – what can be included in the code
- creating a new code
- changing the hierarchical level of a code
- removing a code.

Some of these changes require a reanalysis of all of the cases. This will not be too lengthy a task because the transcripts are coded. It is a much easier task if you are using qualitative analysis software. At all stages you must keep a definitive master template that represents the current template. It is also a good idea to keep a copy of all the earlier versions of the template in case you decide to revert to one of them. If you are not using qualitative data analysis software, a Word document in outline view may represent the template very well. Mind maps can also be used to display the final template – this affords more practicality in exploring the relationships between themes.

Outputs from template analysis are the template, definitions and characteristics of the categories, the scope of the categories, and a reflective account of how the template developed. Excerpts from interviews should be used as evidence to support the characteristics and development of the template. This will lead to a discussion in the findings section related to the categories, the expression of behaviours and concerns, and ideas for easing problems related to categories. In developing the findings of template analysis, it is unlikely that all the themes will be explored – be selective and develop arguments, explanations and recommendations based on the most important themes.

Example of a coding template

Participants' reactions to renal disease	
First-level code	*Second-level code*
Immediate reactions on diagnosis	Strong negative emotion
	Lack of emotion
	Confusion
	Blame, and sense of injustice
Participants' explanations of renal disease	Earlier lack of control
	Lack of information/misinformation from medical staff
	Fate
	Inheritance
Living with renal disease	Impact on lifestyle
	Involvement with the medical system
	Coping strategies
Hopes, fears and expectations for the future	Outlook
	Treatment
	Development of the condition
	Uncertainty

Two integrative themes are *stoicism* and *uncertainty*.
Source: King, N., Carroll, C., Newton, P. and Dornan, T. (2002) 'You can't cure it so you have to endure it: the experience of adaptation to diabetic renal disease', *Qualitative Health Research*, Vol. 12, No. 3: 329–46

CASE STUDY ANALYSIS

Case study analysis is not of itself an analysis technique – it is more a methodological approach that then presents issues for analysis. Case study approaches can vary from the study of one case to the study of cases so numerous that that they require quantitative techniques to make sense of the data. In the dissertation context case studies most often involve research into a low number of cases that provide 'rich', 'thick' detailed data relating to the area under study.

The advantage of the case study method is that it allows multiple perspectives of events, phenomena, or behaviours to be considered. It also allows for in-depth study and analysis. Case study approaches are not superficial surface investigations; they are detailed pluralistic studies of organisational events, phenomena or behaviours. The analysis of one or more case studies involves multiple methods – for instance, interviews, document analysis, questionnaires, focus groups, diaries, and self-accounts. Each of these mini-methods focuses on the phenomenon, event or behaviour identified in the research questions. A range of analysis is needed to cope with these research sources – for example:

- Interviews may use content analysis.
- Self-accounts may use the repertory grid technique.
- Diaries may use critical incident analysis.
- Focus groups may use common mind maps.
- Questionnaires may use inferential statistics.

If these multiple analyses produce findings that confirm some common elements of an event, phenomenon or behaviour, then more confidence can be attributed to the stated outcome.

Sample selection is a critical element in case study analysis. If the research is using a single case, the reasons behind this approach must be set out clearly and logically, and the detailed parameters of why this case has been chosen must be clearly stated. Single-case approaches require extensive reflection and description if they are to create any confidence in the reader. The basis of case selection where two cases only are used requires similarly careful description, reflection and justification. A frequent basis for two-case selection is that the cases represent a comparison. This position has to be justified with data and observations of why these two cases do indeed offer a comparison. Research based on a single or small number of cases is often undermined by weak or non-existent explanation and justification of the chosen cases.

Normal sampling rules should be used once the number of cases has grown beyond the point where the justification is concerned with the uniqueness of the cases. The rationalisation then becomes one which proposes that your sample is typical of a larger population. The research question will indicate how the population should be constructed. A sample is then selected by a random process from the population. There must be a clear statement of how the population was constructed. Typical possibilities are populations of:

- organisations in a geographical area
- people or organisations that have something in common
- staff of different abilities/disabilities
- staff in age groups
- staff with different work–life balance policies
- staff who train and develop using e-learning
- organisations at differing stages of their life cycle
- organisations in a particular industry – eg banking
- organisations of different size – eg small, medium, large.

It is very important in all research to 'construct' the population accurately, but it is particularly so in case study research. It is also important to explain the thought, decision and reflective process that has led you to construct a population in a particular manner.

Cross-case analysis

Cross-case analysis is most often used when there are large numbers of cases. The data from all cases is considered by a predetermined 'type', and the same type is looked at across all cases. Each case has a number of types attributed to it. Imagine that you have a qualitative study of 100 interviews with staff who have been absent from work for more than 15 working days in one year. One group of cases that can be identified as a 'type' 'has had a workplace accident'. Say there are 26 of these in the 100 cases. Once they are identified as a type it is possible to make an extensive examination of the cases looking for patterns or attributes. One outcome might be that the average age of the 'accident at work' type of case is a much lower average age than of all the 100 cases. This is an interesting and useful pattern to observe – but beware of making casual assumptions that accidents tend to happen more to younger staff. Further investigation would be required before any outcome like this could be established as significant.

Cross-case analysis can also follow a pattern by which a researcher examines pairs of cases, creating categories of the similarities and differences in each pair. The researcher then examines similar pairs for differences, and dissimilar pairs for similarities. As patterns begin to emerge, certain outcomes may stand out as being in conflict with the patterns. In those cases, the researcher conducts follow-up research to confirm or correct the initial data in order to create sound research outputs.

The output from case study analysis

The output from case studies can be diverse, just as the analysis is diverse. If there is a numerical aspect to the output, you can use all the normal tables and graphs that would be used in quantitative analysis. Other outputs might include:

- mind maps
- direct quotes
- categories, labels and attributes
- matrix tables of cases and attributes
- themes and theme descriptors, with frequency of occurrence
- cross-case similarities and differences tables
- type tables that summarise cases
- case summaries
- matrix tables of cases and themes or categories.

The most important aspect of research outputs is to ensure that what you present in the final work has some clarity and meaning. If you have to create something new to display your research outputs, do not be afraid to develop a new technique. The aim of any technique of data analysis and output is to explain the story of the data.

REPERTORY GRID TECHNIQUE

Repertory grid analysis is based on the theory of personal constructs, which suggests that individuals interpret the world in terms of their own personal set of constructs, a form of mental model. The original idea and experiments with the technique were conducted by George Kelly (1955). These constructs are bipolar abstractions that people use to distinguish between similar and different elements in the world. The extent to which two individuals, or two groups, share a similar set of constructs indicates the extent to which they experience and understand the world in similar ways. The repertory grid technique is a method for exploring an individual's personal construct system. It provides a way of understanding how people see the world. A lot of business research is concerned with people and how they see other people, products and procedures – for example, how consumers see products, how team members see other team members, or how workers see changes.

Although it is included here in the qualitative methods section because it records rich in-depth and personal data, it is a numerical technique. If you are thinking of using this technique, it will therefore require some foundation mathematics to make the best of the approach. The technique can be used to elicit personal construct systems, but by aggregation it can be used to consider group understandings, albeit in a reductionist fashion. The grid technique can be used as a snapshot of people or events when one grid is administered. But it is also useful in change situations when the same grid can be administered several times over a period of time. This may be appropriate when investigating change, when a grid could be used at the beginning of a change programme, in the middle of the change programme and at the end of the change programme. The three grids produced could then be analysed for changes, and the research could explore how the changes in personal construct systems occurred and what the 'triggers' were for the change. The repertory grid technique could also be used to analyse change from an organisational intervention such as training or development.

The technique is both a method and an analysis technique.

There are four stages to the technique. (Each stage has a number of possible alternatives and it is beyond the scope of this book to cover all the possibilities – consult one of the references in the bibliography if you want to take your studies further.)

- Stage 1: Establishing the list of elements
- Stage 2: Establishing the lists of constructs
- Stage 3: Rating the grid
- Stage 4: Analysis of the grid.

(Throughout the following sections the same simple example of a student or students rating their tutors is used.)

Stage 1: Establishing the list of elements

In our example this was very easy because it was the tutors that teach a certain group of students. If this had been a market research example, products would be the elements. In other cases the elements may come from literature, in that they may be elements of a previous study, or aspects of a theory that is to be tested. Another way of establishing elements is to ask the participants who or what are important in this or that situation.

Stage 2: Establishing the list of constructs

Kelly outlined six different ways to elicit constructs, so if you are using this technique you may have to do some background reading. The original method was to use three elements, normally written on cards (in our case there would be five possible elements, Tutor A to Tutor E). You meet with the participant and firstly show them three cards (let's say Tutor A, Tutor B, Tutor C). You first ask 'How are two of these similar?' Maybe the answer is, 'A and B are approachable!' Then you ask, 'How is the third one different?' Maybe the answer is 'unapproachable' or 'intimidating'. From this you have the first construct and the two poles of the construct, 'approachable' – 'intimidating'. You carry on with this technique until the constructs are being repeated and or no new constructs appear – this point being known as 'construct saturation'. In most cases there will be between 5 and 12 elements and between 7 and 15 constructs. The basic grid may then look like Figure 37, without the numbers in the central block.

Figure 40 Screenshot of a basic repertory grid

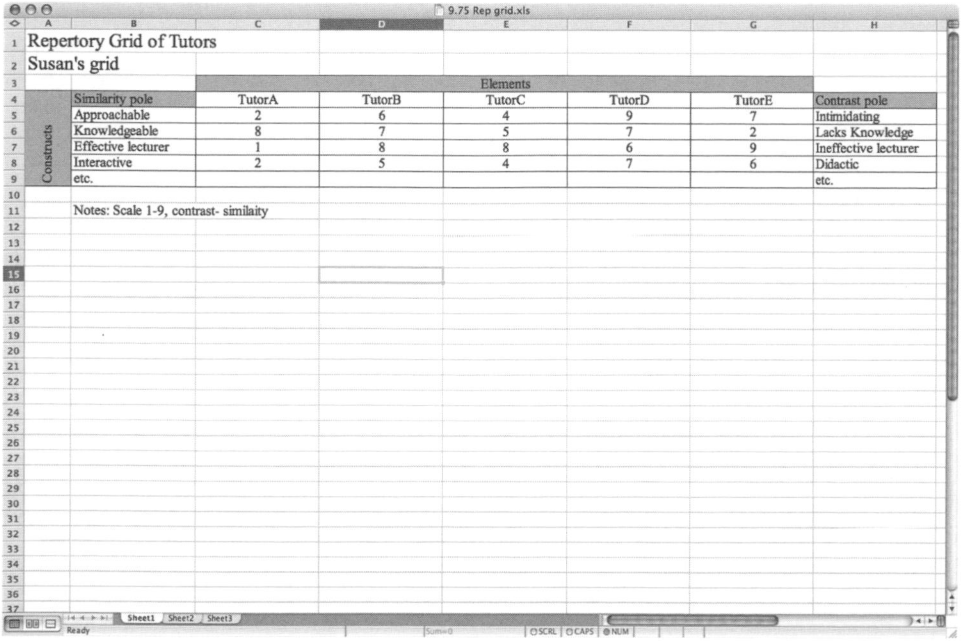

Repertory Grid of Tutors

Susan's grid

		Elements					
Constructs	Similarity pole	TutorA	TutorB	TutorC	TutorD	TutorE	Contrast pole
	Approachable	2	6	4	9	7	Intimidating
	Knowledgeable	8	7	5	7	2	Lacks Knowledge
	Effective lecturer	1	8	8	6	9	Ineffective lecturer
	Interactive	2	5	4	7	6	Didactic
	etc.						etc.

Notes: Scale 1-9, contrast- similaity

Stage 3: Rating the grid

The participant then rates all the elements for each of the constructs, ending up with the basic grid as shown in Figure 40.

Stage 4: Analysis of the grid

There is specialist software that can be used to carry out the analysis of the grid. But it can also be done in SPSS. In SPSS the data is entered into the data sheet – the variables are the elements, although this can be reversed. The tool that is needed to carry out the analysis is the **Clustering** tool. You invoke this analysis by: **Analyse, Classify, Hierarchical cluster**, then put the five tutors into the variable box, in **Plots**. Click on **Dendrogram**, then **OK**.

Figure 41 Dendrogram of the repertory grid of tutors

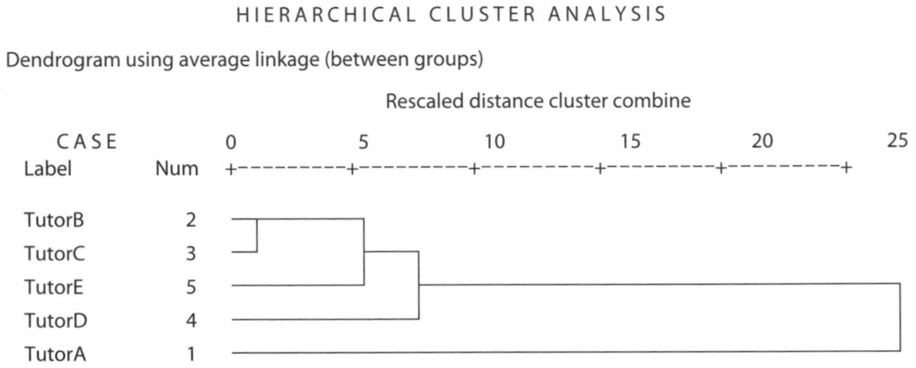

HIERARCHICAL CLUSTER ANALYSIS

Dendrogram using average linkage (between groups)

Rescaled distance cluster combine

C A S E Label	Num	0	5	10	15	20	25

```
   CASE      Num    0         5        10        15        20        25
   Label            +---------+---------+---------+---------+---------+

   TutorB      2     ┌───────────────┐
   TutorC      3     ┘               │
   TutorE      5     ──────────────┐ │
   TutorD      4     ──────────────┴─┘                                │
   TutorA      1     ─────────────────────────────────────────────────┘
```

In the first round of analysis, the dendrogram is the most useful output. It shows the similarities between tutors and indicates the tutors that are different. In Figure 41 you can see by the two tutors clustered in the first round (B and C) that they have been rated in a similar manner, whereas Tutor A is considered to be different from most of the others. You may think this is rather obvious, but our grid is a very simple example. In practice, grids soon grow to be too large to interpret by eye.

The same data analysed with specialist software would produce the output in Figure 42.

Data generated using repertory grid techniques can be analysed in several different ways. The most common methods used include factor analysis, principal component analysis, multidimensional scaling, and cluster analysis. The analyses above have all looked at just one grid – how you compare and combine data will depend on your research questions and the types of output that that you need. It is quite common to compare the grids of groups in order to find the common constructions and the personal constructions.

CRITICAL INCIDENT ANALYSIS

Critical incident analysis is a method that uses procedures to collect, analyse and finally classify incidents that are critical to the research questions. In operations research this might be machine or procedure breakdowns. In human research this may be observation of human behaviour or post-interview analysis of respondents' narrative. Note that the research question could specify the critical incident – maybe a trust relationship breakdown at work. But, importantly, the technique can be used to identify critical incidents in an interview or life narrative: effectively, the critical incident emerges from the respondent and not from the research question (inductive).

Figure 42 Output of elements and constructs on specialist software

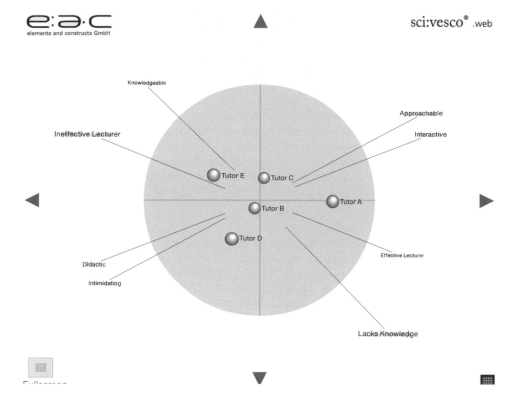

In qualitative research the aim of using the technique is to facilitate the investigation of critical incidents as perceived by the respondents. The technique explores elements of a critical incident and its affects – how people coped and managed to recover from the incident. The aim is to understand the incident's behavioural and cognitive aspects from the perspective of the respondent. Some studies approach this by asking the respondent to talk about, relay, or relive a critical incident or a string of connected incidents. In this approach the critical incident technique is a form of interview.

The technique could also be applied to observations of the way people behave. In this case the research question will contain the critical incident under observation – perhaps (for example) 'the activity of till-dipping in the retail environment: action and confrontation'. In this study the critical incident is the observed act of stealing and the person's reaction when confronted with the accusation. Because such incidents are often recorded for legal reasons, there is a ready-made source of data – you will perceive the huge ethical implications of this research: in criminal circumstances the need for informed consent to participate in a study may be a barrier that is difficult to overcome.

In operational research the incident is also contained in the research question – perhaps (for example) the breakdown and repair of Oracle databases. In this research the incident occurs and is reported to the service provider. Details of the fault and the solutions are recorded; both quantitative and qualitative data may be recorded.

Analysis of critical incidents must firstly deal with classification of the incident.

The inductive approach

Because the critical incident is determined by the participant, it will not be necessary to make a judgement as to the type of incident being discussed. The classification of incidents occurs as an outcome of the analysis. If your research study carried out 24 interviews of self-esteem-damaging events in the respondents' lives, the analysis may place these events in some sort of categories, although it is possible that each event would be unique. Once the categories have been developed, content or template analysis would be used to further classify the data. If your research approach has been to replicate an earlier study, the categories will have already been created by the previous research. The analysis would then classify the data into the predetermined categories, and importantly, report any data that could not be contained in the existing categories. The outcome of the data that could not be classified may be either new categories or a redefinition of the existing categories. The outcomes of the research will be the detailed definitions of the categories and the frequency and patterns of the occurrences. It is also possible that patterns and frequencies of reactions, solutions or actions will be reported.

The deductive approach

Here the categories are formed by the literature and the research questions. The descriptions and definitions of the categories are very important, because the first analysis action is to place any critical incident into a category. The next analysis is to report frequencies, patterns and significances of incidents and the related data – this is predominantly quantitative, but some form of content or template analysis may be needed to report on the non-quantitative issues related to the incident. The outcomes of deductive research are frequency distributions, inferential statistics and relationship indices. It is also possible to use hypotheses and test these, and to make predictions of the likely occurrence of similar incidents in the future.

CRITICAL INCIDENT FORM: AN EXAMPLE

Hardware sales

Category description	Why effective or ineffective	Effective? (Yes/No)
Incident 1	Greeted the customer shortly after customer entered the store and was very friendly. Enabled a connection to be made with the customer shortly after entering the store and let the customer know he was important.	Yes
Incident 2	Took a 'self-service' approach and left the customer alone as she shopped. No opportunity to assess customer's needs and little or no opportunity to suggest additional items or share information with the customer.	No
Incident 3	Completed paperwork successfully, but did not summarise the sale. The end result was a successful transaction, but not summarising the sale created an opportunity for a mistake to not be uncovered.	Yes and No
Incident 4	Gave customer thorough and accurate information and responded well to customer's questions. Came across as an expert with regard to the issue being discussed. Gave the customer confidence that he was making the correct purchase.	Yes

Source: Lorenzet, Cook and Ozeki (2006) 'Improving performance in very small firms through effective assessment and feedback', *Education and Training*, Vol. 48, No. 8/9: 568

GROUNDED THEORY

Grounded theory has been put here at the end of the section in the hope that most readers will not get far enough to read about it. It has become a dominant method and analysis technique for qualitative data in a lot of disciplines, including the social sciences and business. It has been used extensively to conduct and analyse research findings, it is well proven, it works, and although there are critical accounts of its limitations, they do not undermine its academic standing. But it is a very time-consuming process and ought to be carried out without time pressure if the results are to be sound and the output is to actually include some theory development. Normal qualitative dissertation research is carried out more effectively using content or template analysis.

The origin of grounded theory was a perceived need for more theoretically sound techniques for analysing unstructured data. Glaser and Strauss (1967) were the original expounders of the theory and the method. It is often called the constant comparison method, because each interview is compared with the previous interviews. As a theory or theories develop, the interviews are compared with the theory. The pages of transcript are formatted with a wide margin to the right-hand side for notes of this comparison process. If you are using NVivo or other software, similar margins are available in the form of 'panes'. A section at the bottom of the page is set aside for memos.

Grounded theory can commence when you have the first interview transcript. Purists favour building rapport in interviews by not recording or taking notes – they listen out for and record in memory possible themes. This is not really an option for the less experienced researcher, so readers are advised to record and transcribe at least the first five to eight interviews. After this it may be possible to record an interview and code from the audio record, or to follow the purists and record in memory the themes of the interviews. The analysis and the data collection are carried out in parallel. This approach provides important opportunities to compare interviews and develop theory as the research develops.

The process of analysis using grounded theory is:

1   FIRST INTERVIEW. Format the transcript with a large right and bottom margin.

2   Read the transcript carefully two or three times to familiarise yourself with the data.

3   Read the first meaningful sentence, and ask 'What is going on here?', 'What is this?', 'What is the social process?', 'How is the person thinking or acting?' Essentially, you need to tune into the sort of *how* and *why* questions that will help you develop themes and categories and eventually lead you to a theoretical proposition.

4   Carry on to the end of the transcript asking these questions and noting themes and categories and possible theoretical explanations. At this stage you do not have another interview for comparison.

Themes and codes are marked in the right margin, Theoretical ideas are marked on a memo slip (researchers still use index cards for this).

5   SECOND INTERVIEW. Code the second interview with the first interview in mind. Extra questions are: 'Is there anything common to the two interviews?', 'Do the theories from the first interview hold good in this interview?', 'Does this second interview offer a better theoretical and coding base than the first interview?'

6   You will have to make decisions about the level of the categories, and subcategories (see below).

7   THIRD INTERVIEW AND ONWARDS. Now the comparison can be made between the themes/categories and the new interviews, and each interview can be a test bed for any theory that has developed.

8   AFTER FIVE TO EIGHT INTERVIEWS you will probably find that very few new themes

or categories are now being formed, and one theme or category has come to dominate the data analysis – the *core category*. Occasionally more than one core category will be evident. If this happens, code the interviews for each of the core categories in turn. This sits at the top of the hierarchy of categories and is connected to all other categories.

9   CORE CATEGORY: Once the core category has emerged, you only code instances of this category, or subcategories of the core category. This speeds things up greatly, and it is possible to code from recordings.

10   Finally, consider the range of possible theoretical models that might explain the core category and how it interacts in the research context. Develop the characteristics and attributes of this theory or model.

Consider the case study interview transcript (*Carrying out content analysis* earlier this chapter) again.

If you can format it in the manner described above, it will make the analysis easier. I found the following themes in the data (there were lots more):

- entrepreneurial talent
- support my family
- empathy
- intuitive management.

Can you find and code the sections that support these themes?

Under the *entrepreneurial* theme, I developed some subcategories:

- entrepreneurs are born, not made
- you cannot teach entrepreneurism
- types of entrepreneur
- professional prestige.

Under *types of entrepreneur*, I had the following subcategories:

- aggressors
- charismatic
- strategic.

I also made two memos about two possible theories regarding what was going on:

Memo 1
The driver for entrepreneurs may be necessity. The theory goes that they must provide for their family and this is one way they can do this.

Memo 2
Are entrepreneurs forced to do this as a last resort because they cannot get jobs in organisations? No qualifications? Personal habits in conflict with organisational culture? How would I test this? What sort of codes would I need?

What might be the core category?

The outcomes of grounded theory are the core category and an explanation of its characteristics and dimensions, and the hierarchy of categories below the core category – an explanation of a single theoretical model that seems to explain the categories and data. The categories are often in the form of a tree diagram, the particulars of the categories are often displayed in a table, and the theory is often displayed as a model or typology.

9.8 LINKING ANALYSIS TO THEORY

It is important that analysis is linked to theory. The link between theory and analysis will differ depending on the precise circumstance of your research study. It is important that you formally and practically recognise this link. The following sections investigate some common scenarios and the probable links that you must explicitly investigate in your writing.

HYPOTHESIS TESTING OR QUANTITATIVE TECHNIQUES

The developed hypothesis will have been derived from the literature and the available theory. This is the essence of deductive reasoning. The link to theory will be explicit in the hypothesis, but you must still investigate the research areas and theories that have acted as the basis for the hypothesis. This is a vital part of the research reflective process – spell out your thinking regarding how the literature and the theory helped you create the hypothesis. The best way to do this is to create a reflective account of how each hypothesis was developed. This effectively records your thinking steps and should be set out in this manner:

How I developed hypothesis No.1:

1 I noticed it in the literature and theory.

2 It seemed to be confirmed by this research study.

3 This theory reinforced this aspect of the main theory.

4 I could find little research evidence about this aspect so I removed it.

5 Another research study had developed and used this hypothesis (a).

6 I thought this hypothesis wasn't quite right.

7 So I adapted it and combined it with hypothesis (b).

8 Then a further study suggested a slight adaptation.

9 I adapted it like this.

10 I then reversed it in to the null hypothesis: 'male and female students spend the same amount of money on books'.

You would set out the thinking and reasoning behind each of your testable hypotheses.

Theory will also interact with and assist the analysis of the collected data. During your analysis of data phase, be sure to return to the theory, or the main theories, and ask the questions, 'How well does this theory explain my data?', 'What parts of my data does the theory not explain?', 'How could the theory be revised to explain my data better?' Once you start using this process you will begin to realise that published theory is often quite a poor explanatory mechanism. You should feel confident to explore in the analysis why the theory does not seem to be able to explain your data and how the theory could be adapted to explain your data better.

QUALITATIVE DATA

Qualitative approaches more often use an inductive reasoning approach, so the link to theory will be different from that of deductive approaches. Reflective accounts of how theory and other research has influenced the study are still very important, but the mechanism is different. In purely inductive techniques such as grounded theory, there must be no prior connection to any existing theory. The theory must be derived from the data. The reflective explanation of the role of theory will be generated from your research memos. The presentation of theory will be rather like an emerging and sequential story – along the lines of:

1 One of the early things appearing in the data was an idea of entrepreneurship as a necessity.

2 It seemed for many participants that they could not get a job anywhere in an organisational setting.

3 Then some other theories seemed to be more important.

4 Interviews 4, 5, 6 (evidence below) came back to this emerging notion quite strongly.

5 When I went back to the respondents with this emerging theory, every one of them confirmed that it had elements of their experience contained in it.

6 The theory then became the core category and I coded everything else from this core.

In purely inductive research approaches, theory becomes the output of the research. The credibility of the output will depend on the extent and the explicitness of your reflective reasoning.

APPROACHES IN BETWEEN THE PURELY DEDUCTIVE AND THE INDUCTIVE

The two outlines of how theory connects to analysis above are at the ends of a continuum. Your own research will probably lie nearer to the centre of this continuum. You will therefore have to explain both 'faces' of reflective reasoning. First, how the existing theory and literature affected your thinking and how the research question(s) was developed. Secondly, how the inductive or emerging elements of your research have adapted or developed the existing theory.

CASE STUDY

WORK–LIFE BALANCE IN RETAIL STORES

Kash worked in a well-known retail store, part-time, and had noticed that the staff were always asked to work for far longer than they really wanted. This suggested to her that a study of work–life balance would make an excellent dissertation topic. There also seemed to be plenty of literature related to the topic and all the staff she worked with seemed keen to explain how there was always too much work and not enough time to do family- and leisure-related things.

She spoke to the manager at her branch, who said it would be OK to conduct a short interview with any member of staff who was willing to talk to her. Her manager also showed her the company policy on work–life balance and indicated that the head office website had a lot more information. She felt all this was very good and that she would be comfortable doing a dissertation on this topic in her company.

She carried out a literature search and discovered that there had been quite a lot of studies related to work–life balance. It seemed that many of them were interested in what managers thought about work–life balance. The outcomes from them seemed to suggest that:

- Most companies had a policy on work–life balance.

- All staff liked the policy and wanted more control of this aspect of their lives.

- The policy and practice was good for the employer and the employee.

- Everyone seemed to be positive about the approach.

- Employers said the issue was important and they fully supported their staff in creating balance in their lives.

Some other studies suggested that:

- Working hours for retail staff in the sector had risen slightly to 42 hours per week on average.

- Days lost to absence in the retail sector had risen to an average of 10.2 days per person per year.

- The incidence of stress-related problems had doubled in the last three years.

She prepared a dissertation proposal for her supervisor, who was positive and encouraging about the proposal. But the supervisor did raise a few issues:

- The method would have to be chosen carefully and be related to the methodological approach and the literature.

- The number of participants would have to be large enough to give representative data (whatever that was, thought Kash).

- Should the research involve more than one branch or other retail companies?

After this Kash looked at the literature again and had some thoughts of her own:

- How could everyone be so positive about work–life balance? Shouldn't there be some people who thought it wasn't a good thing – managers, maybe?

- If all the retail sector organisations were adopting work–life balance policies, why were the working hours going up?

- Why did stress seem to be on the increase?

- Why was absence going up?

This all seemed very confusing, and she began to think to herself 'There is something wrong here.' Further analysis of the literature showed that most of the studies were questionnaire-based. She thought that this strange situation would not be easily explained by using another quantitative approach. She came to the conclusion that work–life balance and what it means to people ought to be investigated from the point of view of the employee.

After some further consideration she decided to adopt a more qualitative stance on the research and conduct qualitative interviews with as many staff as she could

in the time available to her. Her supervisor endorsed her method and approach, and encouraged her to 'get out in the field' and get some data. This she did, recording interviews and following a very general set of questions designed to let the participants control what was discussed and how long their interviews went on for. After six weeks of hard interviewing she was surprised to find she had carried out 22 interviews and had 26 hours of transcribed material. Luckily, her sister was a great typist and did all the transcription work. She could now turn her attention to analysing the data.

To think about …

1 From what you have read, how thought-out and grounded in the literature was the method that Kash used?

2 What difficulties do you think Kash will have with analysing this data?

3 Advise Kash on the best qualitative method to analyse her data. Justify your selected method with a sound argument.

4 She will need categories of data for the analysis. Where will these categories come from?

5 What sort of categories do you think Kash will eventually use to analyse the data?

6 If you were carrying out this research, what would you do differently?

Once you have answered these questions, it would be useful to discuss them in a tutorial or study group.

SUMMARY

The data analysis chapter was divided into two parts: the first half looked at quantitative data and the second at qualitative data.

- Analysis and explaining an overview. Try to create explanations that:
  - are simple, brief and relevant
  - have a beginning, a middle, an end, and a punchline
  - are specific and appropriate to the research study
  - offer improvements and solutions
  - illustrate the significance to a wider audience.
- When analysing quantitative data, aim to follow these steps:

- describe the data
- investigate trends, distributions and populations
- use inferential statistics to explore relationships.
- Qualitative data can be analysed using:
  - content analysis
  - template analysis
  - case study analysis
  - repertory grid analysis
  - grounded theory.
- Consider how to link analysis to theory, and make those links explicit in your findings chapter.

EXPLORE FURTHER

Fransella, F. and Bannister, D. (1977) *A Manual for Repertory Grid Technique*. London: Academic Press

Glaser, B. and Strauss, A. (1967) *The Discovery of Grounded Theory: Strategies for qualitative research*. Chicago: Aldine

Hassink, H., De Vries, M. and Bollen, L. (2007) 'A content analysis of whistle-blowing policies of leading European companies', *Journal of Business Ethics*, Vol. 75, No. 1: 25

Kelly, G. A. (1955) *The Psychology of Personal Constructs*, Vol. 1: *A theory of personality*. New York: Norton

King, N., Carroll, C., Newton, P. and Dornan, T. (2002) '"You can't cure it so you have to endure it": the experience of adaptation to diabetic renal disease', *Qualitative Health Research*, Vol. 12: 329–46

Locke, K. (2001) *Grounded Theory in Management Research*. London: Sage

Lorenzet, S., Cook, R. and Ozeki, C. (2006) 'Improving performance in very small firms

through effective assessment and feedback', *Education and Training*, Vol. 48, No. 8/9: 568

Moorkamp, M. (2005) 'Women paediatricians: what made them choose their career?', *Journal of Health Organization and Management*, Vol. 19, No. 6: 478

Weblinks

Link to a site displaying a dynamic demonstration of the empirical rule: http://www.stat.sc.edu/~west/applets/ empiricalrule.html

More information on the empirical rule: http://www.nku.edu/~statistics/212_Using_ the_Empirical_Rule.htm

Critical values tables for statistical tests: http://www.wavemetrics.com/products/ igorpro/dataanalysis/statistics/tests.htm

Chi-square critical values: http://www.unc.edu/~farkouh/usefull/chi.html

Nvivo 9 Getting Started Guide: http://download.qsrinternational.com/ Document/NVivo9/NVivo9-Getting-Started-Guide.pdf

CHAPTER 10

The Craft of Writing, and Introductions and Conclusions

What will I learn in this chapter?

- Developing good writing habits
- The macro/micro approach to writing
- How to use creative thinking
- How to write effective sentences and paragraphs
- How to avoid some common errors in writing
- Linking and signposting
- How to structure and format your dissertation
- How to avoid errors in your argument
- Referencing and bibliographies
- Effective introductions and conclusions

10.1 INTRODUCTION

This chapter investigates some important aspects of the writing process. It commences with a 'good writing habits' guide, in the hope of engaging you in the ideas contained in this chapter. There seems little doubt that many students view the writing process with dread – probably for three main reasons. First, creating words on a page is a slow, time-consuming process. Secondly, the writing bit comes towards the end of the dissertation when motivation is often low. But thirdly and most importantly, the craft of writing is not well understood or practised, and many students therefore feel they are not very good at writing. There is also a more commonly-occurring fourth reason: many students are writing their dissertations in a second language.

I hope this chapter will assist you in writing effective dissertations. I would recommend that you read it early in the dissertation process and try to use the ideas it contains. These ideas will need practice if you are to improve your writing skills. As you approach the main writing of the dissertation, use the chapter more extensively to structure and control your writing.

I cannot stress highly enough the need to plan what you write before you start typing. There is a great temptation to just sit down at the computer and start hitting the keys. This is always a big mistake and will lower your final grade. One of the main differentiators of excellent work and average or poor work is the strength and clarity of the argument. Once you have started typing without a clear structure, the clarity and thereby the strength of your argument cannot be improved. So I would recommend that you thoroughly read section 10.3 on *macro writing* and try to develop writing habits that follow the principles therein. In this way you will develop writing that is clear, well-structured and has a strong, clear and compelling argument.

10.2 DEVELOPING GOOD WRITING HABITS

If you look in books and on the Internet, you will find myriad helpful hints for writers. Strangely, they hardly ever say the same things. What follows is my advice on the actual writing process required for a dissertation.

Understand that writing is just like any other skill

Writing is not a magical skill. It is a skill with a standard set of approaches and procedures that can be learned, and learned relatively quickly. If you took up tennis or golf or any new sport when you came to university, you would not expect to become very good without some practice. So it is the same with writing – it can be learned but it takes some time and practice. Most universities have excellent study skills support units that will help you develop your writing skills. Many universities have e-learning and web-based support for writing skills. Many students never get round to involving themselves with developing their writing skills. This is a real shame because poor writing skills can weaken excellent ideas and research.

Develop a writing habit

Writing is a skill and skills must be practised. The best practice for writing is to write. Early in your dissertation there will be very few opportunities for writing large pieces of work. But you should get into the writing habit early. You can create opportunities for writing by reviewing, paraphrasing and critiquing some of the important theory in your subject area. The content will then be useful when you write the critical literature review. Reviewing and critiquing research studies in your subject area will serve a similar purpose. In my view, in the early part of the dissertation you should set aside at least six to eight hours a week to develop your writing skills. The development nature of this writing will be further enhanced if you can arrange for feedback on your writing.

Use feedback to improve your writing

We are often very poor judges of our own writing. To enhance our skills in writing we have to overcome our slight fear of showing our writing to others. Clearly, the uncomfortable feeling can be less when we are getting feedback from others in the same circumstance. This is where a small study group can be really useful. Get feedback on your writing from your study group. You will also get valuable feedback from the skills unit of your university. The added benefit if you use the skills unit is that they will diagnose any weaknesses and point you to development resources to improve that part of your writing. Your tutors may also be willing to assist in helping with writing skills.

Understand that writing takes time

Writing takes time, so you need to plan and organise carefully to ensure that you have enough time to carry out the writing and the reviewing process. Failing to provide the right amount of time to carry out the writing will lead to poor, rushed work. Typically, you will need about six to eight hours to complete (think, write and review) 1,000 words of academic writing. This assumes that you have done the background planning and research. See sections 10.3 and 10.4 below about macro/micro writing.

Read, think, design, write, and reread every day

Writing, thinking, planning, reading, and rereading must become a daily habit when you are completing a dissertation. Unless you have carried out the reading of background material and have been thinking about that material, you will not have anything to write. By 'thinking' I mean understanding, critiquing, analysing, synthesising and evaluating. Once you have written a passage of work you must reread it to make sure that it is correct, makes sense and has clarity of thought and a strong argument. Try to set aside time every day for these tasks.

Develop 'stickability'

You may not have come across the term 'stickability' – it means the ability to concentrate on a task over periods of time, especially when the task seems to be getting increasingly difficult to complete. Stickability is a frame of mind. Successful people are often quite stubborn and will not be beaten by anything. This makes them difficult to live with, sometimes, but they do achieve things. Some people are naturally stubborn and stick at things. If you are not, you may want to think about developing your stickability. Stickability first comes from having goals you believe in and want to achieve – completing a dissertation should be one of those goals. Then plan and organise your time and allocate space to writing. If you plan to spend two hours writing, do only this – stick at it. Gradually, you can increase the scheduled writing periods until a four-hour session is possible. Set session goals – such as 'I will complete 400 words in this writing session' – and do not stop until this goal is achieved. Finally, do not allow distractions when you are writing – no stopping for drinks, or a bit of net surfing, texting, a phone call or snacks.

Think and plan and make notes before you write

Sections 10.3 and 10.4 in this chapter introduce and explore the notion of macro/micro writing. Essentially macro writing is the planning that is done before you start to write. It is a highly structured approach where you plan each chapter, section and paragraph before you start to write. This ensures that when you do write, the process is less daunting in that you simply extend each first sentence in a paragraph to make one full idea of a whole paragraph. You will have to develop and personalise your planning style, but it is essential that you do plan, think and make notes before you start writing.

Get it 'write' first time

Following on from the idea of careful and extensive planning is the notion of writing structured, well-planned and evidenced paragraph. This structured approach means that you are likely to write a paragraph that is 'write' first time. If you type first and think afterwards, you are likely to have to make extensive and time-consuming revisions. The quickest and most effective way to write is to think, plan, structure and organise – and only then WRITE. There will nevertheless always be a need to revise and correct small parts of what you have written.

Understand the necessity to revise your writing

An idea forms in your head and is then transferred to type. While the idea may be well thought through and well evidenced, the writing process will always need review and improvement. You must plan a strategy for reviewing and revising your work. One effective strategy has been outlined in these good writing ideas. The first phase of writing is always clear and detailed planning. Once the words are typed, review each sentence in each paragraph before you go on, then review the whole paragraph. When you have read it several times and made corrections to the English usage, the clarity of idea, and/or the form of words, move on to write the next paragraph. Leave the writing for at least a week and then review whole sections and make revisions and adaptations. If you are able to enlist the help of someone else – friends, family, study group – let them read it and comment. I generally ask them to read it twice, first for the clarity of the meaning of the words and the strength and clarity of the argument; secondly, to check for spelling and grammar errors.

I feel sure that if you are able to follow some of these approaches, you will find the writing process enjoyable and you will produce clear, precise and correct writing.

10.3 THE MACRO APPROACH TO ACADEMIC WRITING

The 'macro/micro' idea of writing is not difficult to grasp, but it is often difficult to remember to accurately switch between the two modes of writing. Macro writing is a form of planning and organising at the macro levels. Note that the term 'macro' applies to *levels* because planning and organising can be carried out at several levels. Micro writing involves close attention to the content and structure of sentences and paragraphs. Most writers switch between these modes in a personalised manner. My argument is that a more focused and strategic approach to macro and micro writing will improve your work.

Planning your macro writing can be done in various ways:

- Make mental models in which each chapter and each sub-point is in a box, with paragraphs leading off the edge. Ordering the chapters and sections is carried out by numbering the boxes and the paragraphs.
- Use pen and paper to set out headings, subheadings and paragraph headings.
- Ordering the chapters is carried out by numbering and renumbering the headings and sections.
- Use Word in outline mode. This allows for structured headings, subheadings and several levels below this. Ordering is done by position in the list, and reordering and reorganising is easy.

Once the headings are organised, try to write one full sentence about the content of each paragraph. This will indicate if the paragraph has any real substance. If you find you are unable to write one full sentence, this heading or paragraph point is not substantial – remove it. The one sentence will be easy to return to later and continue from that starting point. This macro writing is often called *outlining*.

Each point you make in outline mode will become a paragraph. At the first attempt at the macro writing stage you generate ideas for each section and you order those ideas. It is important to reorder those ideas into a logical structure. Logical structures take several attempts before you can be sure you have the most useful logical structure. The question may even arise as to what is a logical structure in the context of your dissertation.

REFLECTIVE ACTIVITY

ORDERING IDEAS

Imagine that you have a literature review section that contains five significant theories. You have already decided that you will keep all five theories in the section but arrange them separately. Yet you cannot decide in which order to present them. It is a problem!

The essence of the problem is to know what would be a logical way to organise these five theories.

Ways you might organise them include:

- historically – the earliest theory first
- by complexity – the most easily understood first, leading finally to the most complex
- by instrumentality – the most frequently-used theory in the literature comes first
- by evaluation – moving from the least useful to the most useful.

Ordering the ideas in the whole dissertation – how chapters and sections flow – will improve the readability and credibility of your writing. The macro-level task of ordering is very important and must be completed from several 'logical' positions. Each position will be evaluated in relation to how readable, credible and plausible it is. As the detail of any section is written, it may be necessary to reconsider the ordering of the points being made. This ordering occurs at many levels in the writing. We looked earlier at ordering theories in a literature review section. Each section relating to each theory will also have to be ordered in paragraphs, and each paragraph will have a set of ordered points in it.

REFLECTIVE ACTIVITY

ORDERING WITHIN AN ACADEMIC THEORY SECTION

Following on from the *Ordering ideas* Reflective Activity, you are now ordering the ideas for each theory. You have the following points that you want to make, but you are not sure of the order in which to write them:

- critique of the theory: three main critical elements
- evaluation of the theory
- research studies that have used the theory as the main research guidance
- description of the theory

- advantages of the use of the theory to understand business research
- limitations of the theory in understanding business research
- practical uses of the theory in management
- description of a related theory developed from the first theory.

Task

Create a logical order for these points so that they build into a strong argument.

From these two Reflective Activities you may be able to see the importance of ordering and reordering. The skills of 'macro' writing will take a little while to develop but they will serve you well in your assignments and dissertations.

When you start macro writing a dissertation, open a new Word document and create this basic structure.

Title – Write your dissertation title and make this Heading 1 (from the Home menu) [You do this by placing the cursor within the title and clicking on Heading 1]

Abstract – Leave this section as a title for now: Heading 2

Acknowledgements – Leave this section as a title for now: Heading 2

Table of contents – This can be added later in Word: Heading 2

Table of figures and illustrations – Leave this section as a title for now: Heading 2

Introduction – A brief introduction to the work. Write this now, but to revise later: Heading 2

Literature review: Heading 2

Methodology: Heading 2

Data collection: Heading 2

Analysis of data: Heading 2

Findings from the data: Heading 2

Conclusion/findings: Heading 2

Bibliography: Heading 2. A complete list of your sources, in alphabetical order and correctly formatted. If you follow the advice later in the chapter, this can be entered automatically at the end

Appendices: Heading 2. Added later

This is the basic structure of your dissertation. The next step is to create macro writing under each of these headings, and go on until you have a starting point for each paragraph.

If we take a look at the next level of headings, for the methodology section, you can see how macro writing works in more detail:

Methodology: Heading 2

Introduction: Heading 3

The general approach of my dissertation: Heading 3

Epistemology: Heading 3

Three possible methods: Heading 3

Method 1: Heading 4
Introduction: Heading 5
History of the use of this method: Heading 5
Literature review of this method: Heading 5
Article 1: Heading 6
Article 2: Heading 6
Article 3: Heading 6
Application of this method to my research: Heading 5
Adaptations required by me to improve the method in my context: Heading 5
Summary: Heading 5

Method 2: Heading 4

Method 3: Heading 4

My one main method: Heading 3

Practical application of my method: Heading 3

Skills required to complete this method: Heading 3

Evaluation of my chosen method: Heading 3

Reflective account of the thinking behind the chosen method: Heading 3

Conclusion: Heading 3

What can we see from this example? Each level of section should have an introduction and a conclusion or summary. The level of headings will proceed down to 5, 6, 7 or 8, depending on the complexity of your work. The macro approach is stepwise logic. Later sections of this chapter will look at how to construct the lower levels of writing, such as paragraphs and sentences.

Figure 43 Word outline

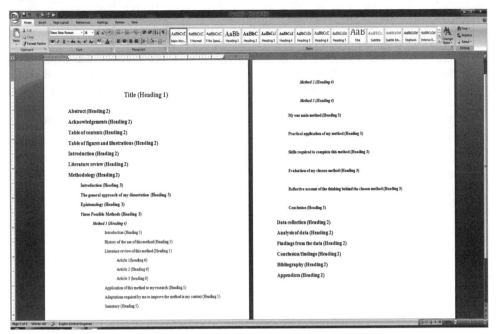

CREATIVE THINKING

In order to generate ideas for inclusion in your dissertation, you will have to develop your ability to think creatively. Creative thinking might be thought of as the ability to generate something new. In your dissertation there will be endless opportunities to create and use new ideas. This is a vital part of the dissertation process, but one that is often forgotten or ignored, leading to rather dull and one-dimensional writing. Creative thinking can be done in a variety of ways, and some of these are considered in the sections below. The ideas that we are looking for in a dissertation are not brilliant, astonishing ideas – they are good, sound ideas for solving problems, creating new theory, using an existing idea in a new way, adapting an existing method to work better in your research.

Everyone can be a creative thinker – it is a state of mind and a set of skills. The following sections should help you to be more creative. Being creative is about spotting ideas and possibilities. It is also a process, and it is these processes – how ideas can be generated – that we will investigate.

Creative evolution

Creative evolution uses an existing idea to develop a better one. Small refinements in methods and theory can generate useful new ideas. Solutions to existing organisational problems can often be refined and improved and used in your dissertation. Research methods are a useful area to consider creative evolution. Published research methods were designed for a different context from that of your research – don't be afraid to engage in creative improvement of a method so that it works better with your context and research questions.

Creative synthesis

Synthesis has already been discussed, and you should be aware that it is the combining of things to create something new. This can be very useful in developing theory, methods, data analysis, and solutions. Try bringing ideas from other areas and applying them in business.

Creative revolution

Creative revolution throws away old ideas and asks 'What about the impossible?' When you are looking for a creative revolution, you do not need to think about what has been used before – only about whether something will work. If your data presents a research problem, finding a creative revolution would require asking many 'What if ... ?' questions. 'What if we ... ?' Or 'What would happen if will did this ... ?' In this way you should try out lots of improbable ideas or solutions until you have a 'eureka' moment. This would be the equivalent of 'brainstorming' ideas.

Creative reapplication

Creative reapplication involves looking at something old in a new way. Clear your expectations of how old ideas can be applied and new opportunities open up. Try to look at your dissertation outcomes in new ways and look for new solutions based on existing solutions. Reapplication in dissertations works well with theory, methods, and solutions.

Creative solutions and breakthroughs occur when we stop trying to implement a solution and start trying to find a solution.

SELECTION

Once you have created a range of ideas, solutions, approaches, you will have to refine them. An important aspect of macro writing action is selection. As you plan and organise the chapters, sections and paragraphs of your dissertation, you will have more ideas, points, theories, opinions and evidence than can be included within the word limit. In the first macro planning stage you will not be selective – you should include all the ideas you generate. In the second macro planning stage you should carry out two tasks:

* Select the points or statements you will make, and the evidence to support those points.
* Then order the points you have selected in a logical manner.
* There is a further section on how to use macro planning in Chapter 11 – take a look at it now!

10.4 EFFECTIVE MICRO WRITING

SENTENCES

When you start to construct the main writing in any of the planned sections, the first layer of building blocks are sentences. Most people write in sentences quite naturally without really knowing what makes a sentence. More importantly, it is possible to write in non-sentences, but although readers can often understand a non-sentence, your writing will have more clarity and punch if you use sentences. Simple sentence structures are often more effective in academic writing than longer sentences. So the building blocks for your work should be short sentences. That leads us to ask, 'What is a sentence?'

It turns out that this is not an easy question to answer. I will try to answer it with a list of the contents of a sentence and a few practical exercises. Sentences should have the following:

* a capital letter at the start
* a full-stop at the end
* a subject – what the sentence is about (short sentences have one subject)
* a verb – a word that describes the action that is being done by or to or for the subject, that tells us what is happening in relation to the subject.

In this form it looks as if we should have no trouble writing in sentences. But there are many variations of this basic structure and requirements. Such as:

- Sentences can be long or short. (Try to write in short sentences – but you are likely to need long ones as well.)
- Sentences can be simple or complex. (Try to write in simple sentences – but you will probably find yourself using complex ones as well.)
- Longer sentences can be broken into smaller parts using commas, semi-colons, brackets or dashes.

Our main aim is to ensure that any collection of words we write is a clear sentence that conveys meaning. The word-checker you use may sometimes 'wiggly-underline' a collection of words in green, and when you right click on this section it will say 'fragment' – unhelpfully, it will often say 'No suggestions'. Green wiggly-underlinings indicate that your sentence is not grammatically correct. Do not submit work that has red or green wiggly-underlining. Words underlined in red are deemed by the spell-checker to be spelled wrong – but watch out, for most spell-checkers do not recognise some of the more specific words related to research and business. Also, check that the spelling and grammar checker is set to UK English – it is surprising how different US English is.

Let's try a few sentences and decide if they are in fact sentences.

- Did the tutor tell you?
  This is a question – but is it a sentence?
  Answer: Yes. (Can you explain why?)
- What a noise they were making.
  Answer: Yes.
- A long curve with a short tail.
  Answer: No.
  Why not? It has no verb – nothing is being done, nothing is happening.

So you should now be able to create effective short sentences. However, it is difficult to express academic issues in short sentences. The problem may then become one of overly long and complex sentences – such as:

> Buying small competitors can be an effective and quick way for a developing organisation to grow its locally-based brand, although it should be pointed out that it is by no means the only way.

This would be improved if the one sentence were split into two shorter sentences. In general, be on the lookout for long sentences, and where possible, shorten them. The same applies to long paragraphs – but we will come to that a bit later.

REFLECTIVE ACTIVITY

USING SHORT SENTENCES

Your paragraph plan shows that you want to express the following points:

- Female students spend £56 per year more than male students on books each year.
- Male students are 22% more likely to buy only the book recommended for a module.

- Female students use their module textbooks for an average of five hours per week, and male students used their module text for only two hours per week.
- There was a roughly equal number of female and male students in the book-buying survey.
- All the analysis outputs from the

study related to male and female trends were significant.

- It appears that female students spend more on books and use those books they buy more often and for longer periods.

- Older students, both male and female, tended to spend more on books.

- If students are employed, they spend more money on books each year – the average spend was £248 for non-employed and £327 for employed.

- The female student employment rate was 67%; the male employment rate was 76%.

Task 1

Use these paragraph points and express in your own words the points in five sentences.

Task 2

Use these paragraph points to express in your own words the points in ten sentences

Task 3

Reflect on:

- the difficulty of Tasks 1 and 2

- the difference in clarity of expression in your responses to Tasks 1 and 2.

Issues of clarity and using short clear statements are connected to sentence punctuation. The following sections look at some of these issues.

THE COMMA

The comma can be used in several ways to improve the clarity and accuracy of your sentences:

- to separate items in a series – as in: oranges, lemons, etc
- after an introductory clause – 'If this data is valid, the two respondents …'
  - after a long introductory phrase – 'During the conduct of this research, …'
  - after an introductory phase comprising just 'to' and a verb – 'To win, …'
  - after a when, where, why, how clause – 'After you complete the dissertation, …'
- to separate a non-essential phrase, clause or brief explanation – 'Peter, the researcher, arranged all the interviews …'
- between coordinate adjectives – 'We met a happy, proactive focus group …'
- to separate parts of a compound sentence – 'Peter read the transcript, but Susie listened to the audio recording.'

THE SEMICOLON

Most commonly, semicolons link two closely related, complete sentences, eliminating the need for a comma and coordinating conjunction (and, but, or, nor, for, so, yet) to join them. You must choose either to use a semicolon or to use the comma and the coordinating conjunction. A comma by itself constitutes a comma splice error or sentence run-on error – avoid these (see the section below). A semicolon with a coordinating conjunction is not grammatically correct.

- I read more than other students; I enjoy books.

Semicolons can also be used to introduce transitional phrases (such as: as a result, even so, for example, in conclusion, on the other hand, in other words) or conjunctive adverbs (such as: consequently, finally, however, indeed, instead, similarly, specifically, therefore) in order to emphasise a pause and the nature of the relationship between two independent clauses.

- Peter did a lot of studying; however, it seemed that he studied the wrong things.

THE COLON

A common use of colons is to introduce a list of items.

- The following are important reasons to write in short sentences:
  clarity
  simplicity of writing
  etc.

(If each item in the equivalent of a bullet list like this is a complete sentence, each should start with a capital letter and end with a full-stop. If the list contains fragments of sentences, each item should start with a lower-case letter and there is no full-stop at the end of each item, but there is a full-stop at the end of the list. If, on the other hand, the list is written continuously across the width of the text as part of one extended sentence, short items comprising one or two words should be separated by a comma; longer items comprising complete phrases or clauses are more often separated by a semicolon.)

Colons can also introduce a more specific or particular statement that amplifies or clarifies the preceding one. The words that follow the colon may be a complete clause or simply a word or phrase – as in:

- I wish it was easier to write sound academic sentences, but such is the nature of good writing: you have to learn as you go along. There is always a lot of rewriting to do.
- Remember: no one reads your first draft.

Colons are also used in academic writing to introduce quotations, especially long ones.

RUN-ON SENTENCES

Run-on sentences represent a particular grammatical error that you should try to avoid. When two (or more) independent statements or complete sentences are joined with a comma, it is described as a run-on error – that is, your sentence has run on when it should have stopped, or should have been punctuated with a semicolon, or should have had a connecting word.

Thus the run-on sentence 'I read more than other students, I really enjoy books' should be corrected to take the form of:

> I read more than other students. I really enjoy books.
> or: I read more than other students; I really enjoy books.
> or: I read more than other students because I really enjoy books.

Avoiding run-on sentences makes your work clearer and more readable. It is also the correct grammatical form. In some instances and some styles of writing, the run-on sentence is acceptable – but in academic work it should be avoided.

UNDERSTANDING THE STRUCTURE OF PARAGRAPHS

A paragraph tends to develop a single idea, statement, finding or line of argument. A series of paragraphs forms a section or a chapter. Try to adopt some of the following ideas related to paragraph use:

- Vary the lengths of paragraphs to maintain the reader's interest.
- Try to avoid very short, one-sentence paragraphs.
- Avoid long paragraphs – there should be a minimum of four or five per page of single-spaced text. Paragraphs longer than this and the reader will get lost and you will lose their attention.
- Paragraphs should have a natural 'flow'.
  The first sentence – introduces the paragraph
  The main points follow on
  The last-but-one sentence summarises the paragraph

The final sentence links to the next paragraph and/or the overall theme of the section or chapter.

- Use link words and phrases such as 'although', 'in contrast', 'however', 'but in this finding', etc.
- Vary your use of common words to avoid monotony. Try to aim never to use the same word twice in any one sentence, and no more than three to five times in any one paragraph.

Statement, analysis and findings paragraphs

In dissertations many paragraphs will be introducing and evidencing statements, analyses and findings. These paragraphs will need a particular structure, as set out below:

Paragraph statement (introduction)
The main claim or statement of the paragraph
FIRST EVIDENCE to support the claim or statement
Warrant – how the evidence supports the claim or statement
Qualification of the evidence (exceptions and anomalies)
SECOND EVIDENCE SOURCE
THIRD EVIDENCE SOURCE, and maybe up to five or six more sources of evidence
Summary sentence
Link sentence to a new paragraph.

REFLECTIVE ACTIVITY

PRACTICE IN ANALYSING

Glenys has produced a range of findings but wants to write a paragraph related to the book-buying habits of students. She has carried out macro planning of the paragraph and has made the following points:

The data suggests that students who work spend £120 more each year on books than students who do not work.

She has a pivot table of spending on books against student income showing a similar relationship.

There were three open statements relating to this aspect of book-buying:

- 'Since I have had a PT job, I have been able to buy all the recommended texts for the modules.'

- 'I don't have a job and I cannot afford any of the course texts – I borrow from the library.'

- 'I work in a bookshop so I can get the texts at trade prices – this is a lifesaver.'

A correlation coefficient shows that the relationship of book spending to income is 0.62 at probability p $\longleftarrow$ 0.005.

Regression analysis shows that 78% of the change in book spending is accounted for in terms of income.

There is some extra data from a website showing that the average student spends £280 per year on books.

There is also data showing that law students spend £424 per annum, and businesses students spend £289.

There is a publisher website that shows that the cheapest form of book buying is from Amazon. But this has a sponsored link to the Amazon website.

The university website has data showing that 61% of students work part-time.

The population in her own data was all business students in her university – 780 – and the sample was 180.

Task

Construct one paragraph, using all the above ideas.

Notes:

- You can embellish the points a little for effect.

- Follow the paragraph structure set out in the text above.

- Reflect on the process of writing this paragraph.

A paragraph must, finally, contain subsequent evidence, warrants and qualifications of evidence. (Depending on your claim or statement, you may wish to add substantial amounts of evidence in support.) You will in any case have to use various sources of evidence to create a convincing argument.

LINKING AND SIGNPOSTING

To improve the clarity of your writing it is important to provide links and signposts. Sentences, paragraphs, sections and chapters can all be linked. Aim to provide extensive links between sentences and paragraphs, and to a lesser extent sections and chapters.

Paragraph links are often provided in the first and/or last line of a paragraph. The last line of a paragraph can link forward (the link is first and the explanation of what is meant comes after the dash) – for example:

However this was not the only issue related to gender – there is another coming up in the next paragraph.

Some issues remain to be resolved in this data – and are explored in the next paragraph.

This evidence brings up some striking points that as yet we have not discussed – but we will be doing so soon.

However, although these points make a compelling argument in favour, there are counterpoints that ought to be explored. (The counter-argument is in the next paragraph.)

The first line of a paragraph can conversely link backwards – for example:

Although we have seen the evidence of a gender-based pattern of behaviour, there is evidence and data that does not support this position – and is in this paragraph.

Although most of the data relates to quantitative measures, we also investigated some qualitative elements, which are coming up in the current paragraph.

There are weaknesses in the argument above that need further exploration (which is forthcoming in this paragraph).

Another way to link paragraphs is to use key words, phrases or closely related words. The link is created by the continuity of the words and phrases. These links add clarity to your argument, and allow the argument to flow onwards in your writing.

Signposting

'Signposts' are a mark of good writing and help the reader to understand the argument more easily. They also provide a sense of where the reader is in the text. The signpost is created with words and phrases such as:

for example, …

however, …
similarly, …
some problems with …
in contrast, …
this programme …
despite this counter-evidence, …
this suggests …
however, in future research …
in the following section …
the next chapter will look at …
in the last chapter we looked at …
whereas this was covered there, that will be covered here …
a recent study reported …
the seminal work in this area was …

In each phrase there is a link to something already mentioned. Signposts can look backwards as well as forwards. Signposts can work at various levels, from sentences and paragraphs to sections and chapters.

ARGUMENTATIVE ERRORS, AND HOW TO AVOID THEM

The goal of your dissertation is to present an original piece of research and convince the markers that your ideas and data are valid by setting out a logical and coherent argument. As you construct each paragraph, try to think about the logic and the evidence you are presenting. The following sections present some of the most common errors that appear in academic writing.

The validity and openness of assumptions

Assumptions are statements or ideas that you have accepted without demonstrating that they are true. If you want to argue that people are motivated mostly by money (a common misconception), you will have to explain the assumptions in this statement and prove that it is the case. You may believe that it is so, but it is not sufficient for you to say you believe it. If you state it, you must confront the assumption and prove it. Most of the statements you make in a dissertation are what we might call 'contestable'. You may argue a point one way; I might argue it another. Without an explicit setting out of the assumption and the provision of evidence to support the statement, the reader will assume that it is an assumption and disregard it. Clearly, if all your statements were unsupported, your whole dissertation could easily be disregarded and would achieve a low mark.

Logical errors

If you do not explore the assumptions in statements, research and theory, you are likely to accept assumptions as facts. When reading others' works, expect the assumptions to be made explicit and the statements to be supported by evidence. If you find writing that does not do this, be critical of the writing, pointing out the unsupported assumptions (critique). Once you have accepted an unsupported assumption, there is a danger of creating illogical arguments and conclusions. These are often called *non sequiturs* (meaning 'it does not follow'). Arguments must be built in a stepwise fashion. Think of an argument as a house; place the foundation building blocks in first, and then build more complex arguments on the foundation ideas. The logical blocks in the argument should build up to the concluding point, so that the critical reader cannot find a *non sequitur* in the argument.

Avoid prejudice and stereotypes

Prejudices and stereotypes exist everywhere in normal conversations, but you must resist repeating them in your academic writing. One technique to avoid prejudice is to create a reflexive account of your beliefs and assumptions about any important area in your dissertation. This can range from believing that all qualitative research is just chatting to personal beliefs about men being less able than women. You must explore your own beliefs and make them explicit to both yourself and the readers of your dissertation.

Unsupported assertions

Asserting something to be true when you do not provide support for that assertion is an argumentative error. Using an unsupported assertion means that the reader has no way of knowing if it is true, because you have offered nothing in support of the statement. The reader or marker will probably disregard the point. Arguments with unsupported statements are weak arguments – strong arguments have support for all the main points of the argument. If you adopt the paragraph style suggested in earlier parts of this book, you will be much less likely to make unsupported assertions.

The same problem occurs when you suppress evidence or provide incomplete evidence. These positions are more difficult because they require you to make a judgement. If you were to state, 'Business is driven by profit', you have to make a judgement about whether this point is universally recognised as being true. If it would be accepted as universally true, you can assert it and it requires no evidence in support. Not every assertion does need supporting evidence – but be careful! Every part of your main argument that might be contested has to have supporting evidence. Failure to do this will weaken your argument.

The suppressing of evidence occurs when you know there is evidence that is counter to your argument but you choose not to include it. Most contested positions need evidence in support and evidence that contradicts. This is what is termed a balanced argument. Balanced evidence is to be expected, so if you use a one-sided argument, it is very likely to be viewed as a weak argument. Strong arguments are always balanced arguments.

PRACTICAL TASKS WHEN CREATING A DISSERTATION

There are two commonly occurring practical tasks that are required when producing a dissertation. First, it is normal to create a table of contents. This is a simple task if you structure your writing and use the contents feature of Word. Second – and not always required – is the creation of an index. This is a more complicated task but is still easy to carry out using the specialist feature of Word.

The table of contents

Dissertations need a table of contents to make navigation easier, and such a table is a normal requirement. It can be created automatically in Word. The contents list is based on the use of Heading 1 style and the second-level entries are based on Heading 2 entries. To ensure that the table of contents works properly you must take care that all the chapter headings are formatted with a Heading 1 style. This is done by placing the cursor in the title and clicking on Heading 1 for the first-level entry. For the second-level entries, headings should be formatted with the Heading 2 style. This would generally cover the major sections in each chapter.

To create a table of contents, place the insertion point where you want the table, and then:

- click on the **References** tab
- then on **Table of Contents**
- and choose the required **Style**.

The table of contents will appear at the insertion point. You can update the table of contents at any point via the **Update Table** button on the **References** tab.

The index

Longer dissertations may require an index. Indexing is a skilled and time-consuming activity, but Word can help manage and create an index. The first phase is to mark each of the index entries in the text. You can mark individual words, phrases or whole sections and chapters.

To mark individual word entries:

- go to the **References** tab
- click on **Mark Entry**
  - the main entry can be changed and a sub-entry added
  - the page number format can also be changed
- then click on **Mark**.

Carry on marking all the index entries you want.

To create multiple page entries:

- select the text that is to form the index entry
- go to the **Insert** tab
- click on **Bookmark**
- enter a name and then click on **Add**
- place the cursor at the end of the text that has just been marked
- go to the **References** tab
- click on the **Mark Entry** button
- add a name for the entry
- click the radio button **Page** range and select the bookmark you have just entered
- click on **Mark**.

Carry on in this manner until all the index entries have been marked.

To create the index:

- place the cursor at the point of insertion
- go to the **References** tab
- click on **Insert Index**
- choose the format of the index and the number of columns and any of the other options
- click on **OK**.

Your index is entered into the document. If you need to add more entries, delete the existing index, mark the additional index points, and then insert the index again.

10.5 THE STRUCTURE OF A DISSERTATION

Check with your university regulations to ensure that the structure of your dissertation meets with the award requirements. A general structure is as follows:

Title page
Title, your name, course name, date, name of supervisor

Abstract
One paragraph summarising the whole dissertation

Acknowledgements
Thanks to those who have assisted you

Table of contents
Chapters and/or sections and subsections with page numbers

Table of figures and illustrations
A list of all the figures and tables used in your dissertation.

Introduction
A presentation of your question/problem/thesis, the context in which the research was undertaken, and a brief outline of the structure of your work

Main chapters:
    Literature review
    Methodology
    Data collection
    Analysis of data – how
    Findings from the data – what

Conclusion/findings
Where you bring it all together, restating clearly your main findings, making recommendations, suggestions, and revisiting and evaluating how well you met the research objectives

Bibliography
A complete list of your sources, in alphabetical order and correctly formatted

Appendices
Any relevant information not central to your main argument – for example, complete questionnaires, copies of letters, maps, etc

Other sections you may be asked to include could be terms of reference, reflective accounts, executive summary, skills development matrix.

FORMATTING YOUR DISSERTATION

Your university may have a detailed set of formatting requirements – check, and comply with them. If, as is more common, there are no formal requirements for dissertation submission, the following list of recommendations should be followed:

- Use A4 paper (or whatever is the standard size in your part of the world).
- Provide a front cover for your dissertation with the title centred about one-third of the way down the page, your own name centred about six lines below, your supervisor's name six lines below that, and with the university name about six lines below that. (Some universities require you to use only your student ID number and not your name.)
- Leave a margin of at least 3 centimetres at the sides and top and about 5 centimetres at the bottom for the marker's comments.
- Use a font size of 11pt or 12pt. Use either Times New Roman or Arial.
- The requirement for dissertations is that they are printed in double-spacing. But because of environmental concerns, many universities will accept single-spacing.
- Align the page on the left only – do not fully justify the text.
- Separate each paragraph with an extra empty line.
- After a full-stop leave (only) one space before the capital letter of the next sentence.
- Do not accidentally leave extra spaces between any of the words.
- Ensure that your pages are numbered using Arabic numerals (1, 2, 3, etc).
- Do not number your points or paragraphs – this is report form and is not suitable for a dissertation.
- Avoid footnotes, unless you are using a numerical referencing system. Avoid too many brackets.

- Use bold and italics sparingly and consistently; avoid underlining, and avoid using 'etc'.
- The bibliography should be listed alphabetically by first author.
- Usc Harvard referencing, unless your university indicates that you should use a different format.

You will normally have to supply two copies of your dissertation. Some universities further specify the binding arrangements. (If nothing is specified, use a glue bind on the left-hand edge.)

10.6 INTRODUCTIONS AND CONCLUSIONS

The first and last chapters of your dissertation are vitally important. They convey the overall purpose and the significance of the dissertation. The introduction sets the context and signposts the argument and conduct of the research. The conclusion defines what the dissertation has achieved.

Introductions and conclusions cannot be formulaic because they all serve different purposes. It is, however, possible to set out some of the main areas that introductions and conclusions must achieve.

THE INTRODUCTION

The introduction is the first section of your work, so it must be well-written and accomplish the following:

- introduce you as a writer and your writing style
- engage the reader – draw him or her into something interesting
- introduce the context of the research
- set the research in the wider context of the literature and other research
- introduce your argument
- scope the research – set the limits of what it will and will not do
- set out the research question(s) to be completed and resolved
- set out the structure of your dissertation – a kind of macro signposting.

The introduction will not be a very long chapter – it will be a chapter on its own. Typically, introductions should not be longer than five to eight pages. I would advise that you write the introduction very early on in the dissertation process – in this form it becomes a thinking and planning process. Do not worry too much about the quality of the writing at this stage. You will have to return and revise the introduction when the dissertation is almost complete.

THE CONCLUSION

Like the introduction, the conclusion brings your central ideas into sharp focus. The aim of the conclusion is to tie up all the loose ends and make the reader (marker) feel that you have fully achieved what you set out to do in the introduction. The conclusion should not just be a summary – that would be a bit dry and dull. The conclusion must summarise, but must also look forward and suggest something new.

The conclusion has to accomplish the following:

- summarise the whole dissertation process
- summarise the findings
- remind the reader of your initial aims and objectives
- evaluate how well your research and this dissertation have achieved those aims
- consider how your research connects to a wider research area
- explain the implications of your research and how they relate to organisational issues and actions

- recommend further research to investigate further aspects of the research or to duplicate aspects of the research
- consider any areas that might be generalised to larger populations.

Remember to review the introduction and the conclusion as your very last writing act before you move on to reviewing your work. The conclusion should be approximately the same length as the introduction, at about five to eight pages (of single-spaced text).

REPORTS

One of the main business forms of communication is the report, mostly required and used for interim dissertation reports or for management reports. There are, however, many different types of report: some are barely one page in length, and others are many hundreds of pages. There is a shift in business towards the one-page report; the argument being that if you cannot communicate the important elements of what you want to say in one page, then the message is not clear enough. Clearly, the implication is that shorter communication is more effective communication.

Reports take a standard form:

- *Title*, author, date
- *Executive summary* – an overview of subject, findings and recommendations
- *Table of contents* – a list of numbered sections in the report and their page numbers
- *Introduction* – terms of reference; an outline of the report's structure
- *The text main body* – including numbered headings and subheadings that convey the message in the argument
- *Conclusion* – which states the major outcomes and recommendations
- *Reference list* – a list of reference material consulted during the writing of the report
- *Appendix* – additional material that supports your argument but is not essential to its explanation.

10.7 REFERENCING

There are several styles of referencing. The most commonly used in business and management is the Harvard style, and this is the only style presented here. The weblinks below provide access to the other referencing styles. Unless your university department requires a specific style, use the Harvard referencing system. What follows is by no means exhaustive and some areas are contested. But if you follow this guide, you will encounter few problems when you submit your work.

All of your ideas will have been based on someone else's ideas or research – it is vital that you acknowledge these ideas. Where you are using quotes, you are acknowledging the use of the actual words. If you fail to correctly acknowledge ideas and quotes, you will have committed the academic offence of plagiarism. There are severe penalties for plagiarism.

There are good academic and practical reasons for getting organised in terms of references and acknowledging the work of others. The credibility of your writing is grounded on the sources you use. Being organised to accurately record and use references was covered in Chapter 5 – take another look at that section before you read on. As you read, take notes of the detail of the theory or research and record the reference to the work.

A *book reference* requires:
- the author's or editor's name (or names)
- the year the book was published
- the title of the book
- the edition (unless the first edition)
- the city the book was published in
- the name of the publisher.

A *journal reference* requires:

- the author's name or (authors') names
- the year in which the journal was published
- the title of the article
- the title of the journal
- the volume and issue number
- the page number or numbers.

A reference to *an electronic source* requires:

- the electronic address or email
- the type of electronic resource
- the date you accessed the source.

A *direct quotation* requires all of the above, as relating to its source, and if from a book, also requires the page number or numbers from which it is quoted.

WORKING PATTERN WITH REFERENCES

If you are following the advice to use the bibliographical features of Word 2007 and above from Chapter 5, you should refer back to that section now. In the Word system you add the reference as you write. Reference lists using the Harvard system are often termed bibliographies. A bibliography is a list of references and a list of works you have consulted generally. Unless your university indicates a different arrangement, compile a complete list of references and works you have consulted, call it a bibliography, and place it at the end of your dissertation but before any appendices.

You must always reference any ideas that you use to develop your argument or your research method. This will require extensive referencing in some parts of the work, most heavily in the literature review section. In this critical chapter most paragraphs will contain five to ten references or direct quotations, where you copy another author's material word-for-word. A direct quotation must have inverted commas placed at the beginning and end of the word-for-word section. Traditionally, double inverted commas were used (" … ") but it is now acceptable, and in some ways preferable, to use single inverted commas (' … ').

Try to avoid using direct quotations: they often waste words and cannot replace your own argument. But sometimes it is difficult to avoid a direct quotation because the author's words may precisely describe the point you are trying to make, or provide evidence of the point you have made. When you use direct quotations, you must reproduce the author's words exactly, including any spelling, capitalisation, and punctuation errors. If you recognise an error, place the word '(sic)' after the error – it indicates that you are aware of the error.

Paraphrasing is when you take another author's ideas and put them into your own words. This is a common and effective approach in dissertations. Be sure to indicate the original author of the idea, however, by correctly referencing the source.

Correctly using references in the body of your work

Using the Harvard system requires the name or names of the author(s) and the year of publication in the main text of your writing.

Imagine that Weick has written and published a book on sense-making in organisations. We could summarise and reference his book with a sentence such as:

Weick (2005) suggests that there are eight distinct ways of making sense in an organisation.

The full reference would then appear in the bibliography.

Reference an idea or paraphrase from a book or journal article with one author like this:

Horn (2009) suggests that we view time using the sweet jar analogy.

(This is where the name forms part of the sentence.)
Or like this:

There have been suggestions that time should be viewed as analogies to other things (Horn, 2009).

The same rules apply when there are two authors:

Horn and Farmer (2009) suggest that we view time using the sweet jar analogy.

There have been suggestions that time should be viewed as analogies to other things (Horn and Farmer, 2009).

When the number of authors goes beyond two, it is best to use the form (Horn *et al*), or as in 'Horn *et al* (2009) suggest …' . *Et al* means 'and others'.
A *direct quote* takes the same form as above but also includes a page number – for example:

'There are many aspects to time management, but at this point it may be helpful to look at just one theory: the sweet jar theory of time management' (Horn, 2009; p.29).

The author's words must be within inverted commas (single or double).
A *corporate source* when referenced looks like this:

The HSE (2008) argues that accidents are in decline …

Or like this:

Accident research (HSE, 2008) suggests that accidents are in decline …

You will encounter situations where authors have written more than one publication in one year. Distinguish between these by placing a lower case 'a' behind the first date and a lower case 'b' behind the second, and so on. Extending the above example we might thus have: Horn (2009a) and Horn (2009b).

When the author you want to quote is *represented in another author's work*, you would reference this as:

Horn and Farmer (in Smith, 2002) argue that …

But try if you can to use the original text for reading, quoting and paraphrasing. Using second-hand ideas often leads to distortion of the original idea.
You will sometimes wish to *quote from anonymous books*. The normal convention is to replace the author with the name of the book:

The cognitive elements of understanding people's action in organisations will always require extensive research (*How to Make Sense of Work*, 2007).

Remember: a direct quotation requires a page number.
Newspaper articles are treated in the same manner as other sources. It is more common for newspaper articles to have no stated author, so we would adapt the technique above:

The Times suggests that illogical and inexplicable behaviour at work is commonplace ('No sense at work', 29 January 2009).

This uses the article name and then the date.
You will find quite commonly that you need to quote more than one source. This is dealt with using punctuation in this way:

The idea of making sense in organisations is not new and there has been extensive and diverse research carried out on this issue (Weick, 2004; O'Connell, 1998; Freeman, 2006).

Lectures or other taught material may be referenced thus:

> No one can make sense of an organisation without reflecting on their own cognitive processes (Horn, 2009: 18).

In this reference the number after the colon represents the slide number in a PowerPoint presentation.

However, quoting from lecture notes is normally a very weak approach to using source material. You should normally be able to access the source material that the lecturer used, so read that and use the argument first-hand.

If the author is unknown, use the technique we have already established – of citing the title or institutional source:

> No one can make sense of an organisation without reflecting on their own cognitive processes (Chilterns University, School of Business, 2009: 18).

Electronic sources are referenced using the author and the date as usual. However, it is sometimes the case that the author is anonymous and there is no date. Web pages often present in this fashion, so we revert to the title of the piece or the organisation and 'n.d.' for no date. For example:

> 'Sense-making: a collaborative enquiry', n.d.

BIBLIOGRAPHY

Every reference you use in the main body of your work must have an entry in the bibliography – most markers check that they do. It is also the convention to list sources that you have used in a more general fashion. This does not necessarily include all your background reading, but there will be a set of resources that do not directly feature in the argument but that have influenced the general location and thrust of your work.

When creating a bibliography, the sources should be listed alphabetically by author's surname, should be ranged left, and should never be preceded by a bullet point or number. Where the author is anonymous or unknown for any one source, insert that source in the alphabetical list using the title of the source instead of an author's name. All sources should be listed in one list – there should not be separate lists for books, journal articles, electronic and newspaper sources. In the printed document ensure that the bibliography commences on a new page. Store the Word file for the bibliography in a separate Word document.

For some awards and some universities, you may be asked to produce an annotated bibliography. This is a bibliography list with an added section that summarises and evaluates the source. This style of bibliography is sometimes used at the proposal stage.

The section below lists the main types of documents you may want to enter into a bibliography.

A book with one author:

Hampson, S. (2002) *The Construction of Personality.* London: Routledge

[Author, Initial. (Year) *Title (italicised).* Place of publication: Publisher]
A book with two authors:

Gentner, D. and Stevens, A. (2006) *Mental Models.* New Jersey: Erlbaum

A book with three or more authors:

Terborg, J., Richardson, P. and Pritchard, R. (2008) *Person–Situation Effects in the Prediction of Performance: An investigation of ability, self-esteem and reward contingencies.* London: Sage

A book that is a second or later edition:

> Fransella, F. and Dalton, P. (2009) *Personal Construct Counselling in Action*, 3rd edition. London: Sage

A book by the same author in the same year:

> Weick, K. (2005a) *Sense-Making in Organisations*. London: Sage
> Weick, K. (2005b) *Establishing Organisational Trust*. London: Sage

A book compiled by an editor (chapters are by different authors):

> Garnham, A. (ed.) (2009) *Thinking and Reasoning*. Oxford: Blackwell

A chapter within a book compiled by an editor:

> Watkins, J. (2009) 'Methodological individualism and social tendencies', in Garnham, A. (ed.) (2009) *Thinking and Reasoning*. Oxford: Blackwell

A book with an anonymous or unknown author:

> *My Best Encyclopaedia* (1985) London: Sage

A journal article:

> Hill, Y. (2007) 'Metaphors and mental models: sense-making and sense-giving in innovative and entrcpreneurial activities', *Journal of Management*, Vol.46, No.6: 1057–74

[Author, Initial. (Year) 'Title', *Journal (italicised)*, Volume number, Issue number; page or page range]

A journal article on CD-ROM or database:

> Hill, Y. (2007) 'Metaphors and mental models: sense-making and sense-giving in innovative and entrepreneurial activities', *Journal of Management [Online]*, Vol.46, No.6; 1057–74. Available: http//www.sage.direct/0670-2398(06)01210-6 [accessed 2 Feb 2009]

'[Online]' refers to the type of media on which the source is located. If it was instead a CD-ROM source, you would put '[CD-ROM]' in the square brackets. As with a normal journal example, the volume number, issue number and page numbers are listed. At the end of this example, note that the name of the database has been listed, along with the identification/access number of the article, and an access date (in square brackets).

Teaching materials:

> Farmer, P. (2009) *Unit 5: Employee Reward*. Chilterns University, Business School.

Teaching material by unnamed author:

> Chilterns University (2009) *Unit 5: Employee Reward*. Business School: Author

'Author' at the end means that the publisher is the same as the author.

A government publication:

> Department for Education and Employment (DfEE) (2009) *Skills for Life: The national strategy for improving adult literacy and numeracy skills*. Nottingham: DfEE Publications

A conference paper:

> Heron, Z. (2008) 'Impressions of the other reality: a co-operative inquiry into altered states of consciousness', Social Realities Conference Proceedings, Chilterns University Conference, High Wycombe; 245–56

A newspaper article:

Fanning, A. (2010) 'I can't make sense of work', *Sunday Mail*, 1 January: 12

A newspaper article by an unknown author:

'I can't make sense of work', *Sunday Mail* (2010) 1 January: 12

 ALISON

CASE STUDY

Alison has done quite a bit of reading and thinks that she knows the subject area quite well. She has many pages of notes about the main sources of her dissertation. She is not quite so sure how to organise the ideas into a meaningful structure. She is carrying out primary research in work–life balance at two local retail stores.

To think about ...

Without worrying about the actual content, prepare a structure for Alison's literature review. You should provide:

- section headings
- paragraph headings
- paragraph points
- word targets for each section.

 TONNA

CASE STUDY

Tonna has progressed her research to the point of having gathered and analysed the data. She is not too sure how to get on and write the findings section. She has conducted primary research in work–life balance at two retail stores. She has questionnaire data from 120 respondents and 14 in-depth semi-structured interviews.

To think about ...

Without worrying about the actual content, prepare a structure of Tonna's findings chapter. You should provide:

- section headings
- paragraph headings
- paragraph points
- word targets for each section.

SUMMARY

If you treat writing as a skill that you can learn and practise, you will enjoy the writing process.

- Develop good writing habits:
    - Understand that writing is a skill.
    - Develop the writing habit.
    - Use feedback to improve your writing.
    - Understand that writing takes time and plan to have time.
    - Read, think, design, write.
    - Develop 'stickability'.
    - Plan before you write.
    - Write it right through accurate planning and precision expression.
    - Understand the necessity for reviewing writing.

- Plan before you write:
    - Use the macro planning idea to structure your writing.

    - Create ideas and then select.
    - Plan chapters, sections, paragraphs and paragraph points.
    - Read and think before you plan.

- Micro writing:
    - Understand the power of sentences.
    - Punctuate accurately.
    - Avoid writing errors.
    - Understand the structure of paragraphs.
    - Use evidence to support statements.
    - Use linking and signposting.
    - Avoid argumentative errors.

- Structure and format your dissertation.
- Use clear and concise introductions and conclusions.
- Be precise about referencing.

EXPLORE FURTHER

Neville, C. (2007) *The Complete Guide to Referencing and Avoiding Plagiarism*. Milton Keynes: Open University Press

Seely, J. (2005) *The Oxford Guide to Effective Writing and Speaking*. Oxford: Oxford University Press

Sinclair, C. (2007) *Grammar: A friendly approach*. Milton Keynes: Open University Press

Weblinks

Creating documents in outline mode: http://edutech.msu.edu/online/Office2007/Word2007/tutorials/WordOutline.pdf

Dr Jay's writing tips: http://www.csun.edu/~vcecn006/

Basic guide to writing at university: http://pam-sissons.suite101.com/returning-student-writing-tools-a15302

CHAPTER 11

Reviewing and Evaluating Your Dissertation

What will I learn in this chapter?

- Techniques for reviewing and proofreading your work
- How to meet the word target
- The fragmentation technique
- How to involve others in your writing
- The role of your supervisor in the review process
- Auditing your work using the assessment criteria
- How your work will be marked
- Reflecting on the experience

11.1 INTRODUCTION

When you have completed the first draft of your dissertation, the whole task is nearly complete – but as this chapter will show there are still a number of tasks to be done before submission of the work. The activities and tasks all focus on what you have written. Adopting some of the ideas in this chapter will improve your work and help you towards a successful grade.

The best way to use this chapter is to skim-read it when you are writing your dissertation, but to return and consider the detail when you have a first draft of your work. It assumes that you will have a document of between 10,000 and 20,000 words.

It is important to realise that all good writing passes through several review processes. You will have to plan to have time before the submission deadline to carry out the review and improvement process. In an ideal scenario you would allow four weeks to complete this phase of the dissertation. 'Reviewing' requires, rereading, reflection and change.

11.2 TECHNIQUES FOR REVIEWING YOUR WORK GENERAL COMMENTS

The process of writing precisely what you mean takes time. Every sentence requires careful rereading and revision to ensure that it expresses precisely what you wanted to say, and importantly communicates your meaning to the reader. I will make that point again – the written word is there to convey a message. While the sentence may look fine, precise and accurate to you, ask what message it conveys to the reader. There is no easy way to know this except by allowing someone else to read your words and asking them what it conveys. Part of the reviewing process must involve someone other than the author of the words.

The good news is that because nearly all writing is completed on a computer, reviewing your work has never been easier. Remember to use the spelling and grammar checking facilities of the software, but do not trust them. They do not pick up every kind of error and they often encourage you to express yourself in very stilted and one-dimensional ways.

The basic reviewing process involves:

- *rereading* – the writing
- *reflecting* – thinking about the writing and the message
- *revising* – changing aspects of sentences, paragraphs, sections and chapters.

The basic process will be used many times for each section of writing. Each sentence of your work may well have been reviewed five to ten times until the point at which you submit it.

The full reviewing process works best when separated into two phases – firstly, reviewing the macro elements of your writing, and then reviewing the micro elements.

MACRO WRITING

At the macro writing stage, you will have started with a set of chapter headings, section headings, and paragraph headings. The level of detail in each section may be different because the writing process is seldom even from beginning to end. Once you have laid out how a chapter or section is to be structured, you can review that chapter or section by itself.

Once the ideas, chapter, sections and paragraphs are laid out, consider:

- Overall structure – does this address what is expected in a dissertation?
- Do the chapters and sections work in a logical fashion?
- Have I missed out a section or chapter?
- What is the main argument running through this work?
- If the sequence was different, would the work be clearer, more logical?
- Does each of the paragraphs develop *one* and only one idea?
- Do the chapter contents all belong together?
- Is this chapter too long? Is it too short?
- Does the sequence of the paragraphs work in a clear and logical way?
- If each of these paragraphs is 100–200 words, will my work be too long? Is it too short?
- Do I have sufficient evidence to support each statement or claim?

If the answer to any of these questions is 'Maybe', then you need to think and reflect more on the structure before proceeding. Macro reviewing is ideally carried out before any micro writing is carried out. You may well review the macro writing 10 or 20 times before you are sure that it is the most appropriate structure. Even when the micro writing process has commenced, you may need to return to the macro writing and review and change things. The micro writing process often throws up problems, anomalies, and/or potential improvements in the overall structure.

This macro review process must involve someone other than the author. In decreasing order of usefulness the macro writing can be reviewed by:

- your supervisor
- another tutor
- the skills unit of your university
- a study group
- a work colleague
- a friend
- a family member.

Macro revisions often involve developing ideas in more detail, finding and including more evidence, developing further critique and more analysis, developing evaluations. All these aspects involve more thinking and research. Macro review is also about reorganising, changing the focus, adapting the argument, and changing the line of argument. These revisions do not need any further research, but they require you to think flexibly and adapt what you already have.

Selection was mentioned in Chapter 10, and revising your work will be about selecting some material and deleting other material. You must be ruthless in this regard. You may have spent time researching an author or theory, but if it does not fit into the argument you are developing, it must be thrown away. Ruthless selection and deletion of material is required to create successful dissertations. Also, do not be afraid to delete a section that is not working. Sometimes sections of writing we have created have flaws that we cannot identify – we know something is not right but cannot quite find it. When this happens, delete the troublesome section and reconstruct it.

Mapping the argument

At this point in the review process it is worth 'mapping the argument', or better still, getting someone else to map the argument. This is done by setting out the steps and evidence in the argument on a sheet of paper. Once mapped, our review should check for the following issues:

- Does the introduction set out the steps of your argument?
- Are the steps in the argument clear?
- Does each step follow logically?
- Is the argument suitably referenced?
- Is each step supported by evidence, illustrations, examples and research?
- Have you signposted the argument? (See the detail later in the chapter about signposting.)
- Have you provided links to different parts of the argument? (See the detail later in this chapter for how to do this.)
- Does your conclusion summarise your argument?
- Is the argument convincing and coherent? Will this argument illicit a good grade?

Once your argument is mapped, you should review and adjust it until it represents the best argument you can produce. Successful dissertations always have a strong, clear argument.

MICRO WRITING

At the micro writing stage, this reviewing process is carried out as you write and after you have written. You will need to return to micro reviewing as one of the last dissertation tasks.

The first reviewing should take place as you write. You will also need to review your writing after a period of time – say, a week or so – and as a final check of the work before submission. Review your writing by asking at least the following questions:

- Have I expressed this point clearly?
- Is this the precise point I want to make?
- Is there any ambiguity?
- Is it doing the correct job at this point in the paragraph? For instance: is it an appropriate statement, evidence, summary or link?
- How does this sentence contribute to the argument?
- Is it in the appropriate academic style?
- What message does this sentence communicate to the reader?
- Is this sentence making one claim, or a carefully constructed complex claim?
- Are there any spelling mistakes?
- Is it grammatically correct?

When you have reviewed, reflected and revised each sentence in a paragraph, ask the following questions of the whole paragraph:

- What main point is this paragraph making?
- Does it try to make more than one point?
- Is the point of the paragraph clear?
- Is the argument strong enough?

- Is it correctly structured? Introduction, statement, evidence (several), summary, link?
- What message does this paragraph send to the reader?
- Does the paragraph flow correctly?
- Is this paragraph in the correct place in the dissertation? (Link back to the macro review.)
- Is this paragraph correctly linked to the one in front and behind?

This immediate reviewing as you write is vital to the writing process, but it is also vital that you return to the work and review it again after a period of time. Many writers open a chapter they are working on and review it by rereading before they write any more material. This is a good warm-up to writing, but it is a time-consuming process. At some point after a week or 10 days you must return to your writing and ask all the above questions. The things you see and the views you form will be quite different from the views you formed at the point of writing. Distance from writing generally lends critical clarity. Remember to involve someone else in the review process.

Two further reviewing thoughts

Using computers for the review process is environmentally friendly and saves you printing costs. However, once or twice in the reviewing process print out what you have written, check it, and have someone else check it. You will spot errors that were not seen when you were reviewing on screen.

At all review stages form the habit of reading your work aloud. It transmits your work by a different medium and you will more easily spot any errors or weaknesses in your work. Better still, if you can bear it, arrange for someone else to read your work to you. A variation on this technique is to read your work to a study group. All these techniques should improve your writing. Most importantly, they also allow you to develop as a writer.

Review your use of words

In introductory sentences, try to use the following types of constructions:

First, … Secondly, … Finally, …
At first, … Later, …
There are four reasons why …
Research studies suggest that the impact of unions will have an change in three main areas. First, …

Use verbs that balance confidence in what you are saying with a reflective stance:
The research suggests …
The research leads us to see …
The evidence indicates …
The data reflects …
The findings support …

Avoid blunt overstatements:
My findings show …
No challenge can be posed to the finding that …
It is obvious that …
This research can be applied in all contexts …
It is clear that …
The evidence proves …
The reader can clearly see that …

You will need forms of words that address others' writings, and you will have to vary them as much as possible to avoid monotony:

As Buckley (2007) points out, ...
Research by Gay and Saunders indicates that ...
Havelock's research findings confirm ...
In her study of Weber, Smith claims that ...
Timson notes that in addition to ...
His study provides an excellent ...
Pretal and Ying state that ...
The study conducted by Stevenson and Smy had similar findings and ...
Varda argues that ...
Sims identifies two reasons why ...
Kasia asserts that ...
According to Frost, ...
Peartree and Mitchell found that ...
McBain contends that ...
A recent study (Mitchell, 2009) maintains that ...

Make only infrequent use of verbs that display too much emotion:

Ali would like us to accept that ...
Jano assumes that ...
Lin presumes that ...
Yg claims that ...
Valenience implies that ...

In concluding sentences try to use summary words and phrases:

This point is evidenced by ...
We may be able to conclude that ...
This may require more analysis ...
The idea will be developed further ...
This may have implications for ...
While this has addressed, ...

During the revision process it is sometimes difficult to focus on all the areas that need revision – the following sections address the most important of these. It may be worthwhile focusing, or asking someone else to focus, on each of the areas separately.

Proofreading

After you have completed these revision processes you will have to proofread your dissertation. After all the effort you have expended reviewing your work, correcting structures, creating arguments and well-evidence statements, you do not want to diminish your work by careless mechanical errors. We all have personal errors in our writing style, and often these go unnoticed by us, no matter how many times we read them. Getting someone else to read your work – a friend, colleague, tutor, professional proofreader – will surface these errors so that you can eliminate them from your writing. Many spelling, grammar and word use issues can be avoided by buying and using a good dictionary and thesaurus.

Structure

Is the structure appropriate for a dissertation? Does the structure provide equally balanced sections and chapters? Is the structure balanced in terms of what is expected for a dissertation? Is the structure logical, and does it allow the argument to flow? Is the structure complete, or are any areas missing?

Content

The content can be reviewed in several ways. Does the content cover all the expected areas for a dissertation? What is the balance of content in relation to the assessment criteria grid? In general, the content should be around 33% knowledge and understanding, 33% analysis, and 33% synthesis and evaluation. Does the content include too many quotes from published works? Is any of the content plagiarised?

English usage

Check for spelling and grammatical errors. But also look at poor sentence and paragraph construction. If specific terminology is used, is it fully explained? Is there any jargon?

Clarity of meaning

Ask someone to read the dissertation and set out on one sheet of paper what each chapter and section communicates. Looking at their notes will display how well you have communicated your meaning.

Argument

As above, ask someone to read your work and set out on one sheet of paper the main argument in your dissertation. This will either confirm that you are succeeding in making the argument you intended or will suggest that your argument is less clear than you intended. If your reader cannot perceive the main argument clearly, your marker will not be able to either.

Links and signposting

Ask someone to read your work and observe only the linking and signposting. Ask them to point out any section where they felt lost or had to read things several times to understand them.

11.3 HOW TO MEET YOUR WORD TARGET

If you use the macro planning reviewing process set out in the writing chapter (Chapter 10) and referred to again in this chapter, you should be able to arrange to write your work so that it meets the word target. To do this you must add word limits to each of the sections in the macro writing phase. It is quite possible to plan to write a 1,000-word introduction in five paragraphs of 200 words, and to plan what will go into each of these paragraphs. It is a little more difficult to plan a 5,000-word literature review in this fashion. But it is vital that you plan both what will be written and the amount that will be written.

CASE STUDY

LITERATURE REVIEW PLAN: AN EXAMPLE

Katie was a very organised person and she was certain that clear planning would help her write her dissertation without going over the word target.

The top-level literature review plan looked like this:

- Introduction (500 words)
- Theory 1 (600) – expanded below
- Theory 2 (500)
- Theory 3 (500)
- Research 1 (500)
- Research 2 (500)
- Professional body website (400)
- Synthesis of these sources (400)
- Evaluation of these sources (400)
- Summary and conclusions (500)

She planned each section in the following manner:

- Theory 1 (600 words)
  - Introduction to the theory (100)
  - The key components of the theory that I can apply to my dissertation (100)
  - Precise application of the theory in my dissertation (100)
  - Other research studies that have used this theory as the guiding theory (100)
  - Critique of the theory (100)
  - Evaluation of the theory (100)

For each of these sections she planned the paragraph points:

- Critique of theory (100)
  (Miles and Burns, 2006) reductionist
  (Harper and Adams, 2005) never been tested by research
  (Smy and Lake, 2009) does not make clear two of the assumptions

You can see from the Literature review plan case study that macro planning is a top-down process. Plan one layer – say, the chapter headings. Then plan the sections in a chapter, and then plan the paragraphs, adding word targets for each area. Katie's example is very highly structured and you may not want to plan in this much detail. However, planning before you write should ensure that your finished work will be spot-on the word target.

What if I am over the word target?

The stated penalties for being over the word target are normally small – around 5% of the total marks. The bigger penalty is borne by the loss of clarity of your argument. Most work that is over the word target is poorly structured and 'wordy'. By 'wordy' I mean that the writing has used far more words than are necessary to make the point. Over-length work is also often structured so poorly that sections are repeated and the points in some sections are made again in different sections. Generally, it is for those reasons that work which is over the word limit receives middling or poor grades.

If you are over the word limit you will clearly have to remove some words, paragraphs and sections – sometimes even entire chapters must be deleted. Where do you start the trimming process? Indiscriminate trimming of words and sections is very likely to remove good, well-organised ideas along with the rubbish and infill. Unfortunately, to effectively reduce the word count you must return to the beginning of the process and carry out the planning that should already have been done. Do not despair – a lot of what you have written will remain once the process is finished.

Follow these steps: (Do not refer to any of your existing writing. Remember to keep in mind your research questions.)

1 Open a new Word document in outline view.

2 At the highest level add chapter titles.

3 Then to each chapter add section titles. (Consider carefully how these sections are ordered.)

4 Then to each section add paragraph titles. (These should make the specific points of argument.) Remember the basic structure of paragraphs.

5 Carry on until every chapter has sections and paragraphs.

Review the structure that you have created, asking all the review questions set out above.

You may have to review and revise this structure many times – perhaps even, 10 to 20 times. At the conclusion of the revision process you should have an outline document setting out the argument for your dissertation.

Now compare the outline plan with what you have written. You may find either of the following situations:

- Your plan is very similar to what you have already written. The problem may be that you are trying to include too much material. The first area in which there may be too much material is theory and literature – this should be between 4,000 and 6,000 words. The second area is in the findings sections, where you may be trying to add all the analysis and findings (or too many of them). This section should be about 4,000–6,000 words too. Select the most important parts of these areas and remove the less important. Judge the importance of a section by how it connects to your research questions.

- Your plan is not similar to the work you have already produced, and you will have to restructure your work. This is done by first selecting parts of your existing work that would fit into the planned paragraphs. Copy these parts from your existing document and paste them in the new outline structure. As you proceed you may find some areas that you have planned but that have no existing writing, these will have to be written. You should also find there are parts of the original document that are not needed. Pay particular attention to the word targets for each section. You may find that some of the paragraphs are too long and wordy. We will deal with that issue in a later section.

What if I am under the word target?

Firstly, remember that this is not necessarily a problem. Word limits are given to indicate the upper limits of your writing. If you have followed and adhered to the writing advice given earlier, you may well find you have expressed all the areas and aspects of your argument in less than the word count. Typically, do not worry if you are up to 2,000 words below a word target of 20,000, or about 10%. But do check that all the required sections have been completed.

If you find you are under the word limit by more than 10%, you may well have not covered some of the expected areas. Show your outline plan to your tutor and ask if all the areas have been covered. If you are covering all the required areas and your work is still well below the word target, then it could well be that your paragraphs are underdeveloped or are not well supported by evidence. Look again at the paragraph structure in Chapter 10 and ensure that your paragraphs follow this type of structure. It is also possible that you are tending to be descriptive rather than critical, analytical or evaluative. Under-length dissertations are often descriptive because the development and revision phases have been rushed.

11.4 OTHER REVIEW TECHNIQUES

FRAGMENTATION TECHNIQUE

This is a review technique to evaluate how effectively you are using sentences. Select a section of your writing – the theory and findings sections are usually suitable – cut and paste around

500–1,000 words into a new Word document. Edit the work so that each sentence starts on a new line, separated by a line break.

THE FRAGMENTATION TECHNIQUE: AN EXAMPLE

This is a rather short section of student writing formatted in the appropriate way to carry out the fragmentation technique.

The preservation approach

The preservation approach stems from comments like 'We love what you guys do and aren't going to be making any changes' (Lesowitz and Knauff, 2003).

The intention is for the target firm to continue to operate relatively independent of the acquiring firm.

The main objective of this approach is to maintain the strategic approach of the target firm with little intrusion from the acquiring firm.

There are four activities that need to be practised to ensure successful integration in this situation (Ellis, 2004):

- Allow differences with the target firm.

- The target firm needs to be given autonomy.

- Allow the target firm to question decisions made by the acquiring firm.

- The acquiring firm needs to provide resources to enable the target firm to fulfil its strategy.

The absorption approach (Ellis, 2004)

As its name suggests, this approach is one where the acquiring firm absorbs the target firm completely into its business.

This approach will have a huge impact on the target firm, and for this approach to work successfully it is necessary to have a detailed integration plan.

If implemented in a regimented and swift manner, it will hopefully minimise disruption and uncertainty within the target firm.

It is recommended to have honest and frequent communication with staff and necessary stakeholders.

Finally, a definitive and shared road map is necessary to highlight the milestones that need to be hit, and when.

Each sentence is then analysed for:

- grammatical and spelling accuracy
- clarity
- contribution to the argument
- whether it is the correct type of sentence for its position in the paragraph.

Also analyse each sentence with these questions:

- How many words does the sentence contain?
- How many sentences are there with 15 or fewer words?
- How many sentences are there containing more than 25 words?
- How many sentences are there with unsupported statements in them?
- What is the average number of words used in a sentence?
- What is the average number of sentences used in a paragraph?

Any sentence that is evaluated as not contributing to the argument should be removed or revised. Using this technique you will reduce the word count of the dissertation and improve the clarity of the argument. In this process you will also discover paragraphs that do not work and need revision. It will also reveal paragraphs that can be removed.

TUTOR HELP WITH REVIEWING YOUR DISSERTATION

At the beginning of this book it was pointed out that your supervisor gets an allocation of time to help and assist you in your research. Although you do not want to waste this time with proofreading, their views on the content of your work would be useful. They will find it easier to be helpful if the volume of work is smaller. First, if you are using the macro writing approach, send them the outline of your dissertation. It is easier for them to read and comment on this small amount of writing, and their views will be far more useful early in the macro writing process. Some supervisors also read sections of the detailed writing – but not all. If you do send them your detailed writing, try to do this in sections and keep the amount you send to a reasonable level. You cannot expect your supervisor to comment on a chapter of writing more than once. So prepare the work carefully and only send detailed work when it is almost complete.

11.5 EVALUATE YOUR WORK USING THE ASSESSMENT CRITERIA

In the final phases of reviewing your work, return to the assessment criteria grid issued by your university and evaluate your work against this grid. Firstly, check the proportions of your writing in relation to the stated amounts of each of the skills. You can do this in sections, by printing out the work and using different-coloured highlighters to indicate when the writing is:

- knowledge
- understanding
- critique
- analysis
- creativity
- synthesis
- evaluation.

These skills are listed in order of difficulty. Poor dissertations tend to display only the skills at the top of the list. To achieve a good grade you have to display all the skills in the correct proportion. In reviewing your work you may find that there is not enough critique, analysis, synthesis, creativity or evaluation. If you do feel that these skills are not displayed in the right proportions, return and revise your work at the macro level by developing and adding these aspects. Then add them at the micro writing stage. You may have to remove some of the descriptive writing to make room for the more analytical writing.

Your work will also be assessed by how well it displays:

- argument
- logic
- clear, precise expression
- the quality and quantity of the data
- validity in the method and findings
- the breadth of research and sources
- the use of English
- adherence to the word count
- reflection
- reflexivity
- correct referencing
- the inclusion of all required sections.

11.6 REFLECTING ON THE EXPERIENCE

You are now at the final section of this book – well done! You may not remember very well your fears and worries when you started your dissertation, but they were probably soon replaced by different fears and worries. You will have developed a considerable set of skills in researching and writing dissertations, and it may be worth reflecting on how you acquired the skills to successfully complete the dissertation.

We could think of reflection as:

A calm, lengthy consideration leading to an expression of personal development for the individual.

Why are we interested in reflection? There are several reasons for focusing on reflection. The completion of your dissertation will probably mark the point where you return to the world of work, or different work. Many professions regard reflective practice and reflective learning as a vital part of what is called 'continuing professional development' (CPD). Recording your reflective thoughts on the dissertation process could be the first entry in your CPD log or file. Reflective logs or diaries aim to trap the personal and emotive feelings of achievement and development. We reflect on our learning and development so that we can learn and develop better in the future. Recording your development throughout the dissertation process may have many parallels for your learning in the future. Some universities ask you to submit a reflective or learning log with your dissertation. The following section considers common ways to be reflective.

We can be reflective by writing reflection records, personal thoughts and emotions related to something – in our case, dissertations. These reflections are often kept in a diary or learning log. A learning diary or learning log is a simple document that records thoughts and emotions over time. Many people simply use a Word document or a paper diary. If you have discovered Microsoft OneNote from earlier sections of the book, this is an excellent and flexible medium for maintaining your reflections. For some people the reflective account is like a melting pot where bits of emotions, knowledge, feelings, ideas, skills, awareness of things are placed. In the act of writing them there can be recognition of how learning has taken place. Committing thoughts and feelings to paper can make them clearer. Don't expect real reflection to be tidy and linear – it is more often messy and confusing. If you are asked to complete a reflective statement, try to tidy up and structure the mess before you submit it.

Imagine you are reflecting on carrying out research interviews for the first time. You might well record your preparations, your anxiety and fears, how effective you thought you had been, what went wrong, what went right, what you would change for next time. Some of these entries may be in the form of reflective questions, such as, 'Why did I do that? – It was so stupid.' You might also enter what you thought the interviewee thought of your performance.

Reflective areas that you might cover in respect of the dissertation process include:

- your fears before starting
- how you decided on a topic
- what you had to give up to do the course and the dissertation
- the effect on your family
- the skills you started out with
- where you think your skills were weak
- the interaction with your supervisor
- difficulties you encountered – family, work and university
- how you think you developed
- career aspirations
- hopes for the outcome of the dissertation
- what you still feel you are weak on
- time allocation issues
- fears about writing such a large work.

Questions often encourage deeper reflection, and the following questions should help you reflect:

- How well did theory explain what happened?
- Has the nature of the dissertation task affected how you reflect?
- What were your motives for doing this thing?
- What were the possible alternatives before you made this decision?
- How did you come to this decision?
- If you had been someone else – a friend, maybe – how would you have done this differently?
- Is there another point of view that you could explore?
- Are there alternative interpretations to consider?
- Are others seeing this issue from different points of view that may be helpful to you to explore?
- Does this issue relate to other contexts? How would it relate to these contexts?
- How have your views on this changed over time?
- Do you notice that your feelings about something have changed over time – or in the course of writing?
- Are there ethical/moral/wider social issues that you would want to explore?

KEY LEARNING POINTS

SUMMARY

Reviewing and revising your work will improve it. This chapter looks at a number of techniques for reviewing and improving your writing.

- Using a revision process – such as:
  - rereading the writing
  - reflecting – thinking about the writing and the message
  - revising, changing aspects of sentences, paragraphs, sections and chapters.
- Review the macro elements before the micro elements.
- Involve others in the review process
  - your supervisor
  - another tutor
  - the skills unit at your university
  - a study group

  - a work colleague
  - a friend
  - a family member.
- Review your use of words, sentences and paragraphs: micro writing.
- Assess your work against the published assessment criteria.
- Learn to be reflective by:
  - describing how something occurred
  - recording feelings
  - thinking and evaluating
  - asking 'What if ... ?' questions
  - looking for other perspectives
  - imagining from other people's positions
  - asking 'How would this work if ...?' questions.

EXPLORE FURTHER

Clark, I. L. (2007) *Writing the Successful Thesis and Dissertation: Entering the conversation*. Harlow: Pearson Education

Langan, J. (2007) *Exploring Writing: Paragraphs and essays*. London: McGraw-Hill Education

Murray, N. and Hughes, G. (2008) *Writing Up Your University Assignments and Research Projects*. Milton Keynes: Open University Press

Index